With Musket & Tomahawk

VOLUME III

The West Point–Hudson Valley Campaign
in the Wilderness War of 1777

Michael O. Logusz

CARREL BOOKS

Carrel Books may be purchased in bulk at special discounts for sales promotion, corporate gifts, fund-raising, or educational purposes. Special editions can also be created to specifications. For details, contact the Special Sales Department, Carrel Books, 307 West 36th Street, 11th Floor, New York, NY 10018 or carrelbooks@skyhorsepublishing.com.

Carrel Books® is a registered trademark of Skyhorse Publishing, Inc.®, a Delaware corporation.

Visit our website at www.carrelbooks.com.

10 9 8 7 6 5 4 3 2 1

Library of Congress Cataloging-in-Publication Data is available on file.

Cover design by Owen Corrigan
Cover painting by Mead, credit: Fort Montgomery collection

ISBN: 978-1-63144-040-3

Ebook ISBN: 978-1-63144-041-0

Printed in the United States of America

Contents

Introduction

1777. In America's history, it is the year which secured independence. Though combat activities had commenced many months earlier in April 1775, at Lexington and Concord, Massachusetts, the final outcome of the newly established American nation had truly hung in the balance until late 1777. Saratoga, deep in the North American wilderness in present day upper New York State, ensured the survival of the newly created American nation. That year in the month of October, a major victory was achieved when over 6,000 soldiers from a proud British army emerged out of a wood line and on a huge field surrendered to the forces of the American Northern Army. Saratoga is regarded as being one of the top twenty decisive battles in military history.

In my first two volumes, *With Musket & Tomahawk: The Saratoga Campaign in the Wilderness War of 1777* and *With Musket & Tomahawk: The Mohawk Valley Campaign in the Wilderness War of 1777,* the military, political, social, economic, and psychological events which evolved and occurred within and around the endless forests of the northeast are presented in depth.

But along with the wilderness events far to the north of New York City, there is the story of the events which occurred in the Northern Army's southern sector. Within the environs of New York City and the region to the immediate north, west, and east of this city, a massive conflict was likewise waged. In themselves, these events also played a role in securing the final victory at Saratoga.

The brave men and women who volunteered for service in the Northern Army's southern sector hailed from various ethnicities, races, religions, and professions. Major Thomas Moffat, who directed scouting operations for the Northern Army's entire southern area-of-operations, hailed from the Catskill region. Issac Franks, a poor Jewish inhabitant of New York City but supportive of the American cause, fled northward when the British occupied the city in 1776. In the vicinity of the Highlands, he joined the Northern Army. George Robert Twelve Hewes, affectionately known as "R.T." and a former participant of the Boston Tea Party, in its aftermath returned to his home in New York City. Fearing arrest with the arrival of the British in 1775, he also fled northward to enlist in the Northern Army. Another soldier " . . . a Colored man . . . born free . . ." was William Stewart. Determined to see the newly established nation succeed in establishing itself, Stewart volunteered for military service. Serving alongside those such as Moffat, Franks, "R.T.," and Stewart was a female soldier named Deborah Sampson. In 1777, she became a recipient of the Purple Heart, a medal awarded to those wounded or injured in a combat activity.

During the Wilderness War of 1777, the Northern Army did not occupy New York City, Long Island, and the city's nearby environs. Yet, this entire region was still officially in the army's operational zone. Via its spies, agents, couriers, saboteurs, and underground fighters, throughout 1777 the Northern Army successfully waged in the dark shadows a triumphant war amidst this populated region.

In this area, the Northern Army was tremendously assisted by the numerous women who resided in British occupied New York City. Agent 355, one of Major Benjamin Tallmadge's best agents along with Lydia Darragh, a Quaker woman who likewise spied for the Northern Army, were just two of the numerous females who not only brought forth vital information but fought a highly successful war of assassination, sabotage, arson, and propaganda.

Initially, my intent was to write a separate Fourth Volume about the role which African Americans, women, and those such as the Mennonites undertook to ensure a victory for the patriots in 1777. Included also would be the political events of 1777 which formally established the State of New York, with Governor George Clinton being elected as the state's very first governor; however, since the bulk of this information ended up being presented in the pages of the first two volumes, the remainder was largely incorporated in the pages of Volume III. Needing to inform my readers about the vital role females and those of black descent played in 1777 along with a few of the other little known but nevertheless vital events, I also included some of this information in separate chapters and very informative footnotes.

In the following pages of *With Musket & Tomahawk: The West Point-Hudson Valley Campaign in the Wilderness War of 1777,* readers will be exposed to the events waged in New York City in conjunction with the military-political events raging to the north of the city such as at West Point in the Highlands, through the Hudson Valley northward to Kingston and Saratoga and into the nearby environs of Danbury, Ridgefield, and other sites in Connecticut, Massachusetts, and New Jersey. As in the previous two volumes, I again tried to capture the importance of the human factor. So in tribute to those who served that crucial year on the southern front during the Wilderness War of 1777, their ideas, goals, hardships, successes, and tragedies are presented.

Chapter 1

The Military Situation on the Southern Front, Late 1777

October, 1777. As General John Burgoyne's army was systematically being destroyed within the forests of Saratoga's region, many miles to the south in New York City General Sir Henry Clinton[1] was putting together an expedition to assist Burgoyne.

Prior to his arrival to New York City on 5 July 1777 from England, Sir Henry's understanding was that Lieutenant-General Sir William Howe would advance northward from New York City to Albany to rendezvous with Major General John "Gentleman Johnny" Burgoyne's army advancing southward from Canada. Arriving in New York City, Sir Henry learned much to his disappointment that Howe was no longer interested in advancing northward. Instead, Howe was now undertaking preparations to commence operations both against Philadelphia— the capital of the newly created American nation—and General Washington's main Continental Army.[2]

Though aware of Burgoyne's military thesis "Thoughts for Conducting the War From the Side of Canada," Howe was convinced that the key to a British victory lay not in a campaign against the New England states but, rather, in the capture of the city of Philadelphia. Certain that Washington would defend the city this, in turn, would afford Howe the opportunity to engage and destroy Washington's army. Possibly, Washington himself would be killed or captured. With Washington eliminated and the city in British hands, the American Revolution would collapse. Assured also that Philadelphia and most of Pennsylvania was a heavy loyalist bastion, the captured city of Philadelphia would be used as a rallying point for the loyalists residing in the other colonies as well.

Sir Henry, however, strongly differed. From his very first meeting with Howe, Sir Henry sought to dissuade him from attacking into Pennsylvania. But Howe would not budge. He was adamant that the key to victory lay in Pennsylvania. Aware, however, of Sir Henry's anxieties and concerns, Howe assured Sir Henry that in the event the campaign against Washington would not be fruitful he would return in time to assist Burgoyne.[3]

WEDNESDAY, 23 JULY

Howe sailed southward. Unknown to him as he sailed away, other key events in the Wilderness War of 1777 were under way. Burgoyne was beginning to experience the first of his many problems, while far away on Carleton Island in the northwestern wilderness, General Barry St. Leger was undertaking his final preparations for a thrust to Albany via eastern Lake Ontario, Oswego, and the Mohawk Valley. And in Oquaga,[4] a mixed loyalist-Indian force commanded by a Captain John McDonell and Adam Crysler with attached British military advisors was finishing its preparations to commence a northeastward thrust through the Schoharie Valley to link up in due time with both St. Leger[5] and Burgoyne. Sailing away with no less than 18,000 troops[6] which encompassed the brunt of the New York City – based army, Howe left Sir Henry behind with no more than 7,000 English, German, and loyalist soldiers.[7] Though this strength might have appeared to be significant—in consideration that Sir Henry was holding the entire area of Long Island, Staten Island, Manhattan Island, and the other islands encompassing

New York City, as well as the eastern region of New Jersey and the area immediately to the north of New York City, encompassing the Bronx and a part of southern Westchester County, up to the southern banks of the Croton River and Cross River—Sir Henry's troops were actually spread quite thin.

From the outset, commanding New York City's occupational forces proved to be a very difficult assignment. A combination of health issues stemming from obesity and an old battle wound suffered fifteen years previously at Friedberg, Germany,[8] also affected Sir Henry. Compounding Sir Henry's position was that he had little control over Lord William Tryon, England's Royal Governor of the Colony of New York and Richard Cunningham, New York City's brutal Provost Marshal, individuals directly appointed by England's king; furthermore, by mid-1777, the Wilderness War had worked its way into the city. An exceptionally strong pro-patriot underground was under way. New York City had become the main spy center for those rebelling and, along with the anti-British propaganda warfare being waged by the patriots, frequent gunfights, sniping incidents, arson, bombings, sabotage and attempts to assassinate high ranking English and loyalist officials were likewise now the norm. Crime and corruption were rampant, a strong black market existed, the usage of opium (especially by British officials and military officers) was widespread and a secret but lucrative slave trade was under way. Food and fuel shortages along with the lack of sufficient housing for both military personnel and civilians plagued the city. What especially compounded this situation were the two huge fires which had mysteriously erupted in 1776 resulting in much destruction, of which little had been repaired or rebuilt. Numerous loyalists, especially those fleeing from the north, flocked into the city seeking British assistance and protection. Frequently accompanied by entire families, they further burdened England's officials with their numerous demands.

But New York City's sad state of affairs was not the only problem Sir Henry faced. Throughout the remainder of the summer and early fall he seldom heard anything from either Burgoyne in the north or from Howe in the south. Though on occasion a runner did appear, what news received was usually scant and weeks old. For those attempting to reach Sir Henry, distance and time was always against them. In some cases messengers dispatched either to New York City or out of the city to Burgoyne or Howe simply disappeared. Yet, it always seemed as if the patriots knew what was going on within and around the city. Their numerous agents, spies, and the so-called "eyes and ears" continuously fed the patriots much accurate information.[9]

With each passing day, Sir Henry knew that the grand plan to bring the American revolt to its knees was rapidly deteriorating. Though little was heard from Howe and Burgoyne, Sir Henry feared that neither of the commanders was encountering much success. Continuing to ponder on the sequence of events now occurring, the city's commander once again reflected to that day when, on 20 December 1776, Howe first wrote to Lord Germain citing that he would now shift his military operations into Pennsylvania proper. Though Howe was not fully explicit as to how this would be done, Germain voiced no immediate opposition or concerns about the change of plans. Shortly after, on 3 March 1777, Germain even responded favorably to Howe's request to attack Philadelphia.[10] Satisfied with Germain's response, on 2 April, Howe again wrote to Germain. In his letter Howe provided additional details on how he (Howe) would take an army into Pennsylvania by sea rather than by land.

On 8 May, Germain received Howe's letter of 2 April. Meeting immediately with King George III, Germain discussed Howe's proposal to attack Pennsylvania via a sea route. During their meeting the king neither supported nor opposed Howe's proposal. Though Germain was informed by the king to respond to Howe, for unknown reasons Germain failed to immediately respond to Howe's letter of 2 April until 18 May. And in his response of 18 May, Germain informed Howe that the king was confident of Howe's judgment and had approved of the changes. Germain did, however, emphasize:

".. . trusting, however, that whatever you may mediate, it will be executed in time for you to cooperate with the army ordered to proceed from Canada and put itself under your command."

Unfortunately for Howe, Germain's letter of 18 May did not reach Howe until 16 August 1777.[11] By then, Howe was en route to Pennsylvania and it was too late for Howe to simply turn around and rush back to New York City to renew a major offensive toward Albany.[12] After sailing up the Chesapeake Bay and landing on 25 August at the Head of Elk (Elkton) in Delaware, Howe advanced very cautiously against both Philadelphia and Washington. Speed was not a factor. Rumors circulated that Howe actually feared Washington's Continental Army.

In the meantime, as these events were unfolding, Sir Henry was still occupying New York City. Informed of Germain's letter of 18 May to Howe, Sir Henry anticipated a return of Howe's fleet. But as one day turned into another and the summer weeks turned into fall, Sir Henry's hopes and expectations diminished ever so.

MID-AUGUST, 1777

In a message dated 6 August that Sir Henry had received from Burgoyne, Burgoyne wrote that he expected to be in Albany by 23 August. In the aftermath of this message Sir Henry once again heard little. As for the few additional messages which arrived, the information was by and large of little military value.

FRIDAY, 22 AUGUST

Three well-coordinated raids, simultaneously undertaken by the patriots on this day, shattered the region far and wide. Raiders from Connecticut, New Jersey, and upstate New York struck British outposts in eastern Long Island, at Kingsbridge, and Staten Island. The fighting on Staten Island was especially heavy. In conjunction with the raids, sniping incidents, bombings, and several large arson fires erupted within the city proper. With troops spread far and wide, Sir Henry was unable to effectively counter the patriot activity of 22 August. This day may also be cited as being the date when Sir Henry was officially dragged into the Wilderness War of 1777.

SEPTEMBER 1777

Though still operating in the dark, by September, Sir Henry was fully aware of St. Leger's defeat at Fort Stanwix and his retreat from the western region, the defeat of the McDonell-Crysler raiders southwest of Albany, and Burgoyne's defeat at Bennington. Knowing that Burgoyne was advancing at a snail's pace toward Albany within the forests of the wilderness and confident that the rebels would defend the provincial town, Sir Henry began to formulate plans to assist Burgoyne. In itself, this would not be an easy task because right from the outset Sir Henry never properly understood what, exactly, his mission was to be in relation to the British campaign of 1777. In General Burgoyne's "Thoughts . . ." the role that a New York City commander was to specifically undertake in relation to the British campaign of 1777 is not clearly presented; likewise, prior to the commencement of Burgoyne's offensive, Sir Henry never had the opportunity to meet and speak directly with Burgoyne. And no one from England's military high command ever dictated any direct and specific orders to Sir Henry on what he, as a commander, was to undertake in 1777.

Though in "Thoughts . . ." Albany is identified as an objective to be secured for a commander advancing southward from Canada, beyond Albany nothing is specific. In the final analysis "Thoughts . . ." is actually nothing but a discussion of possibilities and alternatives. While Burgoyne does at one point speculate a possible junction with Howe in Albany in order to secure in entirety the Hudson River, nothing in "Thoughts . . ." specifically reveals that a New York City commander should move northward to Albany via the Hudson River or, even, conduct a flanking action via New England. Perhaps Burgoyne assumed that King George and his Ministry would develop a more detailed plan for the conduct of the 1777 campaign and the Ministry would instruct Howe (or whoever would be the New York City commander) on what, exactly, the city's commander was to undertake in relation to this campaign. Regardless, by mid-August Burgoyne was bogged down deep inside the wilderness. Unfortunately for Burgoyne, Canada's Governor-General, Guy Carleton, was very inept in supporting him. Supplies and reinforcement from Canada were barely trickling down to Burgoyne. Suffering from a phobia that the Americans would again invade Canada, Carleton kept strong elements of the British army within Canada proper for its internal defense. Carleton also despised Lord Germain who, in actuality, was Carleton's superior officer. Since Germain was based in London, England, Carleton was not very keen on obeying orders and directives coming from thousands of miles away. Though solely a personal matter, in the end the Carleton-Germain feud would impact itself very negatively upon the entire British campaign of 1777.

Unable to obtain the support he so needed from the north, Burgoyne began to increasingly look southward for assistance; simultaneously, as he searched southward Sir Henry, still an advocate of some type of offensive action to be directed against the patriots amassing to the north of New York City, was looking increasingly northward. Despite his reduced strength, Sir Henry was still willing to undertake a military action to attack the Northern Army's southern front. If successful, such a thrust would benefit not only Burgoyne but, likewise, Sir Henry himself. And as he readied to strike northward through an area just recently proclaimed as West Point, simultaneously, by his actions Sir Henry created an entirely new chapter for the Wilderness War of 1777.

Chapter 2

West Point

Located on the easterly edge of the Appalachian Mountains' Catskill region in a high hill area known as the Hudson High-lands, West Point's name derives from a westerly point protruding eastward into the Hudson River. Shaped millions of years earlier by a massive ice age moving chunks of land into various directions, the area which eventually would make its dramatic impact upon both American and world history stood silent for countless eons. Here, amid the massive, lofty granite rock peaks covered in vegetation and massive trees of a mixed forest, flowed a river southward. Prior to emptying into the Atlantic Ocean its waters circled around a series of islands. In time a major city, known as New York, would arise upon these rocky islands.

For many centuries, the Highlands had solely been the home of numerous species of animals, birds, and fish until, suddenly, one day, human beings appeared. Respecting the flowing waters the first Native American Indian inhabitants of this region named the majestic river as "Great River That Runs Two Ways." Three hundred fifteen miles in length, the origins of this river lie in a tiny lake located in the northwest Adirondack Mountains. Dubbed by the Indians as "Lake Tear of the Clouds," its name remains to this day. As for the mountain which overlooks this lake it was named as "the Cloud Splitter." At 5,344 feet in height, it is now known as Mount Marcy and is the highest peak in New York State.

In the mid-summer of 1609 an English explorer, Henry Hudson, sailing under a Dutch contract and seeking a passage to the South Seas, traveled up this river. In time, this waterway would bear his name. Sailing up the river, the entire crew was awed by the scenic beauty of the river's countryside. Approximately 50 miles to the north the *Half Moon* was forced to negotiate a sharp, 90-degree turn around an island in order to continue its explorative voyage. As the *Half Moon* executed its turn undoubtedly some of its crew, former army and naval military men, noted not only the island but more so the jagged heights overlooking both the river and island. Surely expressions on how this site would be an ideal place for a fort or, even, an entire fortifications system, were heralded.

Exactly how far north Henry Hudson sailed upriver is unknown. Perhaps he reached the site where the present day city of Albany is located; possibly Hudson and some of his crewmen boarded smaller boats and oared farther west on a river presently known as the Mohawk, which flows eastward and is the Hudson River's largest tributary.[1] Other members of the expedition might have even traveled northward into present day Lake Champlain. Failing to find a westward passage, after approximately one month of exploration the *Half Moon* sailed back down the river. As before, it again had to negotiate the 90-degree turn. In future years the river would be known as the "Mauritius" River[2] and "North" River. Despite its various names, by the mid-18th century the river was internationally known as the Hudson River.

In the 17th and 18th centuries Europeans of various ethnicities and people of African heritage began to settle along both banks of the river and the lands adjacent the Hudson's waters. Sizable towns such as Poughkeepsie, Newburgh, Kingston, Hudson, and Albany, along with villages and settlements, appeared. Within a valley referred to as the Hudson Valley[3] many farms, estates, and commercial trading centers came into being and the Hudson River was recognized as being a major transportation and trading route.

Prior to the outbreak of the American Revolutionary War of 1775, excluding a few small forts and block house – type positions built on the Hudson River mostly in the vicinity of Albany, no sizable military fortifications existed. Simply put, no one had ever bothered to construct an elaborate military defensive system anywhere along the river. But within weeks of the first shots being fired at Lexington and Concord in April 1775, this would quickly change. Now, America's patriots and England's ruling officials began to eye the area with increasing concern.

On 25 May 1775, America's recently formed Continental Congress issued six resolutions.[4] Resolution number 2 stated:

> ["Military] Posts be also taken in the Highlands on each side of Hudson's River and batteries erected in such manner as will most effectively prevent any vessels passing up the river."

Along with the Continental Congress' assessment, General George Washington and the newly established New York State Provincial Convention[5] were also eyeing the location. For them, this was the ideal location to establish military fortifications. Indeed, at the outset of the Revolutionary War, General Louis Le Begue Presle Duportail (an officer with engineering skills) warned General Washington "that if the British gained control of the Hudson River, the Americans could not maintain an Army in the field for more than three months."[6] Duportail especially identified the site where the Hudson River takes its sharp 90-degree turn. According to Duportail, this particular location was one of the most critical sites to the entire American Revolutionary War effort. As Duportail emphasized, whoever controlled this terrain would possess such—"the key to the Continent."[7]

In addition to the propaganda and psychological advantages gained by controlling the Hudson River and its valley, the Americans had four other key concerns: military, economic, communications/transportation, and political. Needless to say, each reason was equally important as the other.

Militarily, the British supplied their Iroquois allies, especially the Mohawks, with military and non-military goods and supplies. Usually, these items were delivered into the Mohawk Valley from Canada. But when during a severe winter much of the St. Lawrence River and the shoreline of Lake Ontario froze, a different route was utilized. Now, from New York City, a British port city in colonial America, military cargo destined for the Indians was carried by ship up to Albany and once there, the cargo was transferred onto smaller boats which, in turn, floated up the Mohawk River to pre-selected locations to deliver the supplies.

Economically, British control of the Hudson Valley (along with the Mohawk and Schoharie Valleys) would deny the patriots another vital agricultural region. Various food and fish products; livestock, horses, oxen, lumber and other items essential for livelihood and the newly established American nation, would be in British hands.[8]

Communication/transportation—British control of the Hudson River would deny the patriots a critical communication and transportation route. With the loss of the Hudson River, even if the Mohawk River was still somehow retained by the patriots, it would, nonetheless, be impossible to move critical items for the patriot cause to the other colonies. British control of the Hudson River would also deny the patriots New England's manufactured goods, agricultural products, and its light industrial base.[9]

Politically, British control of the Hudson River-Lake Champlain-Richelieu River complex would totally cut off New England, the bastion of the American Revolution. New England was regarded as the "heart and soul" of the revolution.[10] With the loss of this vital region, America's Revolutionary War effort would be tremendously compromised.

The importance of the river can be seen as evidenced in a 1775 Provincial Congress of New York Report which was also submitted to the Continental Congress:[11]

"If the enemy persists in their plan of subjugating these States to the yoke of Great Britain, they must, in proportion to their knowledge of the country, be more and more convinced of the necessity of their becoming masters of the Hudson River, which will give them the entire command of the water communication with the Indian nations, effectually prevent all intercourse between eastern and southern confederates, divide our strength, and enfeeble every effort for our common preservation and security."

Simultaneously, as the Americans viewed the importance of the Hudson River so, too, did the British Military and its Ministry. In 1775, the British concluded that it was imperative to maintain the Hudson for its operations. Thus, the so-called "Hudson Valley plan" came into existence.[12]

"Isolate her, and the rest of the colonies will come to their senses. Isolate her, therefore, by striking north from New York and south from Lake Champlain to seize control of the crossings of the Hudson. Then the [British] army in Canada can be used in an offensive role. Afterwards New England may be invaded on a broad front from the rear, in conjunction with a force from Rhode Island."

Despite patriot efforts to fortify the Hudson River in the vicinity of West Point, in the opening years of the Revolutionary War very little was done. A lack of time, resources, money, manpower, and skilled military engineers hampered, for the time being, all efforts. Critical events outside of the area, such as those on Long Island, New Jersey, Pennsylvania, the Lake Champlain area, and Canada, also tremendously slowed and, even, sometimes totally suspended any efforts to properly fortify West Point.

SEPTEMBER 1775

Early that month Mr. Bernard Romans,[13] a botanist and engineer by profession, was tasked to design a fortification system for West Point. Accompanied by several New York Commissioners, the four journeyed to the Highlands. Obtaining a boat, they rowed up and down the river in the vicinity of present day West Point to study the area. Needing a place to stay overnight, the four moved into an abandoned farmhouse[14] on Martalaer's Rock[15] which is actually a sizable rock island[16] on the Hudson River and where the river takes its 90-degree turn. By the time the Wilderness War of 1777 would erupt, Martalaer's Rock would be renamed as Constitution Island.[17]

Despite Romans' best efforts, his designs were largely useless. Romans totally ignored the idea of placing any type of obstacles into the water. He chose Constitution Island to be the center of the main fortress. On and adjacent to this island a huge fort, a so-called "Grand Bastion" was to be constructed. Sixty-one cannons and twenty swivel guns were to be integrated into a total of eleven batteries and blockhouses within this "Grand Bastion."[18] These various defensive positions would be constructed on the island and on the eastern and western sides of the Hudson River adjacent the island. Barracks, storerooms, a guard house, and an ammunition magazine were also to be established.[19] Romans calculated that 150 men, within a period of four months, would be able to construct the defensive system he planned[20] at a cost of 6,000 pounds.[21]

Clearly, Romans' calculations revealed his lack of knowledge on what it truly takes to construct an effective fortifications system. Because his "Grand Bastion" was to be protected by an outer rock wall measuring 30 feet in thickness, 18 feet in height and about 500 feet in length[22] this, in itself, would take many months to construct. Upon departure, the three commissioners expressed serious reservations about Romans' abilities.

NOVEMBER 1775

Throughout the fall of 1775, as Romans was busy putting his fortifications into place and was requesting from the Continental Congress a direct promotion to a colonel's rank,[23] others were also viewing West Point and its area. Various New York Provincial Convention State members[24] along with individuals authorized by the American Continental Congress arrived into the area. These visitors wanted to determine what, exactly, was going on and what, exactly, was needed to be done. Such was the case on 17 November 1775 when three members of the Continental Congress arrived on Constitution Island to investigate the situation.[25]

Encountering Romans and approximately 200 soldiers and laborers[26] the three noted that other than one completed blockhouse and some barracks on Constitution Island, nothing else had been done. As for the "Grand Bastion," at best it was only in its rudimentary stage. Embarrassed that so little had been done Romans assured the three "that only a little more time was needed."[27] But clearly, this would not be the case.

Though none of the three were military men,[28] they immediately identified serious weaknesses in Romans' defensive system. Of the approximately 71 cannons of various calibers found,[29] the inspectors noted that of the guns positioned on Constitution Island not one was capable of engaging an enemy vessel until the ship was almost upon the island; furthermore, though Constitution Island's center mass rose about 40 feet in height above the river, the terrain lying directly westward across the river overlooked the entire island. Though previously Romans had proposed to establish some small batteries across on the higher terrain to protect both the island and that part of the river, as of this date none had been built. The investigating commissioners also concluded that even if any batteries had been constructed it would not matter because such weakly manned and unsupported batteries could easily be overrun. In reality, it would actually require a fort and not just some batteries to effectively protect both the river and the so-called "Grand Bastion" or, otherwise, the "Grand Bastion" would be exposed to massive fire from the overlooking heights.

Though Romans insisted on defending Constitution Island, from local residents the commissioners learned that just several miles to the south of Constitution Island where the Hudson River first narrows into a southwesterly and, then, suddenly veers into a southeasterly direction, the location is much more suitable for constructing defensive positions. One particular sight identified stood just to the northeast of a hill named as Bear Hill. Adjacent this hill flows a creek. Named as the Popolopen Creek, the waters of this creek flowed eastward and tumbled over the Hudson River's western bank directly into the river. And here, right above the creek, a fort would effectively block an entire stretch of the river. As the proponents of this location stated:[30]

> "At Pooploop's Kill [Popolopen Creek], opposite Anthony's Nose, it is a very important pass: the river narrow, commanded a way up and down, full of counter currents, and subject to almost constant fall winds; nor is there any anchorage at all, except close under the works to be erected."

That same month, the investigating team submitted a very disturbing report to America's Continental Congress. Citing that Romans' fortification designs were totally ineffective[31] the investigators also specified that an engineer with military knowledge was needed.

In response, Congress immediately dispatched a quick message to Colonel Henry Knox, General George Washington's Chief of Artillery, to take a closer look at the fortifications. But before the message was delivered to where Knox was staying in New York City, the artillery colonel had just passed through the Highlands en route to Fort Ticonderoga.

DECEMBER 1775

The Continental Congress decided on three courses of action: 1) Constitution Island would be fortified but on a reduced scale; 2) a large fort would be constructed on the northern side of Popolopen Creek and, 3) Bernard Romans was to be immediately relieved of duty.[32]

JANUARY 1776

On 5 January, the Continental Congress resolved that "no farther fortifications be erected at Marter's Rock, on Hudson's River, and that a point at Popolopen's Kill [creek] on the said [Popolopen] river, be without delay effectually fortified [with a fort]."[33] As for the new fort to be erected, it was to be named Fort Montgomery in honor of the American Continental Army general, Richard Montgomery, who was killed in action on 31 December 1775 while attacking Quebec. Other than the one fort to be constructed, nothing else was to be built. This explains why when the Wilderness War of 1777 raged along much of the lower Hudson River "there was not much at West Point."[34]

Chapter 3

The First Battles of the Wilderness War of 1777

Prior to examining Sir Henry's northerly thrust against the patriot Northern Army in October, 1777, it is important to first understand the sequence of events which occurred in and around the Highlands, New York City, Westchester, and Orange Counties, and the regions to the west and east of New York City.[1]

OCTOBER 1776

Directly to the north of New York City was located Fort Independence.[2] In October, this fort[3] was abandoned by the retreating patriots.[4] Occupied by the British, it was strengthened and incorporated into the British defense system ringing New York City.

JANUARY 1777

Major General William Heath, a Reserve Continental Army officer accompanied with militia General John Morin Scott, launched a sizable attack against British positions to the north of New York City. What motivated these two generals to attack is not known because neither General George Washington, the Commander in Chief of all of the continental, militia, and irregular forces, nor the Northern Army's headquarters in Albany, had ordered any kind of offensive action against the city. Perhaps, General Washington's winter offensive against Trenton and Princeton was a stimulating factor; possibly, the attack was conducted for psychological reasons. Or, simply, maybe at the very moment the two generals had nothing better to do and decided to harass the British in New York City.

Two objectives were targeted by the patriots—Fort Independence and Valentine Hill upon which stood the Valentine mansion. Valentine's home,[5] a sizable and comfortable mansion, stood not far from Fort Independence. Valentine Mansion was also occupied with British and Hessian troops and several outposts ringed the hill.

Moving rapidly, General Scott overran Valentine Hill, captured the outposts, and secured the mansion; simultaneously, General Heath attacked Fort Independence. Though repulsed at Fort Independence, the generals laid siege to it. Day and night for several days they pounded the fort with their several cannons. Unable to capture the fort and noting that the British were bringing up a strong reinforcement, Generals Scott and Heath withdrew. As for Valentine Hill, the captured site was abandoned and the mansion was reoccupied by British forces.

It is recorded that when the patriots withdrew they could hear the taunts of the British defenders mocking them. Regardless, the British also heard the patriot cry of "WE'LL BE BACK!" Of historical significance is that the shots fired by the American patriots in January 1777, were not only the very first ones to be fired that year in the soon to be created New York State but, likewise, these shots heralded the beginning of the Wilderness War of 1777.

MARCH 1777

Before the last snows of 1777 had melted, Howe undertook a series of minor—but quite significant—military raids against the patriots. These raids were undertaken to weaken the patriots, secure vital food stuffs, and deceive General Washington as to what the British were up to. Commencing in March, such raids would characterize much of the activities of 1777.

THURSDAY, 6 MARCH

Meeting in Kingston, an old quaint town located between the Highlands and Albany and designated to be the state's capital, the Convention of Representatives of the State of New York passed an act allowing state officials to confiscate the properties of all known loyalists. Seized properties would be put up for sale and all proceeds would be used to help finance the war for independence.

One of those affected by this act was the loyalist Beverley Robinson. Until recently, Robinson had been residing in his stately manor house very near West Point in the Highlands. Patriot activities, however, had forced him to flee with his family down to New York City. For his loyalty to the King, Robinson was commissioned as a colonel and he began to raise a loyalist combat unit titled as "The New York Volunteers." In the meantime, as this was happening, Robinson's home was being utilized as a headquarters for the Northern Army's Highland – based forces.

SATURDAY, 22 MARCH

Forty miles to the immediate north of New York City on the right bank of the Hudson River in the vicinity of the Highlands lay the town of Peekskill. Knowing that patriot arms were stored at that location and informed that the garrison's troop strength was low, General Howe ordered a raid against the site. Approximately 500 British soldiers augmented with loyalists moved upriver via boat against the targeted area.[6]

SUNDAY, 23 MARCH

After disembarking in Lents Cove to the south of Peekskill and securing the strategic high ground known as Drum Hill which overlooked both the Hudson River and Peekskill, the raiders attacked the town.[7] At this time Peekskill was under the jurisdiction of the Highlands command. Brigadier General Alexander McDougall, who assumed command of the

Highlands just days before on 12 March,[8] held responsibility for the entire region. But with only about 220 continental soldiers in Peekskill comprised from McDougall's headquarters, the 2nd and 4th New York Continental Regiments and one independent detachment,[9] General McDougall ordered them to retreat northward.[10] Though not tremendously outnumbered McDougall feared that in the event the continentals would be destroyed, the Highlands would lose a valuable force. Prior to pulling out, the patriots destroyed a large portion of the supplies.[11]

One of the key players in this engagement was Lieutenant–Colonel Marinus Willett. When the British attacked, Willett, along with the 3rd New York Continental Regiment, was stationed at Fort Constitution. Because the regiment's commanding officer, Colonel Peter Gansevoort, was absent during this period, Willett, who was second in command, led.

According to Willett, as his troops were parading for a review[12] an express rider suddenly galloped in with an urgent message from General McDougall. Informing Willett that a very large enemy force had just landed near Peekskill and was advancing against that town, the general ordered Willett to rendezvous with him in the vicinity of Peekskill. Without even breaking formation, Willett's troops immediately departed the parade ground and marched in McDougall's direction. En route, Willett spotted several burning houses in the distance while his scouts reported that the British had positioned one of their units far forward of Peekskill. Linking up with the Highlands commander, Willett proposed to immediately attack the forward unit and, once overrun, engage the entire British force jointly with the troops McDougall had on hand.

McDougall, however, refused. Citing that he would not attack until the local militia unit which he had ordered would appear to reinforce his Highland force, McDougall just sat and observed the enemy from a safe distance. As for the militiamen, they never appeared.

Finally, at sunset, McDougall consented to an attack. Though successfully undertaken little time was left, and the heavy darkness settling in masked the fleeing enemy. In the ensuing engagement the patriots inflicted 15 casualties.[13] Regarding the action, Willett remained forever convinced that had an attack been launched sooner, the entire British force could have been routed. By waiting for the militia reinforcement, valuable time had been lost.

Of interest is that during the attack a blue Camelot cloak cape, belonging to a British army officer, was found by Captain Abraham Swarthout, one of Willett's company commanders.[14] Returning back to Fort Constitution, they took this cloak with them. Shortly after, when the 3rd New York Regiment deployed to Fort Stanwix the cloak was brought along as well. And on 3 August 1777, when the British and their allied forces began to besiege Fort Stanwix and its patriot defenders suddenly realized that no American flag was on hand, Fort Stanwix's female defenders immediately sewed one together. Among the material utilized for the flag was the blue cloth from the Camelot cloak secured previously at Peekskill.[15]

TUESDAY, 25 MARCH

Angry about their losses and inability to destroy the Americans, the British withdrew to New York City. Prior to leaving Peekskill the raiders swarmed over much of the countryside torching various sites and looting indiscriminately.[16] Of historical significance was that in the Colony of New York, Peekskill would be the first settled area to undergo a vicious attack in 1777. But by no means would Peekskill be an exception. Before the Wilderness War of 1777 would conclude, there would be many more Peekskills.

MONDAY, 7 APRIL

In a letter dated 7 April and titled "Complaints of the Commissioners that Westchester County is in a Dismal

Condition and the Continental has Suffered in Consequence," Mr. Richard Hatfield, a New York State Secretary to Brigadier General George Clinton (soon to be elected as the first governor of New York State), wrote to Clinton how "Our [Westchester] county is in a Dismal situation." Mr. Hatfield was referring to the lawlessness and cattle rustling and food thievery undertaken by criminal gangs such as the so-called "Cowboys" and "Skinners" operating in the region between New York City and the Highlands:[17]

> "The Tories our Inveterate foes have been busy for the space of a fortnight in driving off Cattle and horses; last Friday night a drove of 40 fatt Cattle were driven thro' Rye. We doubt not during the above mentioned space of time 500 Cattle and horses have been driven to the Enemy; ourselves and good friends are much exposed to the Cruel and merciless outrages of the Enemy."

Mr. Hatfield also warned:

> "We doubt not that many of a week [weak] Resolution have Desrted to the Enemy from the weakness of our forces that would otherwise have been of service to our Cause."[18]

Seeking assistance to curb this lawlessness, the secretary stated that members of the State Commission were in need of military assistance. As Hatfield cited in his letter:

> "We, therefore, hope and earnestly Intreat, the favour of your affording us and the well affected inhabitants, Relief, by ordering down Immediately [from West Point and the Northern Army] a sufficient Number of Forces to Enable us to do our duty, and to Cutt of all Communication from the Enemy."[19]

TUESDAY, 15 APRIL

Mr. Philip Field, a resident of Dutchess County and a patriot of African descent, appeared at West Point to join the Northern Army. That day, he was placed into the newly forming 2nd New York Regiment. During this time another black male, recruit Peter Williams, defied his loyalist master and fled into the ranks of the patriots. In the case of Williams, he possessed an intimate knowledge about the various pro-British loyalist units and gangs such as the "Cowboys" and "Skinners" operating in the region to the south of West Point, including their personalities, strengths, and thievery tactics. Armed with the vital information brought in by Williams, West Point's patriots would soon conduct a series of very successful operations in the region between New York City and West Point to destroy this loyalist and criminal threat.

FRIDAY, 18 APRIL

On this day, the Highlands, patriot defenders placed an iron chain across the Hudson River between Fort Montgomery and a piece of ground dubbed as Anthony's Nose. Approximately 1,650 feet in length, the chain's iron links were held together and reinforced by cables, log buoys, sizable eyelets which the chain links were inserted through, and anchors. In itself, the chain floated on a series of rafts tied tightly together but loose enough to float and bounce on the river's water. Since an obstacle is totally useless if not protected by covering fire, this entire chain was protected by cannons positioned on the higher terrain overlooking the river.

WEDNESDAY, 23 APRIL

Escorted by two British war ships, a combined British-loyalist force departed for the area of Fairfield, Connecticut. Their main target was the town of Danbury, a vital patriot depot.

FRIDAY, 25 APRIL

In the evening hours between 9 p.m. and 11 p.m., a British force of 2,000 strong comprised of 300 loyalists from Brown's

Provincial Regiment, 250 British troops from each of the following units: 4th Foot, 5th Foot, 23rd Foot, 27th Foot, 44th Foot, and the 64th Foot, along with about 200 dragoon and cannoner soldiers,[20] landed near Fairfield, Connecticut. Howe's actions were also based on orders received from Lord Germain stipulating that King George III wanted a series of attacks into New England.[21] The intent of these attacks was to slow the recruiting of manpower for the Continental Armies, put a halt to the patriot privateers who, by 1777, were creating serious problems for both the Royal Navy and England's merchant fleet, to tie down sizable rebel (patriot) forces along or near the coast, destroy military targets, and secure food and animals needed by the British, German, and loyalist occupants of New York City. As a result of this directive another—but much larger—British raid was launched against the Connecticut towns of Ridgefield and Danbury. Ridgefield stood about 1 mile across the New York border and Danbury several miles farther up, and about 30 miles to the northeast of West Point. Here, within this Ridgefield-Danbury area, heavy fighting took place from 25–28 April.

SATURDAY, 26 – SUNDAY, 27 APRIL

By the morning of 2 a.m. on 27 April, a force of 100 continentals and 500 militia fighters including a small company of continental artillerymen with 3 cannons led by Colonel John Lamb[22] had assembled in Bethel,[23] a village approximately 4 miles southeast of Danbury and 60 miles northeast of New York City. At the crack of dawn on Saturday, the raiders commenced a quick march of about 23 miles to the town of Danbury. The commanding officer of the Danbury raid was Governor General Tryon. Two British army generals, General James Agnew, and General Sir William "Woolly" Erskine, accompanied Tryon. Occupying Danbury with 50 continental soldiers and elements of the 16th Connecticut Militia was Colonel Jedediah Huntington. Noting the strength of the incoming enemy force, Huntington immediately ordered a retreat into the nearby hills;

however, seven militia volunteer fighters remained behind to buy time for Huntington's retreat. Concealing themselves in various buildings, they engaged the raiders with sniper fire and for a short time succeeded in harassing and slowing the raiders. Eventually, all seven were killed. Among the fallen was a militia fighter registered as "Ned." Of African descent and armed with a rifle, Ned was one of those who requested to stay behind to engage the British.

In a related operation, a number of British ships sailed up the Hudson River to Dobbs Ferry. Located about 30 miles to the south of West Point, Dobbs Ferry was a critical ferry point connecting together New York, Connecticut, and New Jersey. But upon arrival to this site no one was disembarked and, for a couple of days, the British naval force just stood in place. Possibly, it was just a diversionary action undertaken to keep West Point's military in place.

As news of the British attack reached far and wide one of the most notable and colorful figures of the Wilderness War of 1777, Brigadier General Benedict Arnold, came galloping in on his horse. Prior to his sudden appearance, General Arnold had been in New Haven, Connecticut. Upset and angry about being denied a promotion, Arnold was actually contemplating resigning from patriot service. Encountering militia Generals David Wooster, Connecticut's top commanding militia officer, and Gold S. Silliman, a regional militia commander in Bethel, the three formulated a battle plan.

Informed of the British raid into Connecticut, 16-year-old Sybil Ludington, the daughter of Northern Army Colonel Henry Ludington, immediately saddled her horse and throughout the very rainy and late evening and night hours of 26–27 April, rode a distance of over 40 miles to warn the local populace and various militia units of the incoming raiders. Her actions resulted in a quick mobilization of the region's manpower.[24]

In the meantime General McDougall, with 1,200 continentals from West Point,[25] crossed the Hudson and Croton Rivers. Suspecting that the Danbury raiding force might possibly withdraw to the ships off Dobbs Ferry, near the town of Bedford, McDougall commenced a forced march toward that location. Located on the edge of New York State, Bedford was situated to the southwest of Ridgefield but just northeast of Dobbs Ferry. McDougall reasoned that from Bedford he would be able to intercept any retiring enemy force. In the event the British decided to bypass Bedford and withdraw to the port towns of Norwalk, Greenwich, or Rye Neck, from Bedford McDougall would also be within striking range to intercept them.

In his attempt to seize and destroy the British force General Arnold, accompanying Silliman's 400 militiamen, blocked a narrow road to the south of Danbury; simultaneously, Wooster and 200 militiamen established a blocking position on an adjacent road also leading to the coast.[26]

Unknown to the patriots was that Tryon was no longer in Danbury. After seizing Danbury and destroying 19 dwellings, 22 barns and storehouses, and various military stores such as its 1,600 tents,[27] Tryon quickly withdrew. Utilizing a different route than the one selected to approach Danbury, Tryon's force fell back via Ridgefield. When the patriot generals realized that Tryon was actually to their south and retiring back to the coast, Generals Arnold, Silliman, and Wooster commenced a vigorous pursuit to overtake and capture Tryon. Being the aggressive commander that he was, Arnold took the brunt of Silliman's force and, by marching rapidly around the British, reached Ridgefield and quickly established here a blocking position to hold the raiders in place. In the meantime Silliman began to flank the British from both sides while Wooster approached from behind to attack the enemy rear. En route to Ridgefield, Arnold was joined by another 100 local militiamen.[28] Reinforced to a strength of nearly five hundred,[29] Arnold was now blocking the main road to Ridgefield. As for Tryon, he was retiring very slowly because his force was burdened with a sizable herd of cattle, sheep, goats, and horses secured in and around Danbury. Fresh meat, after all, was desperately needed in New York City.

North of Ridgefield, Silliman and Wooster finally caught up with the raiding force and a running gun battle ensued. As gunfire raged between the raiders and the patriots Tryon's leading element made contact with Arnold's force which was blocking the road, and more militiamen and even armed women poured into the battle area. Sniping from houses, barns, rooftops, trees, and from behind rock walls, they harassed the raiders.

The fighting became close-in. Animals scattered. Others, struck by gunfire, collapsed to the ground. Here and there a building burned. Amidst the constant shouts of orders and the massive sounds of gunfire the screams of the dying—both men and animals—were heard far and wide.

Struck in the head, General Wooster went down. Galloping right up to the British vanguard, Arnold's horse was shot.[30] Collapsing to the ground, the horse pinned the patriot general underneath its weight. As he worked to free himself, Arnold noted a scream and glancing upward, spotted a British soldier with a bayonet mounted on his musket charging rapidly toward him. Quickly reaching for the pistol tucked underneath his cape Arnold raised it up and fired a red hot ball deep into the charging mass. Falling instantly, the soldier never again stood up. Finally extracting himself from underneath the horse, Arnold stood up and began to command on foot.

With fixed bayonets, the British pressed forward and struck with true élan! Breaking through the patriot defense line, the British continued forward. Unable to hold them, Arnold ordered a retreat to Norwalk.

With Wooster's death at the rear, no other leader assumed command and a collapse ensued in that sector. Sensing a weakness, the British shifted much of their rear guard toward their front and flanks. Keeping Silliman's militia at bay, the raiders entered Ridgefield and decided to stay overnight. Intermittent gunfire raged through the night. It had truly been an exhaustive affair.

MONDAY, 28 APRIL

At the crack of dawn, Tryon's force continued its retreat southward. Undoubtedly, Tryon now had his regrets that he had ventured so far from New York City, for he knew that if the patriots ever caught him he probably would be executed. Knowing that the nearest British outpost was still many miles away and during the previous evening and night hours more patriots had appeared, the raiding force retired hastily. Connecticut's governor, Mr. Jonathan Trumbull, Sr., who played an instrumental role in recruiting Connecticut volunteers for the Northern Army, ordered all militiamen west of the Connecticut River[31] to immediately mobilize. Colonel Huntington reappeared with his continentals[32] and many more armed men and women, individually or in small groups, likewise made their presence. These fighters hailed from various parts of Connecticut, eastern New York, and from as far as Hartford. By 28 April, an estimated strength of no less than 2,500 to 4,000 continentals, militiamen, and armed citizens were on hand.[33] This strength, however, did not include McDougall's 1,200 continentals approaching rapidly from the west. Concluding correctly on 28 April that the British ships off Dobbs Ferry were solely there to create a diversion and they posed no threat, McDougall abandoned Bedford and commenced a forced march to reach the main battle area.

Despite General Arnold's best efforts, he could not halt the British force from reaching the shoreline. As the raiders neared the beach to board their ships, they were met by a group of Royal Marines well-positioned with cannons upon Compo Hill, a terrain feature overlooking the debarkation site, just west of present day Westport, Connecticut; simultaneously, cannon fire from the guns of the ships provided additional covering fire for Tryon's withdrawing force. Realizing that the key to capturing the retiring British force, now rowing back to their ships, was the seizure of Compo Hill, General Arnold ordered an immediate attack upon it. But as the militiamen fell under the combined fire of those positioned upon Compo Hill, those manning the ships and a spirited bayonet counterattack charge by 400 regular British troops under General Erskine, they lost their will to attack. Satisfied that they had repulsed the raiders and seeking no further action, the militiamen even began to retire. As Arnold raved, the British rowed away and the Great Raid against Danbury was now history.[34] Other than some minor skirmishing and the war between the Cowboys and Skinners to the north of New York City, for the time being both the New England and southern fronts remained quiet until the fall of 1777.

TUESDAY, 29 APRIL

Marching into Danbury, McDougall learned that the raiders had departed and were somewhere on Long Island Sound. Realizing there was nothing more that he could do, McDougall issued the order to retire back to the Highlands and West Point.

THURSDAY, 1 MAY – SATURDAY, 31 MAY

Fed up with the criminality and the lawlessness exhibited by the various criminal gangs operating between New York City and the Northern Army's positions in the vicinity of West Point, the Highlands–based patriot army command decided to intervene.[35] Throughout that month a series of anti-gang operations were undertaken to annihilate once and for all the region's criminals but especially the Cowboys and Skinners. By these actions the patriots would restore law and order into a lawless region, eliminate the gangs terrorizing their fellow countrymen who were simply trying to live in a crime–free environment, restore an honest trading economy which would benefit not only the local residents and the newly established nation but, likewise, the military garrison at West Point and, a

military action against the gangs would afford the army continental and militia units stationed in the Highlands some combat
experience. Of historical significance is that 1777 was the year
when the United States Army utilized for the very first time its
forces in combating lawlessness and organized crime syndicates.

In conjunction with local militia forces and armed citizens,
the Northern Army's regular Continental Army regiments based
in West Point commenced their operations within a region
referred to as the "Neutral Ground." Among the participants
who fought the outlaws was a continental soldier named George
Robert Twelve Hewes. Affectionately known as R.T., nearly
twenty years earlier, in 1758, R.T. wanted to join the British
army. Physical health problems, however, precluded him from
doing so. Adopting the patriot cause, R.T. was a participant of
the Boston Tea Party. In its aftermath, he returned to his home
in New York City. When the city fell to the British in 1776
R.T., fearing arrest, fled northward to Albany where he joined
the Northern Army. Soon after, he was assigned to West Point.
Serving alongside R.T. was a corporal by the name of "Robert
Shurtleff." Shurtleff's real name, however, was Deborah Sampson.
Marching into the so-called "No Man's Land" with her continental compatriots to battle the Cowboys, Deborah's regiment
engaged a group of outlaws not far from Peekskill. Firing her
musket, she shot and killed one of the outlaws. Noting another
outlaw standing nearby and lacking time to reload, she charged
him with the bayonet. In the ensuing fight, she suffered a saber
blow to her left cheek. She recovered and won the Purple Heart
award but a facial scar remained for life.[36] Another soldier who
set off to engage and destroy the gangs was William Stewart, "a
Colored man" born about 1759 in Brunswick County, Virginia.
Enlisting in 1777 in North Carolina, soon after Stewart marched
off to West Point where he began his military service, he was
among a number of other African Americans who voluntarily
served and fought that year in the Northern Army.[37]

By the conclusion of 1777, both the Cowboys and Skinners were finished. Greed and internal gang rivalry, along with measures taken by the Northern Army, shattered the gangs. Its survivors fled to New York City or scattered to other regions. The meat and food products were preserved for the patriot effort and in the aftermath of the anti-crime operations, very little meat or other food products came into New York City from the northern region.[38]

That month, West Point was visited by Margaretha Farges. Born in poor health, Margaretha barely survived her childhood. At a very young age, Farges quickly adopted the Revolutionary cause. In the 1760's she was affiliated with the so-called "Daughters of Liberty," a loose-knit women's organization espousing total separation from England and the establishment of an independent American nation. From the vicinity of the Highlands at West Point to Fort Edward at the base of the Adirondack Mountains, and westward into the Mohawk Valley, throughout the summer and fall of 1777 Margaretha hitched rides in wagons, walked, and travelled on horseback. Carrying a large leather suitcase filled with copies of the Declaration of Independence and literature supportive of the American Revolution and Independence, wherever Margaretha journeyed she distributed her material. Throughout the towns and settlements within and near the wilderness areas, her voice was often heard as she read the Declaration of Independence in public. A fiery patriot, she encouraged one-and-all to support the patriot cause, to render whatever support they could and never to waver . . . "FOR VICTORY IS NEAR!" A strong supporter of the Northern Army, Margaretha frequently promoted the new nation's ideals and aspirations to its soldiers.

Though she witnessed the wilderness victory of 1777 and lived to see the final victory of 1783, her health continued to decline. In 1783, she passed away at the age of 29.

As the Wilderness War of 1777 raged and the Cowboys and Skinners fought amongst themselves prior to being finished off by the Northern Army, another war was also under way: the so-called "Yankee-Pennamite War."[39] Commencing in 1769, it finally concluded in 1807.

The background of this conflict stemmed from Connecticut's claim of transcontinental control from the Atlantic to the Pacific Ocean or, as many put it at the time "from sea to sea." Along with its claim, Connecticut also imposed various restrictions, rules, and frontier regulations.

Yet, despite Connecticut's best efforts to impose its authority, neither the inhabitants of southern New York State nor those of Pennsylvania accepted Connecticut's authority. This was especially so with those residing in the region of the Susquehanna River and the Wyoming Valley.[40]

Another contributing factor to this conflict was the Susquehanna Company. Organized in 1753 in Connecticut to exploit Connecticut's land claims, in 1754 the company purchased the Wyoming Valley from the Six Nation Iroquois Indian Confederacy.

Pennsylvania, however, refused to acknowledge this land purchase. Pennsylvania claimed the Wyoming Valley territory belonged to them as a result of a land grant made in 1681 by the founder of Pennsylvania, William Penn, and that in 1768, Pennsylvania had also negotiated a treaty with the Six Nation Iroquois; therefore, Pennsylvania's officials cited that its 1768 treaty had voided any treaties previously made by Connecticut such as the one in 1754.[41] Pennsylvania also formally announced that as of 1768, Connecticut no longer held any authority either in the Wyoming Valley or in southern New York State.

Determined to enforce what they felt was their territory, Connecticut, via its Susquehanna Company, refused to honor Pennsylvania's claims. Various disputes arose between the two states, especially pertaining to the issue of how Connecticut was bringing in so-called "Yankee" settlers to reside in the disputed region and take land away from the so-called "Pennamite" residents of Pennsylvania. Though most of these settlers hailed from Connecticut, others also arrived from New Jersey, eastern Pennsylvania and New York.

In 1769, determined to halt Connecticut's expansion and to demonstrate its authority, Pennsylvania's officials formed a military force to halt the intrusion of Connecticut's desires; in turn, to counter Pennsylvania's force, Connecticut organized military forces under the command of Captain Zebulon Butler, a seasoned veteran of the French-Indian War who served as a representative of the Wyoming Valley in the Connecticut Assembly and was one of the directors of the Susquehanna Company. From the period of 1769 to 1775 heated disputes marked with occasional violence characterized the region.[42]

For America's young Continental Congress, the Yankee-Pennamite War was a very serious matter. The newly established American nation could not afford an internal conflict within its midst. With Connecticut and Pennsylvania at war, America's Continental Armies would be denied manpower and critical resources; likewise, England could exploit this conflict to their military-political advantage. Approaching the disputing parties Congress succeeded, for the time being, in establishing a temporary ceasefire and truce.

In 1777, the Yankee-Pennamite War was not fought. Between the critical events wrapped around the Wilderness War and Howe's invasion of Pennsylvania, for the time being such activities overshadowed the Connecticut-Pennsylvania conflict. Tensions, however, remained strong.[43]

Chapter 4

June-July-August-September, 1777

In early June the 1st[1], 2nd[2], 4th[3], and 5th[4] New York Continental Regiments were based in the Highlands.[5] These regiments encompassed the 1st New York Continental Brigade.[6] As for Colonel Peter Gansevoort's 3rd New York Regiment,[7] weeks earlier the Northern Army had ordered this regiment to deploy to Fort Stanwix to assist in the defense of the western frontier. It also deployed because skirmishing between pro-American settlers versus loyalists and Indians allied for[8] or against[9] the revolution was on the rise. Another unit in place was the 14th Massachusetts Regiment. This regiment, however, was not a part of the 1st New York Continental Brigade.

That same month Generals George Clinton and Israel Putnam proceeded to establish a strong river flotilla. Three ships were quickly organized: the *Congress, Montgomery,* and *Shark.* The mission of these ships was to protect the chain spanning the Hudson River, support the forts on shore, protect patriot shipping, counter enemy shipping, and prevent enemy vessels from sailing far up the Hudson River. But problems immediately arose.

Congress was still in Poughkeepsie. The *Montgomery* had no guns. And the *Shark* lacked a captain. All three ships lacked qualified crewmen. A vigorous recruitment effort was undertaken in an attempt to obtain competent river seamen and continental and militiamen were screened for river duty.[10]

The month of June was characterized by recruiting military personnel and civilian workers (especially blacksmiths and carpenters) for the defense and construction of the Highlands. Needing more military personnel, nine militia units were mobilized for the time being to assist.[11] The construction of Fort Montgomery, along with the establishment of a river fleet and the laying of the very first river chain obstacle from the shoreline below Fort Montgomery across the river, took on a priority. Money matters, for pay purposes and to buy iron for additional chains, were addressed and that same month General George Clinton was campaigning for governor of the newly established New York State with the election scheduled for mid-June.[12]

MONDAY, 30 JUNE

General George Washington ordered General Israel "Old Put" Putnam, who had assumed command of the Highlands on 12 May 1777, to "let no pains be spared to complete the Booms."[13] Though one river chain obstacle was already in place, Washington wanted more river obstacles. To what extent General Washington was conferring with the commander of the Northern Army, General Philip Schuyler, about blocking the Hudson River, is not known. But it is known that Schuyler, very concerned about the Northern Army's southern sector, upon receiving reports that the ideal site for impeding the Hudson River was in the vicinity of Fort Montgomery, immediately ordered that the Hudson River be blocked at this location.[14]

THURSDAY, 3 JULY

A final tally of the votes revealed that General George Clinton won the governor's election. On 7 July, just one day after the fall of Fort Ticonderoga, General George Clinton formally learned that he had been elected as governor of the state.[15] On 30 July, General Clinton was summoned to Kingston to take the oath of office as the first governor of New York. Of historical significance is that although the election was held under very difficult circumstances amidst the Wilderness War of 1777, it was still successfully accomplished.[16]

SATURDAY, 12 JULY

Militia Brigadier General John Nixon with his 600 fighters arrived in Albany from Peekskill. Soon, he would be followed with General John Glover's 14th Massachusetts Continental Regiment. Previously referred to as the 21st Massachusetts (Sailor) Regiment,[17] this crack Continental Army regiment had been transferred in the spring of 1777 from Washington's main army into the Northern Army and initially was posted into the Highlands. Needless to say, the transfer of these two units from the Highlands to the northern front only further weakened the patriot defense system in the Highlands.[18]

THURSDAY, 17 JULY

Informed of Burgoyne's success, General Howe dispatched a congratulatory letter to Burgoyne. But Howe also stipulated that he would be heading southward into Pennsylvania. Orders were issued to load the boats. The date of departure was set for 23 July.

MONDAY, 21 JULY

A messenger with a letter from Burgoyne arrived in New York City with news and details on how Fort Ticonderoga had been captured.[19] Howe was delighted. But Sir Henry feared that this would only further intensify Howe's desire to attack into Pennsylvania. Since everything was supposedly going well for Burgoyne, for the moment there was no urgent need to conduct a northerly advance toward Burgoyne and Albany. Needless to say, Sir Henry's fears were not unwarranted. Responding to Burgoyne's letter, Howe again congratulated him but, as he did four days previously on 17 July, Howe again reiterated that he would be heading southward.

WEDNESDAY, 23 JULY

On this day a number of key events occurred.

While roaming through the countryside of Popolopen Creek,[20] General (and Governor) George Clinton came upon a hilly knoll overlooking the Hudson River. Climbing upon the knoll, the patriot leader turned to the north and, immediately, was shocked! Approximately half-a-mile directly to his front stood Fort Montgomery. Though the fort was being constructed on rugged terrain rising 100 feet above the western edge of the Hudson River, from where Clinton stood he was actually looking down upon the fort.[21] Returning to Fort Montgomery, General Clinton immediately tasked 167 soldiers to begin clearing the hilltop in preparation for the construction of a new fort, and the governor dispatched a letter to General George Washington of the flaw.[22] As for the new fort, it would be named as Fort Clinton.

On this same day, a patriot troop strength revealed these figures: Fort Clinton registered a strength of 167; Fort Montgomery 174; Fort Constitution 180; and Fort Independence 112.[23] These figures, however, did not include the sick, those on furlough, those absent with or without authorization, the deserted, or those attached for a period of time to some other unit outside the area. These figures also changed on a daily basis.

As the sun set over the peaceful Atlantic Ocean on 23 July, General Howe's army was sailing southward. Howe was off to destroy Washington and capture Pennsylvania, leaving Sir Henry behind with only a token force to garrison a sizable city and the area adjacent to it. The moment the first ships pulled away Sir Henry, perhaps, sensed that this would not only commence the beginning of the end of the British campaign of 1777 but, worse, the end of England's Imperial rule in the New World.[24]

SATURDAY, 26 JULY

General Washington wrote to General George Clinton in response to his letter of 23 July. Regarding Clinton's observation,

Washington added "...the Hill, which overlooks the Fort [Montgomery], I think it ought to be taken possession of Immediately." To support this project, Washington also wrote that "I have sent up Lieutenant Machin[25] to lay out and oversee such Works as shall be tho't necessary by the officers there ..." and "I must leave it with you to erect such Works as you, with Col. Clinton's and the Engineer [Machin] may think necessary."[26]

MONDAY, 28 JULY

General Washington ordered General Putnam to immediately dispatch some troops into New Jersey.[27] Within several days, they set forth. Now, even fewer personnel were on hand to continue the critically required work.

WEDNESDAY, 30 JULY

Far away from New York City, General Howe dispatched a letter to Sir Henry. Howe added:

"If you can make a diversion in favor of General Burgoyne's approaching Albany, I need not point out the utility of such a measure."[28]

Howe, who was off to engage Washington, undoubtedly began to suspect that perhaps Burgoyne would require some assistance. Even a simple diversion would help.

FRIDAY, 1 AUGUST

General George Washington, who had been closely monitoring the events taking place in the northern theater of operations since early 1777, dispatched a short letter to Governor Clinton. Washington wrote:

"...I received the provoking account, that the enemy's fleet left the Cape of Delaware yesterday, and sterred eastward again. I shall return again with the utmost expedition to the North [Hudson] River; but as a sudden stroke is certainly intended by this manoeuvre, I beg you will immediately call in every man of the militia that you possibly can, to strengthen the highland posts. The importance of Fort Montgomery is such, that I wish you to repair immediately to it if you possibly can, consistent with the duties of the office upon which you have entered."[29]

That same day Governor George Clinton ordered Colonels Pawling and Snyder to immediately transfer 180 militiamen from their militia units to Colonel Morris Graham's regiment which, in turn, was to reinforce the Northern Army in the vicinity of Albany.[30]

SATURDAY, 2 AUGUST

Governor George Clinton's older brother, James Clinton, who served in the rank of Brigadier General, assumed overall command of both Forts Montgomery and Clinton though Colonel John Lamb was appointed to command Fort Montgomery.[31] Clinton's headquarters would be in Fort Clinton. Also on this day a mobilization decree was issued by Governor Clinton. Brigadier General Abraham Ten Broeck, the highest ranking militia general in the newly created State of New York, was ordered to mobilize additional manpower for the Northern Army. This mobilization decree was issued in response to General Burgoyne's advance to Fort Edward and because Schuyler's Northern Army was retreating to Saratoga.[32]

SUNDAY, 3 AUGUST

General Burgoyne received Howe's response message of 17 July. To ensure secrecy, the message was concealed in a small, hollow silver bullet. This was done in the event the messenger had to swallow the message.

Unraveling the paper, Burgoyne was shocked! This was, indeed, terrible news. Worse, by now almost everyone knew that a messenger had appeared and the troops were waiting for information.[33] Folding up the letter, Burgoyne decided that for the time being he would keep the contents of the message just to himself. He would not even confide its content to his second in command. Should someone ask, Burgoyne would simply respond that it was nothing of concern. As for the troops, he would make something up.

Reopening the letter, Burgoyne once again viewed it. Until now he had been counting on Howe's support.[34] Realizing that this would no longer be the case, Burgoyne feared that hard times could now lie ahead.

TUESDAY, 5 AUGUST

Receiving a letter from George Washington warning that British Army General Sir Henry Clinton might be planning to attack the Highlands, patriot General George Clinton immediately mobilized a number of militiamen and dispatched them to the Highlands. Realizing that the Northern Army needed to communicate more rapidly and effectively with Washington, the governor also established an express route. Select individuals, serving as messengers, would race on horseback back and forth between Albany, Kingston, the Highlands, and General Washington's main headquarters.[35]

WEDNESDAY, 6 AUGUST

Burgoyne dispatched a quick note to New York City citing that he expected to reach Albany by 23 August.

THURSDAY, 7 AUGUST

Excitement reigned in the air when a British ship, the *Mercury*, appeared off Verplanck's Point. Verplanck's Point was located almost 2 miles to the south/southwest of Peekskill on the eastern bank of the Hudson River. Dispatching a boat under a large white flag of truce, upon landing the young English officer immediately stated that he is carrying a message, personally written by Sir Henry, for General Putnam. The issue at stake was the fate of a loyalist lieutenant named Edmund Palmer who had been caught spying in the Highlands and was sentenced to be hanged.

Upon reading Sir Henry's message, Putnam flew into a rage! What especially angered Putnam was Sir Henry's demand to know on what grounds Putnam had authorized the execution of Palmer. Insisting that Lieutenant Palmer's sentence be commuted, the British commander also warned the old patriot general that in the event Palmer was executed, the Americans could expect similar reprisals.

Sir Henry's effort to have Palmer released ended in vain. In reply, General Putnam did two things: he provided a short hand-written response to the officer who, in turn, would bring it back to Sir Henry, and "Old Put" ordered that Palmer be immediately hung. For extra sensationalism, the loyalist officer was hung from a tree overlooking the Hudson River's eastern bank. En route back to New York City, the British witnessed the condemned swaying gently in the river's breeze.

THURSDAY, 14 AUGUST – SATURDAY, 16 AUGUST

The Battle of Bennington was fought. Burgoyne's forces suffered a major defeat. Nearly a fourth of Burgoyne's army was lost. Morale plummeted. Sensing defeat and fearing for their lives, the first sizable desertions commenced, especially amongst the non-English personnel.[36]

Chapter 5

West Point Prepares for War

TUESDAY, 19 AUGUST

On this day, General Schuyler was relieved of command. General Horatio Gates assumed command of the Northern Army. Despite the fact that just several days before the British had been defeated at Bennington, and were being systematically destroyed both at Fort Stanwix and in the Schoharie Valley. . . and Burgoyne was in the process of being methodically annihilated by Schuyler's tactics, America's Continental Congress, still upset about the fiasco at Fort Ticonderoga, decided to remove Schuyler.

By the end of August, the patriot defense system within the area soon to be etched in America's history as West Point began to take on some semblance of order. On the east side of the Hudson River extending northward the 2nd and 4th New York Continental Regiments were based in Peekskill. The 2nd was commanded by Colonel Philip Van Cortlandt and the 4th by Colonel Henry B. Livingston. One mile above Peekskill, Lieutenant-Colonel Roswell Hopkins manned Fort Independence.[1] Eight miles farther up the Hudson River lay Fort Constitution. Manned by Lieutenant-Colonel Jotham Loring's detachment of 131 officers and militiamen, it was supported with Major Maurice Pleas' battalion of 72 officers and militiamen and Captain Gershom Mott's artillery company of 5 officers and 15 cannoneers.[2]

On the west side of the river (again extending northward) stood Fort Clinton now commanded by Colonel Levi Pawling; approximately half-a-mile to the immediate north of Fort Clinton stood Fort Montgomery. This fort was manned by the 5th New York Continental Regiment commanded by Colonel Lewis Dubois; second in command was Lieutenant-Colonel Jacobus Bruyn. However, the 5th was reinforced with a militia unit commanded by Colonel Johannis Snyder.

In addition to the regular Continental Army units, a total of sixteen various militia battalions and militia regiments were spread throughout Peekskill, the various forts, and the newly established Continental Village[3] found in the Highlands. These units were commanded by Colonels Wigglesworth, Paterson, Pawling, Snyder, Shepherd, Huntington, Webb, Wyllys, Durkee, Douglas, Bradley, Swift, Chandler, Graham, and Greaton.[4] In all, a troop strength of 3,000 was registered.[5] All of these forces fell under the command of General Israel "Old Put" Putnam.[6] Among those proudly serving his newly born nation at West Point was Issac Franks, a veteran of the Long Island and New York City battles.

Along with the army units, a river flotilla began to make its appearance. Two frigates, the *Congress* and *Montgomery* (the *Montgomery* had eight 12-pound guns); one sloop, the *Camden* with ten guns; two galleys, the *Shark* with four 9-pounders and the *Lady Washington* with one heavy 32-pound gun and eight light 3-pound guns, were found.[7] Various boats ranging from canoes, row boats, sailboats, and river bateaux, were also utilized.

THURSDAY, 21 AUGUST

Despite Burgoyne's defeat at Bennington, the British remained a serious threat. To counter this, on 21 August[8] Putnam transferred the entire 2nd New York Regiment commanded by Colonel Van Cortlandt and the entire 4th New York Regiment commanded by Colonel Livingston, northward to assist in repelling Burgoyne's army. Prior to their departure, both of these regular army continental regiments had been based in the vicinity of Peekskill.[9] Now, the patriot defense in the Highlands was further weakened. Despite warnings from General Washington and the patriot spies operating in New York City that the Highlands were in danger of being attacked, neither General Putnam nor the Northern Army's high command had a choice because, at this time, the top military priority was to halt Burgoyne.[10] So until some other continental troop unit arrived, the only remaining continental unit left in the Highlands was the 5th New York Regiment. But unlike the continental regiments which had departed, the 5th New York was not even close to being in full regimental strength. Of the five New York continental regiments previously based in the Highlands, the 5th was the weakest;[11] hence, it could not be deployed. Along with the 5th most (if not all) of the militia units were understrength as well.

To cite an example of what the 5th New York Regiment was experiencing: though it had a commanding officer and an assistant commander, it lacked a major. A senior captain, James Rosekrans, who commanded the 1st Company,[12] was third in the chain of command. Another captain was Jean Francois Hamtramck. A fiery patriot and one of the very first volunteers for the Revolutionary War, Jean Francois was born in Canada to a father who, in 1749, had emigrated from Treves (Trier), Germany,[13] and a French-Canadian mother. By age 18, Jean Francois had had a good schooling and was fluent in English, French, German, and Latin. Though born in Canada and a British citizen, Jean Francois opposed England's dominance of Canada and with many other Canadians, sympathized with the colonists in rebellion. When the Americans invaded Canada in 1775, on 15 September Jean Francois joined the patriots. Enlisting in the town of Pointe Olivier not far from Chambly and a Canadian town occupied by the patriots, Jean Francois was initially posted into a supply section. Along with distributing supplies, he kept an accountability of the supplies previously captured by patriot leaders such as Major John Brown and Ethan Allen in their raids and ambushes upon wagons and boats en route to various British forts and outposts.

On 6 February 1776, Colonel Jeremiah Duggan, who was in charge of organizing additional units, promoted Jean Francois Hamtramck to the rank of captain[14] and assigned Captain Hamtramck to command an infantry company.[15]

In the following months, Captain Hamtramck would experience nothing but hardship, capture, and release.[16] Returning in due time to the American colonies, on 11 July 1776 Captain Hamtramck, now known as "John Francis," appeared to the Continental Congress where he provided firsthand testimony on the events of the American performance in Canada. Among the members of the investigating committee was Thomas Jefferson. What, exactly, "John Hamtramck, a Canadian" did in the aftermath is not known but he never returned to Canada.[17]

In early 1777 "John Francis" Hamtramck rejoined the Northern Army in Albany. Shortly after in February, he appealed to the state committee to have his former rank restored. On 17 March[18] it was reinstated and Captain Hamtramck was ordered to report to the 5th New York Continental Regiment in the Highlands.

Despite some additional incoming volunteers such as Captain Hamtramck, serious manpower shortages continued to plague the patriots serving in the Highlands. The 5th Regiment, which on paper was authorized a strength of 640, had only 267 on active duty among its eight companies.[19] As for the remaining militia units posted in the Highlands, all remained tremendously under-strength.[20] Part of the problem stemmed from the necessity of rotating the militiamen in and out so that they could take care of their personal affairs, such as their farms. Though on occasion a unit could somehow be brought up to near or full strength, this could still take days and the combat efficiency of the unit remained questionable. So until more personnel could some-how be rotated in, understrength units were the norm for the Highlands in 1777.

SATURDAY, 23 AUGUST

General St. Leger lifted the siege of Fort Stanwix. Unable to overrun the fort, stalemated at the Battle of Oriskany, taking casualties, experiencing desertions, and now warned of a very strong incoming patriot force commanded by no less than General Arnold himself, St. Leger commenced a rapid retreat back to Canada via Oswego.

TUESDAY, 26 AUGUST

Oswego. From here, General St. Leger submitted an official report to Burgoyne.[21] Initially started in the evening hours of 23 August, St. Leger's writing was interrupted by the sudden arrival of Hon Yost escorted by Oneida Indians who quickly spread fear and panic amongst St. Leger's force resulting in a mass flight.

In his report, St. Leger denounced the Indians and gave examples of poor behavior;[22] however, St. Leger emphasized that upon his return to Montreal he would immediately regroup to soon link up with Burgoyne. St. Leger planned to do this by going down the Richelieu River-Lake Champlain water system as previously did Burgoyne. Passing the message onto one of the few remaining Indian warriors still serving, St. Leger instructed him to find Burgoyne and deliver the message directly to him.

The key to the defense of the Highlands and its valley was the Hudson River itself. If successfully blocked, all enemy movements would be halted. Because previously it had been conceived that one of the best ways to close the river was with a strong chain strung across it, in late spring the first chain obstacle had been positioned. Now, any enemy ship running up against this chain would be stopped and targeted by gunners firing their cannons from the overlooking forts and redoubts.

Despite the placement of the one chain, in actuality the work progressed very slowly. On a typical day everything moved at a snail's pace. Indecisions, a weak garrison, uncoordinated efforts, ineptness, inefficiency, lack of priorities, and the lack of equipment and material along with a lack of urgency to accomplish anything specific—such factors took their toll. Complicating the situation was General Putnam himself. Exhibiting no strong leadership, he left too many of the key decisions to his subordinates. Days turned into weeks, weeks into months and soon the summer was over. As the leaves of early September began to slowly change color, the Highlands remained unprepared for war.

THURSDAY, 28 AUGUST[23]

St. Leger's Indian messenger reached Burgoyne. Along with Howe's message of 23 August Burgoyne surely must have sensed that the entire military situation was deteriorating.

Yet Burgoyne knew that a sizable military force advancing northward from New York City in support of his southward advance could reverse the recent sequence of disastrous events. Still determined to reach Albany, with the capture of this provincial town a significant change in his favor was bound to occur. But in order to achieve this, Burgoyne would need assistance from the south. In fact, the key to victory now lay with those in New York City.

WEDNESDAY, 10 SEPTEMBER

General and Governor Clinton met with his legislators. Confident of what had been going on, Clinton assured everyone that all was well. As for the Highland forts, they "are in so respectable a state of defense as to promise us security against any attack in their quarter."[24]

Why the governor stated this is not known. With his absence from the Highlands (he was, after all, in addition to being an army general, also the elected governor and was now in Kingston, the capital of New York State) it is possible he was not being properly briefed on what, in actuality, was occurring. Perhaps Clinton had too much trust and confidence in Putnam; possibly, the Highlands were no longer the governor's priority because at this very moment Burgoyne was still regarded as the main threat. Regardless, the governor's assessment of 10 September was very incorrect because as of this date none of the forts had yet been completed, a weak garrison was fortifying the entire site and though the first boom and chain had been inserted into the river it was almost halfway into September and West Point was still totally unprepared for war.

Fearing a possible British thrust into New Jersey, on this same day General Washington ordered General Putnam to immediately shift 1,500 troops into that region.[25] The Highlands were now further weakened.

THURSDAY, 11 SEPTEMBER

From his headquarters in New York City, Sir Henry dispatched Lieutenant Daniel Taylor, a very competent runner, to General Burgoyne. Hearing little from Burgoyne, Sir Henry needed to know directly from Burgoyne what, truly, was happening. Well before the disastrous Battle of Bennington and the British retreat from Fort Stanwix, Sir Henry had concluded that the British campaign strategy for 1777 was in serious trouble. Mentally cursing Howe for creating such a situation, Sir Henry wrote:

> "You know my good will and are not ignorant of my poverty. If you think two thousand men can assist you effectually, I will make a push at [Fort] Montgomery in about ten days, but ever jealous of my flanks. If they make a move in force on either of them, I must return to save this important post. I expect reinforcement every day. Let me know what you wish."[26]

Though Sir Henry had been informed by Burgoyne's letter of 6 August that he expected to be in Albany by 23 August, by mid-September it was obvious that Burgoyne's advance had been halted. The last Sir Henry knew was that Burgoyne was still in the vicinity of Saratoga, 40 straight line miles to the north of Albany. In military terms, this is a tremendous distance and the days were becoming shorter, the nights cooler, the first cold rains were coming down and winter, with its heavy snows, was just around the corner.

On this day, 35 miles to the west of Philadelphia, the Battle of Brandywine was fought. Skillfully, Howe outmaneuvered the Americans and forced the patriots back toward Philadelphia. Washington lost approximately 1,000 troops that day.[27] Flush with victory, the British continued to march rapidly toward Philadelphia, the capital of the newly established American nation.

That same evening, Sir Henry launched an evening raid into New Jersey. Though the main mission of the raiders was to secure additional food supplies for a city growing increasingly hungry, New York City's commander was also hoping to tie down as many of New Jersey's militia units from reinforcing either the Highlands or the Albany front. Perhaps, some of the Highlands' defenders would even be re-shifted southwestward into New Jersey, thus further weakening the Highlands for any future attack from New York City. Attempting to assist Burgoyne in any way that he could, Sir Henry contacted Major General Robert Pigot, the commanding British officer of Rhode Island and with whom Sir Henry had served at Bunker Hill, to launch a sizable demonstration northwestward into central Massachusetts and southern Vermont. If conducted, Pigot's actions would possibly alleviate much of the pressure against Burgoyne because the patriots would have to counter Pigot's thrust. But as it turned out, Pigot had no desire to either assist Sir Henry or Burgoyne. Perhaps, the Battle of Bunker Hill was still too fresh on Pigot's mind where, in addition to losing many of his soldiers, Pigot himself was wounded. Secure in his quarters and seeking no trouble, Pigot simply replied, "My hands are full and I cannot do anything." It was, of course, a weak excuse and everyone, including Pigot, knew it.

FRIDAY, 12 SEPTEMBER

Sir Henry's raiders returned. But little was gained. Excluding some horses, several hundred head of cattle and sheep along with twenty milking cows[28] nothing more was procured.

SATURDAY, 13 SEPTEMBER

Continuing his push toward Albany, Burgoyne crossed the Hudson River onto its west bank. His next objective—Saratoga.

SUNDAY, 14 SEPTEMBER

Yet, perhaps, Sir Henry's raid of 11 September had not been totally unproductive. Fearing the loss of New Jersey, and that its unprotected citizens could switch their allegiance back to the King, General Washington ordered General Putnam to dispatch General McDougall with a strength of no less than 1,000 militiamen and as many continental soldiers as possible from the Highlands to New Jersey.[29] By 23 September, 2,500 troops headed by McDougall were inserted into Washington's main army.[30] However, as Washington's army gained strength, Putnam's Highland defenders were further weakened.

Anticipating a British occupation of Philadelphia, America's Continental Congress fled from that city and established itself in York, Pennsylvania. For the time being, York would serve as the nation's temporary capital.

SUNDAY, 21 SEPTEMBER

In the early dark hours, the British launched a successful night attack against the patriots at Paoli, about 17 miles to the west of Philadelphia. Shattering "Mad" Anthony Wayne's brigade, the attackers opened the road to Philadelphia.

Via Lieutenant Daniel Taylor, Burgoyne received Sir Henry's letter of 11 September.[31] It had taken the Lieutenant ten days to deliver the crucial message. After personally briefing the Lieutenant on what he was to report back to Sir Henry, the Lieutenant set forth. Burgoyne fully realized the danger of Lieutenant Taylor's mission. But if everything went well, Sir Henry would soon receive Burgoyne's response that he would value any push from the south.

MONDAY, 22 SEPTEMBER

Early that morning, Burgoyne dispatched another message to Sir Henry appealing for assistance.

TUESDAY, 23 SEPTEMBER

Two more messengers were dispatched to New York City. Surely, reasoned Burgoyne, someone should get through.

WEDNESDAY, 24 SEPTEMBER

A large British fleet arrived to New York City from England. In addition to bringing in critical foodstuffs to a city already experiencing food shortages, the ships also delivered arms, ammunition, powder, cannons, horses, and other war material. But most importantly, 1,700 British and Hessian troops came in.[32] Among the arrivals was a Polish nobleman, Count Grabowski. Seeking adventure and being very fond of the English king, Grabowski volunteered to serve the English cause. Posted to Sir Henry, Grabowski served as his Aide-de-Camp. Duly noting the incoming fleet, the city's spies quickly dispatched warnings to Governor Clinton, Generals Putnam, Washington, the Northern Army High Command and, even, to the Continental Congress based in York. The warning, however, was inflated with its report that "3,000 British and German troops had arrived." Regardless, at least the defenders of the Highlands had been warned.

FRIDAY, 26 SEPTEMBER

General Howe took Philadelphia. In a coordinated action his brother, Admiral Richard Howe, cleared the Delaware River. The British would remain in that city until 18 June 1778.

Despite Howe's triumphs and his occupation of Philadelphia, no true victory had yet been achieved. Washington's army was still operating in the field. Unlike in Europe where usually the capture and occupation of a nation's capital marked the end of a war or conflict, this was not so in America. In fact, in his effort to seek a decisive victory in Pennsylvania, Howe had blundered tremendously by not dispensing with Washington. Unable at the moment to redeploy back to New York City, excluding the 27th Foot ordered to return to New York City, the brunt of Howe's army remained, for the time being, in Philadelphia. In the end, Howe's blunder would prove to be a major factor in enabling the patriots to achieve a victory in the Wilderness War of 1777.[33]

Soon after, in faraway France, Benjamin Franklin, who was pleading the American cause to Europe's dignitaries, was attending an evening dinner party. During the event a Frenchman who held the Americans in low esteem remarked sarcastically to Franklin, "Well, Howe has taken Philadelphia." Looking over to the individual, Franklin simply responded, "I beg your pardon, Sir. But Philadelphia has taken Howe!"[34]

SATURDAY, 27 SEPTEMBER – SUNDAY, 28 SEPTEMBER

Over the weekend, Burgoyne dispatched additional messengers to Sir Henry. Captain Alexander Campbell was one of the runners. Dressed in civilian attire, until recently Campbell had served as a liaison officer between Burgoyne and Howe. Of interest is that Burgoyne's message of 28 September urged not only assistance but also a request for orders from Sir Henry on what to do.[35]

By the end of September Sir Henry concluded that the campaign of 1777 had gone astray. But if Howe could return in due time to New York City and if Burgoyne could at least secure Albany and obtain enough food supplies to sustain his army through the winter months, all would not be lost. Later, in the spring of 1778, a major two-pronged thrust could be resumed forcing General Washington to march into Albany's vicinity only to encounter England's combined forces which would, once and for all, shatter Washington's main continental army. But prior to anything occurring in 1778, certain actions would first have to be undertaken in the fall of 1777, especially in the Highlands region. By attacking and occupying West Point, the consequences of such an attack would prove productive for both the immediate and distant future. Even a limited offensive

operation could prove invaluable. A thrust northward would
destroy the patriots, capture their forts, alleviate the patriot
pressure against Burgoyne, demonstrate British strengths and
capabilities, halt patriot shipping on the lower Hudson River,
and secure the Highlands as a springboard for any offensive
actions to be launched in 1778 against the patriots in the Albany,
Vermont, and New England regions.[36]

MONDAY, 29 SEPTEMBER

Receiving a response from Burgoyne in regard to Sir Henry's
proposal of 11 September, Burgoyne's message stated:

"It will draw away great part of their force, and I will
follow them close. Do it, my friend, directly."[37]

Sir Henry, however, did not just read the message. Seeking
information, he thoroughly debriefed the messenger. Assuring
him that he had nothing to fear by speaking openly, the
messenger spoke directly.

From him Sir Henry learned that just recently Burgoyne
had cut the daily food quota. There was only about thirty days
of salt provisions left and supplies were barely trickling in.
Communications with Canada were scant. Rebel raiders were
constantly harassing Burgoyne's rear, and just recently had struck
Fort Ticonderoga. Burgoyne's irregulars, along with some of the
regulars, had begun to desert.

But it was not all negative. Regarding Burgoyne, the messenger
emphasized that he was still determined "to force Gates at any
time and get to Albany. It seemed to be his intentions to come
down to rejoin the southern [New York City–based] army."[38]

This was all the news Sir Henry needed to hear. If Burgoyne
was willing to take a risk then so, too, would Sir Henry. The stakes
were simply too high to be ignored. Something had to be done.
Since Howe was far away and unable to assist, it was now up to
Sir Henry.

Informed of the British reinforcement of 24 September and fearing that recently arrived troops would possibly be committed against the Northern Army's southern front located in the Highlands, Governor Clinton dispatched orders to various colonels for them to mobilize their militia units and "march to reinforce the Posts in the Highlands."[39] Clinton wrote:

> "... there is the utmost Reason to apprehend that the Enemy stationed at New York and Kingsbridge are much more numerous than was generally expected, and that they are making great and speedy Preparations for an Expedition which there can be little Doubt must be intended against the county of W. Chester [Westchester] and the Posts and Passes in the Highlands ...."

Governor Clinton also acknowledged that Highlands' posts had been:

> "... induced by the weakness of the Posts by the large Reinforcements lately ordered from thence for Genl. Washington."[40]

TUESDAY, 30 SEPTEMBER

Mr. Abraham Leggett, a Chairman in Westchester County's General Committee, dispatched a letter to Governor Clinton. In his letter, Leggett predicted the enemy would attack northward and he appealed for assistance in countering any British thrust. Leggett wrote:

> "We have received certain Intelligence that the Enemy are making the greatest Preparations to advance into our County and sweep all the [cattle and animal] Stock from [the] Croton River to Kings Bridge before them.

"We beg that your Excellency may take our Case into your serious Consideration and be pleased to order into our County some further Relief . . ., as what Militia we can muster will neither be Sufficient to retard the Progress of the Enemy in case they advance, nor prove numerous enough to drive the stock out of their Reach."

In conclusion, Mr. Leggett added that he is enclosing a letter from Brigadier General Parsons which just recently had been submitted to the committee. As the general emphasized:

"A dark and gloomy Cloud seems to hang hovering over us, the Enemy preparing to Make their Incursions into the Country where Depradations and savage Barbarity will be the Consequence."[41]

Both Mr. Leggett's and General Parsons' warnings were more than correct because on this very same day Sir Henry, after consulting with his staff and key commanders, issued the order to march. Sir Henry was going to war. His immediate objective: the Highlands.

Chapter 6

Sir Henry Attacks!

For Sir Henry, the key to the reduction of the Highlands was the capture of Forts Clinton and Montgomery. To accomplish his mission, from the occupational forces stationed in New York City, Long Island, Staten Island, and other sites adjacent the city, Sir Henry selected these British, German, and loyalist units: the British 7th Royal Fusilier of Foot,[1] the 26th Foot,[2] 27th Foot,[3] 52nd Foot,[4] 57th Foot,[5] 63rd Foot Regiments;[6] one company from the 71st Foot;[7] a troop from the 17th Light Dragoons;[8] Colonel Andreas Von Emmerich's Hessian Jagers;[9] the Koehle[10] and Anspach Grenadiers;[11] the Trumbach Hessian Regiment;[12] and loyalist units[13] such as Colonel Beverley Robinson's Loyal American Regiment;[14] the Emmerich's Chasseurs;[15] the Guides and Pioneers;[16] the King's American Regiment;[17] one company of the King's Orange Rangers;[18] and the New York Volunteers.[19]

Along with army units, Sir Henry committed a naval force.[20] River bateaux[21] would transport and supply the army troops while naval ships would assist the ground troops in reducing any patriot resistance encountered on or near the banks of the Hudson River. Several galleys, under the command of Captain James Wallace, would probe ahead with the bateaux. Behind this force, farther downriver three larger and more powerful frigate ships—the *Mercury, Tartar,* and *Preston,* would assist. Commodore William Hotham, commanding from the *Preston,* would direct the entire naval force.[22]

Both Hotham and Wallace were from the Royal Navy. In all, no less than 3,000 to about 4,000 ground soldiers, including loyalists, would participate in Sir Henry's attack.[23] This figure, however, excluded the navy's personnel.[24]

FRIDAY, 3 OCTOBER. SPUYTEN DUYVIL CREEK[25]

Early this morning 1,100 British soldiers[26] moved by water and land from New York City to Fort Independence, which overlooked the Spuyten Duyvil Creek. Here, the troops were initially placed into specially designated assembly areas. Later on in the evening hours, Sir Henry loaded these soldiers, which represented his first contingent, into bateaux. Rowing quietly into and up the Hudson River, this contingent reached Tarrytown by daybreak. Located on the eastern bank of the Hudson, Tarrytown was almost halfway up to Peekskill; simultaneously, as the watercraft edged northward, a second contingent of equal strength[27] marched northward on a road from the Kings Bridge on the eastern side of the Hudson River.

This action was a diversionary measure undertaken by Sir Henry to deceive the patriot commander, General Putnam, into believing that Peekskill and its area would again be targeted as previously. By evening, the waterborne and land marching forces had linked up together and Tarrytown was occupied. For Sir Henry this was ideal because he wanted the British force to be spotted and reported. Noting this British activity and to warn his brother on what was transpiring, late that afternoon General James Clinton dispatched a military runner directly to his governor brother. On this day, the estimated combat strength of the Highlands stood at about 1,200 continentals and militiamen all serving in understrength units.[28]

SATURDAY, 4 OCTOBER

Sir Henry's third contingent, like his first, proceeded up the river in transports. Excluding the naval personnel, the third contingent was the largest with a strength of approximately 1,500.[29]

Arriving at British occupied Tarrytown on that very same day, the brunt of its soldiers remained on board their transports floating in the Tappan Zee (Tarrytown Bay) on the Hudson River. The third contingent also included the frigates *Preston, Mercury*, and *Tartar.* The mission of these frigates was to protect the troop laden transports and assist in the destruction of any forts and batteries on and near any shoreline.

North of Tarrytown in Peekskill, General Putnam concluded that Peekskill was Sir Henry's main objective. Wanting to increase his combat strength in and around Peekskill, Putnam ordered Forts Clinton, Montgomery, and Constitution to dispatch some troops immediately to Peekskill. Putnam also dispatched express riders with messages to Governor Clinton who, at the moment, was farther up north in Kingston. Along with Putnam, General James Clinton dispatched another quick letter to his governor brother.

By his movements, Sir Henry succeeded in truly deceiving Putnam that Peekskill was his main target; simultaneously, by drawing additional troops farther to the northeast, Putnam further weakened a defensive system already weak in the first place.

2100 (9 P.M.)

In the evening hours of 4 October, Governor George Clinton was conducting a legislative meeting. Interrupted by the arrival of Putnam's and Clinton's messengers who brought news about the sizable British force advancing up the Hudson River, Governor Clinton informed his legislatures on what was reported,[30]suspended the meeting, issued an order for the Orange Militia to mobilize immediately, and departed for the Highlands.

Miles away in Pennsylvania, the Battle of Germantown had been fought. Throughout that sweltering hot day Washington's army bravely engaged Howe's forces with true élan. Though by the end of the day the patriots had been defeated, Washington's troops retired in order. Each and every soldier serving in

Washington's Main Continental Army was very proud that on this day they had succeeded in holding their own against a much stronger and experienced British force. Even Howe and his commanders acknowledged that the American Army had performed well.

SUNDAY, 5 OCTOBER

Loading his forces positioned on the eastern side of the Hudson River upon bateaux and ships, Sir Henry issued the order to move rapidly upriver. His next objective—Verplanck's Point. Located about 13 miles upriver to the north of the Tappan Zee on the east side of the Hudson River, Verplanck's Point is a piece of rocky land jutting into the Hudson River. Across and slightly downriver on the Hudson's western bank is another piece of rocky ground jutting into the river. In 1777 it was known as Stony Point. On a clear day as one stands on the edge of Stony Point and looks into a northeasterly direction, Verplanck's Point may be seen. About 4 miles to the northeast of Verplanck's Point lay Peekskill which headquartered General Putnam. Another 2 miles directly to the north of Peekskill stood a major continental supply point dubbed as "Continental Village." Besides being a supply point, it contained buildings to garrison troops.

Enroute to reach Fort Montgomery in the Highlands, Governor Clinton was mobilizing as many militiamen as he could. Though initially he believed that the British were just targeting Peekskill, Clinton now began to fear that perhaps, something much bigger was actually in the making.

1200–1500 (12 P.M.– 3 P.M.)

Sailing past Stony Point,[31] that afternoon Sir Henry reached Verplanck's Point where he disembarked 1,000 troops.[32] Mostly, these were loyalists accompanied by some British officers serving as advisors.[33] By landing this strength at this location, the patriots would indeed be deceived into believing that Peekskill—and possibly even Continental Village—were the main objectives.

At Verplanck's Point a small two-gun battery was in place. Terrified of the superior strength approaching them, the crew abandoned their position and fled into the interior. In their haste to escape, they did not even attempt to fire any of the two cannons as a warning to those farther upriver and inland.[34] Informed of the landing and believing that Peekskill was truly the British objective, General Putnam ordered its garrison to retreat four miles farther inland. Abandoning Peekskill, 1,000 soldiers[35] immediately began to move northward toward the vicinity of Annsville Creek and its higher terrain.

By late Sunday morning, Governor Clinton was about a mile to the north of Fort Constitution, located on Constitution Island, in a boat headed downriver. Suddenly, from the distance, he first heard a faint boom followed by a series of booms. Clearly, it was the boom of cannons. Governor Clinton now knew what was happening. The British were coming!

Previously that summer, the patriots had developed an early warning system. In the event a British force would be observed heading upriver and northward from Verplanck's Point, a cannon would be fired. In turn, any shore battery or boat outfitted with cannons would, upon hearing the blast, also fire a cannon. Via a network of cannon blasts echoing northward, everyone would be warned that a sizable enemy force was en route.

Though not very far away, Governor Clinton was traveling at an exceptionally slow pace. His movement was hindered by the strong winds blowing northward and the river's current moving ever so slowly southward. Unfortunately for the defenders of the Highlands, this wind was actually pushing Sir Henry's force rapidly northward.[36]

Reaching the site where the river takes its 90-degree turn and wraps itself around Constitution Island, Governor Clinton disembarked on its western bank where, presently, is located the

United States Military Academy. The governor was now about 6 miles to the north of Fort Montgomery. Noting the one dwelling standing almost directly across Constitution Island, the governor might have possibly stopped at this residence. Privately owned, it stood not far from the river's bank and the house was known as "Moore's House."[37] Unable to secure a horse at this location, he proceeded as quickly as possible to Fort Montgomery on foot.

In 1777, other than Forts Clinton and Montgomery, almost nothing else existed on the western side of the Hudson River. As for the present day military academy, the various forts, redoubts, and batteries which are now evident, these positions did not exist in 1777.[38] Excluding Forts Independence, Clinton, Montgomery, Constitution, and a handful of batteries, nothing else existed. Regarding the forts, none were completed.[39] Simply put, despite various efforts in establishing a strong defensive system, one had not yet been developed. It was only in the aftermath of 1777 that a strong defensive system came into being. So when Sir Henry attacked in October 1777, all in all, West Point was solely in its early stage of development.[40]

As Sir Henry was unloading his loyalists at Verplanck's Point, Captain James Wallace, who was commanding the galleys, proceeded upriver toward Fort Independence. Situated on the Hudson River's eastern bank about one mile to the northwest of Peekskill, the fort overlooked and protected both the river and Peekskill Bay.

Firing a barrage upon the fort and sinking a sizable boat moored in the river, the British pressed closer to the fort. Fearful of the flotilla, the defenders of Fort Independence fled and retreated inland where, deeper in the Highlands, they linked up with Putnam's retreating militiamen. The British, however, neither stormed the fort nor attempted a landing. Following the bombardment, Captain Wallace's galleys withdrew slightly back down the river.

1500 (3 P.M.)

Finally arriving at Fort Montgomery, Governor Clinton was met by his brother, Brigadier General James Clinton. Noting how the two forts stood in disrepair, the governor later lamented, "I found the garrison weaker than when I left it!"[41]

The entire force defending both Forts Clinton and Montgomery possessed a fighting strength of around 500 to, at most, 550.[42] As for Fort Montgomery, its weakest point was in its rear, facing the west. Lieutenant Machin was more than correct when earlier he had noted: "Part of the walls of the fort were not more than half raised."[43] Regarding the artillery, there was a lack of cannons. And most of the cannons in Fort Montgomery were pointed in the direction of the river. Being the senior commander, the governor instructed his brother, James, to assume command of Fort Clinton while he would command Fort Montgomery.

From the town of Rampage Clove, Major Thomas Moffat, a scout leader,[44] dispatched a runner with a letter for General James Clinton, which reached General James at Fort Clinton. Written hours earlier, on 5 October, Major Moffat warned Clinton: ". . . the Enemy are in Motion . . . ." Major Moffat knew what was happening because he had scouts probing both sides of the Hudson River as far south as New York City. And his scouts were bringing back timely and accurate information.[45] As Major Moffat reported:

> "That the enemy were in Haverstraw Bay Standing up the River. Their Van [advance guard] near Stony Point and that their fleet consisted of 9 Topsail Vessels a Number of Sloops, Gallies etc. with about 50 flat Bottomed Boats and appeared to have a considerable Number of Troops on Board."

Major Moffat also added:

"I have wrote to Major Gutches [Goetchius] desiring he would afford me what assistance he can in case of Necessity."

But in addition to submitting an intelligence report, Major Moffat indicated that one of his captains had already engaged the enemy in the vicinity of Suffern.[46] Moffat wrote:

"Captain Wood with about 20 Men... had the good fortune about Two in the Morning to fall in with a party of those Villans to the number of about 8 or 10 and forced them (after Challenging properly and they refused to Stand), Killed one dead on the Spot wounded another so Badly he Died Next Morning about 9 o'Clock."[47]

Whether these loyalists had anything to do with Sir Henry's movement is uncertain. Regardless, of historical significance is that these opening shots were actually the very first ones to be fired on the southern front in October, 1777. Although only a brief night skirmish the event at Suffern was significant because it was a patriot victory.

At approximately the same time that Verplanck's Point was being secured Captain Campbell, Burgoyne's messenger of 28 September, suddenly made his appearance. Initially, Campbell was to go all the way down to New York City. Encountering British forces penetrating into the Highlands enabled Campbell to rendezvous with Sir Henry sooner.

Besides delivering Burgoyne's written message, Campbell emphasized to Sir Henry that Burgoyne needed to know if Sir Henry could reach Albany and provision it by river from New York. And if so, Campbell also inquired as to when Sir Henry could arrive. Directing the captain to get some food and rest, Sir Henry stated that he would soon respond.

So far, from the British side, Sir Henry's handling of the expedition had been conducted with much skill. He succeeded in totally deceiving General Putnam as to what his real intent was, and he developed a situation which misled General Putnam into retreating farther inland and away from the objectives Sir Henry was actually targeting. By repositioning his troops farther inland General Putnam, as already mentioned, further weakened his entire defensive system.

In the evening hours of 5 October much confusion and uncertainty existed amongst the patriots. "Will the British advance further?"..."What are they up to?"..."Will they also land at Stony Point, across from Verplanck's Point?"..."What, if any, is their real goal?"..."Is this the beginning of a major push to Albany?"..."Or Burgoyne?"..., etc...., etc....Surely, such questions were pondered by the patriot defenders.

2300 (11 P.M.)

Desperate for information, the Clinton brothers began to take action. General James Clinton ordered Major Samuel Logan to conduct a strong reconnaissance. A continental officer from the 5th Continental Regiment, Major Logan was "an alert officer who was well acquainted with the ground."[48] Though in recent days the major had been ill, he continued to serve. With approximately 100 soldiers[49] the major was ordered to proceed into Timp Pass to reconnoiter the area as far south as Stony Point. Prior to moving out, Major Logan was explicitly instructed that he was not to engage the enemy under any circumstances. His troops were only to observe, monitor, and report back to Fort Montgomery pertaining to enemy movements up the river as well as any landings on the Hudson River's western or eastern banks. Along with Major Logan came Captain Stewart[50] who served as second in command. A veteran of the French-Indian War, Stewart was noted for his aggressiveness and quick thinking, especially under difficult circumstances.

MONDAY, 6 OCTOBER

Midnight. General Putnam requested that Governor Clinton immediately dispatch 60 soldiers under a captain "to secure the pass between Fort Independence and Anthony's Nose"[51] on the eastern side of the Hudson River. Still convinced that Peekskill and Fort Independence were the primary objectives of the British attack, Putnam wanted additional troops in that sector. Clinton dispatched the 60.

0200 (2 A.M.)

Sir Henry dispatched several ships along with some bateaux shortly after midnight from Verplanck's Point northward to Fort Independence. With lights blazing and loud crews, the noisy ships gave the appearance that a landing would be taking place in the vicinity of Fort Independence; simultaneously, as the ships proceeded upriver, further confusion set in. So far, Sir Henry's diversions were working.[52]

At the very moment the diversion was under way, Major Logan reached Timp Pass. A long and rocky pass, it is surrounded by very high and steep terrain on both sides. As for the narrow road within the pass it is, in some places, at best a foot path.

Originating at the base of a sizable hill known at that time as Bear Hill, the pass leads southward toward Stony Point. Enroute southward, to the immediate left lies Bald Mountain and a series of steep rocky hills known at the time as the Dunderberg Mountains.[53] This hill mass also borders on the Hudson River's western bank and overlooks the river.

To the right of the pass (again, as one continues southward) lies a series of very high and steep rocky hills. Some were unnamed but West Mountain and Buckberg Mountain were a couple of the named features at the time. A small hamlet, known as Doodletown,[54] existed at that time and was tucked in between Bear Hill, Bald Mountain, and West Mountain. This hamlet lay at the entrance or exit way of Timp Pass and was connected by several roads. Anyone entering or exiting Timp Pass had to first pass through Doodletown. En route to the entry of this pass, Major Logan also proceeded through Doodletown.

As presented, in 1777 a number of the high hills adjacent the pass were not identified by name. Various small creeks and streams, some intermittent although others flowed year-round, intersected through this pass. The vegetation was exceptionally heavy. Huge thick trees, rising many feet, were found. The trees and vegetation also shielded much of the light. In daytime most of Timp Pass was well shaded and at night was virtually pitch-black. Despite some settlement, the region was sparsely populated. That year it could rightfully be classified as a semi-wilderness region.[55]

Exiting Doodletown, Major Logan entered Timp Pass and probed cautiously forward. In the virtual pitch-black darkness, his men moved southward in single file. What further complicated the situation was the very thick fog rolling into the pass.

Approximately halfway into the mountains and about 3 miles to the south of Fort Clinton, Major Logan halted. Unsure of what lay ahead, he decided to remain in place. A combination of pitch-black darkness with heavy and thick fog slowed their efforts. Realizing, though, the need for intelligence, Major Logan dispatched several patrols into various directions. One, commanded by Lieutenant Samuel English, probed farther southward toward Stony Point in near total darkness.

0500 (5 A.M.)

Reaching Stony Point, English positioned his men all around the site, and several of his troops even climbed into the trees. From where Lieutenant English and his men were positioned, at the crack of dawn they would be able to see Stony Point, the Hudson River, Verplanck's Point and, hopefully, the British force. Provided, of course, the fog lifted.

0600 (6 A.M.)

Shortly before dawn in very thick fog General Putnam, accompanied with a couple of staff officers and a handful of security personnel, neared Fort Independence. Indeed, so thick was the fog that nothing could be seen. Noting no activity and still convinced that Peekskill was the enemy's chief objective, General Putnam turned his horse around and proceeded back to Peekskill.

As General Putnam was seeking any sign of any British activity, approximately four miles to the southwest of Fort Independence on the Hudson River's western bank, the first British row boats began to land at Stony Point. After quickly discharging their troops, its two to four crewmen rowed rapidly back to their transports to pick up another batch of soldiers. In addition to the row boats shuffling back and forth, bateaux were also landing. Sir Henry's intent was to exploit the advantage provided by the intense fog. After landing some scouts, and informed that no patriot forces were on site, Sir Henry issued orders to proceed swiftly with the landings.

En route to Peekskill, Putnam and his party encountered a local resident. Noting the continentals, the local immediately informed Putnam that moments before he had observed British troops being ferried on boats to Stony Point. Concluding that the man who claimed to have witnessed the landing was either wrong or, possibly, was a loyalist and still convinced that Peekskill was the true British objective, Putnam did nothing.

Across the river from where Putnam had been told that a landing was under way Lieutenant English, standing totally engulfed in a thick carpet of fog near the Hudson River's river bank, began to note activity. So dense was the fog that the river's waterline could not even be seen. But suddenly a strong gust of wind blew momentarily against the heavy fog. As the wind pushed much of the fog backwards, Lieutenant English and his men were awed at what they suddenly saw.

An awesome fleet, encompassed by puffs of fog, stood on the river. It actually appeared as if the entire British fleet was out there! Numerous row boats, bateaux and sizable ships were suddenly observed. Some of the watercraft were already beached and discarding soldiers while others, loaded with troops, were either nearing the shoreline or were rowing back to the larger ships to pick up the many seen standing upon the decks. Clearly, the British would yet be ferrying many hundreds, if not thousands, of additional troops. Noting the situation, Lieutenant English immediately ordered everyone to fall back to Major Logan.

The key to the capture of the Highlands were Forts Clinton and Montgomery. Knowing this, Sir Henry chose a rapid movement to capture them. Because a direct frontal thrust would be suicidal, Sir Henry decided on utilizing the indirect approach. He would attack both forts, simultaneously, from behind.

To accomplish this, Sir Henry ordered an attack with his most elite troops; therefore, of the approximately 2,100 British, German, and loyalist soldiers who landed at Stony Point,[56] most hailed from the better units. Sir Henry also divided them into three main groups: an advance guard, a main body, and the rear guard.

The advance guard was commanded by Lieutenant-Colonel Mungo Campbell, a highly aggressive, brave, and resourceful soldier; second in command was Colonel Robinson.[57] Campbell's force was comprised of elements of the 52nd and 57th Foot Regiments, Colonel Andreas Von Emmerich's Hessian Chasseurs jagers, the New York Volunteers, and Colonel Beverley Robinson's Loyal Americans. In all, no less than 900 to 1,000 strong[58] of which 400 were American loyalists.[59] Possibly, Robinson's well-trained unit was committed into the vanguard for psychological reasons. Along with Burgoyne and the other British commanders operating to the north, Sir

Henry likewise was counting on additional loyalist support. So if a well-armed and sizable loyalist unit would appear, it was thought that perhaps it would induce others to support the British effort.

The main body, possessing a troop strength of 1,200,[60] was commanded by General Sir John Vaughan. The 26th and 63rd Foot Regiments, one company from the 71st Foot, one troop of dismounted grenadiers from the 17th Light Dragoons, the Koehle and Anspach grenadier units, and some Hessian jager soldiers, comprised this force.[61]

The rear was commanded by General William Tryon who still served as the infamous Royal Governor of New York. For Tryon, this expedition was a personal affair because Tryon harbored a fiery hatred of the patriots. First, they had forced him into exile from his majestic and comfortable estate near Albany into New York City which, by 1777, had turned into an over-crowded, crime-ridden cesspool; secondly, just several weeks before, another near assassination attempt had almost taken his life. When en route to the piers to board Sir Henry's ship for this upcoming expedition, Tryon could not fail to note the KILL TRYON! graffiti splattered upon a brick wall. And, of course, there was the Danbury raid which had turned into a fiasco. Thirsting for revenge, Tryon wanted to kill each and every patriot. He would burn their homes, steal their cattle, violate their women, and stomp their revolutionary effort. Tryon would make the patriots pay.

Unfortunately for Tryon, unlike in New York City where he could—and did—dictate over a general, up here Sir Henry was strictly in command. It was no secret that Tryon loathed Sir Henry. As long as Sir Henry was in the Highlands, Tryon could not do as he pleased. But at least Tryon was engaging the patriots. Although he brought up the rear with the 7th British Foot and the Trumbach Hessians,[62] Tryon actually had no formal command over them. Only Sir Henry would dictate as to when and where these regiments were to be committed.

For tactical efficiency and control, Sir Henry positioned himself in the center with the main body. Accompanying him was his friend and aide, Count Grabowski. Soon, Sir Henry would be battling his two blood cousins.[63]

"Major, they're coming! They are coming! I don't know how many! But there's a lot! Easily, many hundreds!" Barely able to speak following his quick run through approximately 2 miles of rough terrain Lieutenant English, amid moments of panting and gasping for air, revealed what he and his men had seen.

Immediately, a debate arose as to what should be done. Captain Stewart proposed to establish an ambush. At this particular location, Timp Pass was exceptionally narrow and rough and the sides of the pass were especially steep. Since it was obvious that Forts Clinton and Montgomery were the objectives and the entire British force would have to march through this pass, Stewart proposed that the hundred soldiers, positioned behind and amid the trees, boulders, brush, and rocks, would effectively hold the pass. Firing down and screaming like demons, they would easily portray the impression of a much larger force. Citing how such an ambush in similar terrain defeated Braddock on 9 July 1755 during the French-Indian War just several miles in front of Fort Duquesne, and a fort Braddock sought to capture, success was achieved when Braddock's leading element was shattered by a numerically smaller force. As its survivors reeled back, amid the noise and gunfire confusion set in; in turn, confusion led to panic and collapse. And here, at Timp Pass, argued Captain Stewart, a similar opportunity now existed.

Major Logan, however, disagreed. Ill, suffering from a fever, his stomach churning from ulcer pains, the major was not seeking a fight. Besides, Governor Clinton's orders were explicit: Major Logan was only to reconnoiter the area and obtain information on British movements. Under no circumstances was he to engage the enemy. Confident that he had accomplished his mission, Major Logan reassembled his men, dispatched a sergeant with news of the British landing directly to Governor Clinton, and proceeded to retire upon the very same route which, just hours before, he had taken during the dark night hours.

Falling in with the others was a very disappointed and frustrated Captain Stewart. For the rest of his life he remained convinced that the British could have been halted and defeated at Timp Pass.[64]

0800 (8 A.M.)

After assembling his troops, Sir Henry issued the order to advance forward. Leading the way was Lieutenant-Colonel Campbell. Campbell's force was to march as rapidly as possible northward along the narrow road from Stony Point to secure Timp Pass. Distance-wise, it was about 3 miles to Timp Pass. Sir Henry regarded this pass as a vital feature. Once secured, Campbell's next objective would be Doodletown, almost 1.5 miles farther up beyond the pass and on the pass's northern edge.

As mentioned, Doodletown lay at an intersection. From this intersection one road veered to the left toward the west/northwest and the other road veered directly to the right and eastward toward the Hudson River. Near the cliffs overlooking the river, the easterly road took a sharp, almost 90-degree northerly turn directly to Fort Clinton.

As for the road which veered to the left, it brought a traveler around and over to the northwestern corner of Bear Hill. At this location, the road parted. The main road continued directly northward, while another smaller secondary road turned directly eastward and circled around the entire rear or northern slope of Bear Hill. As for Bear Hill, it was overshadowed by another hill directly to its north. Known as "The Torne," this sizable hill lay virtually adjacent to Bear Hill.

Tucked in between Bear Hill and The Torne was a lengthy ravine. Spanning from the west to the east, this ravine lies between the base of the northern slope of Bear Hill and the southern slope of The Torne. This ravine is referred to as the Popolopen Ravine. Though somewhat sizable, in some places it, too, is very narrow. Through this ravine also flows a year-round creek. Known as Popolopen Creek,[65] its southern bank borders on the northern slope or edge of Bear Hill and its northern bank borders on The Torne's southern slope or edge. Watered from the various streams, springs, and the runoff waters from Bear Hill, the Torne and the various other terrain features of the Highlands, the creek flows eastward until it empties into the Hudson River. But as the creek nears the cliffs overlooking the Hudson River, it widens, and the creek is characterized with swampy marsh on both sides though in a few places natural fields existed. Popolopen Creek also flowed between Forts Montgomery and Clinton. North of the creek stood Fort Montgomery; to the south stood Fort Clinton. To maintain easier communications between the two forts the patriots constructed a footbridge about four feet in width and three feet above the ground, and this wooden path also spanned over the creek which flowed between the two forts.

As for the road which circles around Bear Hill and passes through the Popolopen Ravine, it weaves alongside Popolopen Creek; however, here and there, it crosses the creek. Small footbridges located along the way enabled a traveler to cross over the creek's waters.

From the road intersection at Doodletown, if a traveler took the western fork to reach Fort Montgomery by going around the entire Bear Hill, the distance was about 5–6 miles; if a traveler took the eastern fork toward the Hudson River and Fort Clinton, the distance was considerably shorter, only about 2 miles. Because of this, much of Sir Henry's planning was centered on the distance factor.

After reaching Doodletown, Lieutenant-Colonel Campbell's force was to immediately veer to the west (left) and take the long route around the western side of Bear Hill; then, via the secondary road which travels through the Popolopen Ravine (again tucked in between Bear Hill and The Torne), Campbell's force was to march eastward to reach Fort Montgomery over-looking the Hudson River. Campbell's mission was to capture Fort Montgomery. Since speed was a vital component of Campbell's mission, he was also to march as rapidly as possible.

In the meantime, as Campbell's force would be working its way around Bear Hill toward Fort Montgomery, General Vaughan's force, upon reaching Doodletown, would veer to the east (right) and after a short march would turn northward to proceed directly to Fort Clinton. His mission was to capture Fort Clinton. Because Sir Henry wanted to attack the two forts simultaneously, Vaughan was to slow the pace of his march to give Campbell additional time.

As for General Tryon, his mission was to occupy and defend Timp Pass from Doodletown to Stony Point, maintain a com-munications line with the British fleet and, on order, be prepared to immediately dispatch additional troops to support either the attack on Fort Montgomery, Fort Clinton, or both.[66]

To ensure swiftness, Sir Henry ordered that all of the cannons and heavy equipment remain on board. Of interest, however, is that although Sir Henry characterized that speed was of the essence to attack the forts, it appears that little or no thought was given to the individual soldier. From the outset, the typical British soldier carried a weight of around 60 pounds of gear and equipment while the Germans carried loads exceeding that. And these weights did not include the weight of each soldier's personal musket.

Needing to know what lay ahead, Lieutenant-Colonel Campbell positioned his scouts to the front and ordered them to immediately set forth. Leading the way was Brom Springster. Born and raised in the Lower Highlands, Springster knew the lay of the land thoroughly. A proud loyalist, he was serving in Col-onel Robinson's regiment. Along with some other loyalists from the same unit, they were inserted amongst the various units to serve as guides. Springster also knew all of the local loyalists. En route to Fort Montgomery he was to point out the homes and properties of the loyalists and non-loyalists. Those identified as being disloyal to the King were to have their properties torched.

With the fog slowly dissipating, from where he stood across the Hudson River on its eastern bank General Putnam finally began to see the first signs of British activity on the river's western bank. A short ways up from Stony Point a boat launching basin was fully engulfed in flames. Perhaps the man who claimed that the British were landing at Stony Point was, after all, correct. Dismounting from his horse, Putnam quickly dispatched a letter to Governor Clinton. Handing the letter to a military runner, he informed him to immediately proceed across the river directly to Governor Clinton. Putnam also wanted to know if Governor Clinton was aware of any British landings at Stony Point and did the governor feel that Fort Montgomery was going to be attacked by land.

When the sergeant dispatched by Major Logan delivered his message to Governor Clinton the governor, wanting to inform General Putnam on what was happening, immediately began to write a message for Putnam. But in the midst of writing, Putnam's runner suddenly appeared. Wanting to know if "the enemy mean to attack fort Montgomery by land"[67] and should this be the case, Putnam cited that he would immediately dispatch reinforcement if reinforcement was requested.

Delighted that a messenger had arrived from Putnam, Governor Clinton immediately wrote out a message on the back of the same paper used by Putnam. Citing the report of Lieutenant English, Governor Clinton acknowledged that the British had, in fact, landed and undoubtedly, their objectives were both Forts Clinton and Montgomery. As for the rein-forcement, Clinton urged that they be dispatched immediately. Governor Clinton also jotted down a time of 8 a.m.[68]

But then, the governor did a most unfortunate thing. Instead of handing his response to Putnam's runner, Governor Clinton instead gave it to Mr. Silvester Waterbury. Waterbury was a non-Northern Army member who simply was a civilian residing in the area and, by profession, was a trader who right at that moment happened to be on the scene. Handing Waterbury the message, the governor reminded Waterbury of the importance of this message and urged him to hurry.

By now, things were moving very rapidly. British troops were advancing into Timp Pass, Putnam was gearing up for action, Governor Clinton was issuing various orders and the British flotilla was edging closer to engage the patriot river fleet and its shoreline defenses. Anticipating reinforcement from General Putnam and not wanting to waste any time, Clinton dispatched some of the fort's personnel in boats over to Robinson's Landing located on the Hudson River's eastern bank to await Putnam's reinforcement. The governor also ordered the frigate *Congress,* docked at Robinson's Landing, to immediately sail to Constitution Island to bolster Fort Constitution's defense.

Despite the rough terrain, Lieutenant-Colonel Campbell's advance guard was proceeding forward at a fast pace. Almost immediately beyond Stony Point, the terrain starts to rise significantly upwards. Reaching the entrance to Timp Pass, Campbell's leading element was now about 500 feet above the river. Proceeding into the pass, in future days those serving alongside Campbell remarked how their commanding officer was amazed that the patriots had made no effort to defend it. Campbell knew that the Americans had just been there because his scouts had reported signs of enemy activity. Delighted that so far all had gone well, Campbell began to advance his entire force into the rough pass. In the meantime his scouts, still accompanied by Brom Springster, had exited Timp Pass and reached Doodletown. But they did not exit the settlement. Instead, they concealed themselves behind some rock walls, trees, and brush to simply observe.

0900 (9 A.M.)[69]

Returning with his troops, Major Logan submitted a report. Unfortunately for Governor Clinton, Major Logan had nothing more to add to Lieutenant English's previous report.

Seeking additional information, Clinton immediately dispatched 20 soldiers, under the command of Lieutenant Paton Jackson, to return immediately to Timp Pass via Doodletown.[70] Though at best only several hours had passed since the first British soldier had landed at Stony Point, much had happened. In fact, the circle of events was rapidly leading to a full scale battle.

As Jackson and his men were rapidly heading for Timp Pass, Lieutenant-Colonel Campbell's force, excluding his scouts, was still within the pass. Huge roots, numerous rocks and boulders and the heavy vegetation, combined with the steep terrain, slowed their march. Initially, Campbell wanted to keep his columns three abreast. But in many places the road was so narrow that his troops could only march in single file.[71] Despite the difficulties, progress was made and Campbell's force was approaching Doodletown. Once through the settlement and around the western slopes of Bear Hill, it was anticipated that the march would proceed without difficulties because though the terrain was still somewhat rough with much vegetation, at least it was not so steep. As for the valley through which flowed the Popolopen Creek, it was significantly wider than Timp Pass and along the way some natural fields existed.

0930–1000 (9:30–10 A.M.)

Proceeding rapidly, Lieutenant Jackson and his men reached the edge of Doodletown. Suddenly, muskets roared and three patriots fell into eternal rest. Unable to recover the bodies, the lieutenant and his survivors fled back to Fort Montgomery.

Hearing the shots, Sir Henry momentarily halted. The shots which echoed through the pass announced to everyone that finally, contact had been made. Standing beside Sir Henry was his aide, Count Grabowski. With a smile upon his face, the Count assured Sir Henry that it soon would be over.

Sir Henry, however, was not the only one who heard the shots. So, too, did Governor Clinton. Ceasing his discussion, he turned into the direction of the shots. Noting that the shots had come from the vicinity of Doodletown, the governor now knew that the British had exited out of Timp Pass. Without even waiting for Lieutenant Jackson's return, Governor Clinton called for an officers meeting.

Distance-wise, it was less than half-a-mile between Fort Clinton and Fort Montgomery. As mentioned, to maintain swifter communications, a wooden footbridge had been constructed to link the two forts together. Light supplies could also be carted by wheelbarrow or hand carried from one fort to the other upon this footbridge. Knowing that the two forts were not in the best condition, Governor Clinton decided to first engage the advancing British forces beyond the forts. Once Putnam's reinforcements appeared, the two forts would be strengthened with fresh troops and the patriots would be in a much better position to engage the incoming enemy.

In response to the British movement, two separate forces were dispatched. The first, from Fort Clinton, consisted of 100 soldiers—50 continentals from the 5th New York Regiment[72] and 50 militiamen. The militia soldiers were commanded by Lieutenant-Colonel James McLaughry; Lieutenant-Colonel Jacobus Bruyn, a continental commander, commanded the continentals and was appointed as overall commander.[73] Bruyn's and McLaughry's mission was to proceed back down the road to Doodletown and somewhere in its vicinity, link up with Lieutenant Jackson. Once united, the combined group was to engage and delay the enemy and report back continuously. Accompanying the two Lieutenant-Colonels was Captain Hamtramck. On that hot day, the two senior officers would need aggressive commanders. Though all of the men were armed with muskets, a number of McLaughry's militiamen did possess a rifle and tomahawk. Those armed with these weapons were also very proficient with them.

The second group, comprising 60 artillerymen now serving as infantrymen and operating out of Fort Montgomery, proceeded west into the pass through which flowed the Popolopen Creek. Commanded by Major Newkirk[74] this group also brought along one 3-pound cannon. Captain Ephraim Fenno was in charge of the gun. Realizing that perhaps an engineer officer would benefit the group Governor Clinton ordered Lieutenant Thomas Machin to accompany the group. As with the other group, their mission likewise was to engage and delay the enemy within the pass.

Pondering what was holding up Putnam or if he had even received the message, Governor Clinton's worries rose. Suddenly, the noise of some force approaching Fort Montgomery from a nearby forest was heard. Fearing that an enemy force was probing in, the defenders of Fort Montgomery readied for action.

Suddenly, an officer emerged from the wood line. Sitting upon a horse, adorned with the hat of a nobleman, and draped in a flowing dark blue cape, he was accompanied by several servants and a small group of militiamen.

It was Lieutenant-Colonel William S. Livingston. Wealthy aristocrats who sided with the American patriots during the Wilderness War of 1777, each and every Livingston male served in the Northern Army and most saw combat from the vicinity of Fort Ticonderoga down to the Highlands; their women nursed the wounded, assisted and housed refugees, and gathered and delivered supplies for the patriot cause. Riding up to the governor, Livingston dismounted, saluted smartly and immediately he and his volunteers were gladly welcomed.[75]

1330 (1:30 P.M.)

Looking at his watch, the governor noted that it was getting late. And still no sign of Putnam. Staring over to Robinson's

Landing from Fort Montgomery, the governor noted the men previously tasked to transport the troops via rowboats and bateaux were still standing by on the shoreline awaiting Put- nam's reinforcement. Anxious and worried that perhaps Putnam had not received the 8 a.m. morning message, Governor Clin- ton quickly wrote out another message informing Putnam what was happening and that reinforcement was of immediate essence. Handing the message to one of Livingston's servants, the governor also instructed him to report immediately to Gen- eral Putnam. Unfortunately for Governor Clinton, his failure to once again utilize a military runner would soon prove to be fatal.

Proceeding toward Doodletown, Lieutenant-Colonels Bruyn and McLaughry encountered Lieutenant Jackson and his withdrawing soldiers. Immediately, Jackson reported to the two patriot commanders that he had lost several men and that a strong enemy force was right behind them. Other than that, Jack- son and the others knew nothing more. Incorporating Jackson and his troops into Bruyn's group, the patriot force dispatched a runner back to Governor Clinton and continued to proceed forward. Not knowing what was up ahead, they probed forward very cautiously.

By now, the bulk of Lieutenant-Colonel Campbell's force had passed through Doodletown. After entering the settlement, Campbell's force immediately veered to the left to proceed around Bear Hill. Campbell was pushing fast and hard. Not- ing the bodies of the slain patriots, Campbell sensed that their compatriots would probably fight for the forts.

As Campbell and his troops were veering around Bear Hill, Major Newkirk, Captain Fenno, and Lieutenant Machin reached a spot which Machin immediately reasoned was worth defending.

Slightly over one mile to the west of Fort Montgom- ery, Popolopen Creek flows through a very narrow gap filled with rocks and boulders. At this particular location, Bear Hill almost links with The Torne. Indeed, the gap here is so narrow that the trail, surrounded by thick brush as the creek's waters flow through it, is very difficult to negotiate. A small group of men effectively utilizing the numerous trees, rocks, and boulders, could easily hold off a much larger force. Lieutenant Machin also knew that once the British exited out of this gap, they would be on far more suitable terrain and Fort Montgomery would be their next stop.

In the meantime, in Fort Montgomery, Governor Clinton was gearing up for battle. Fortunately for the patriots, there was much powder in Fort Montgomery. To effectively defend the fort, the governor removed some of the troops out of Fort Clinton and dispersed them around the three redoubts located to the west (and rear) of Fort Montgomery.[76] The governor reasoned that between those holding the redoubts and the two delaying forces already committed, the others remaining in Forts Clinton and Montgomery would have ample time to prepare for battle as they awaited Putnam's reinforcement. Again looking across the river, the governor was disappointed to see no reinforcement en route. Surely, he must have wondered for the hundredth time "Putnam, where are you?"

Probing cautiously into Doodletown, Lieutenant-Colonels Bruyn and McLaughry's leading troops carefully filtered into the settlement. So far, they had seen nothing of the enemy force previously reported by Lieutenant Jackson. But as the patriot force edged slowly forward, the remainder of Campbell's force suddenly appeared. Shocked in encountering one another, both sides at first just scattered but then, someone fired and a brisk firefight commenced.

Hearing the shots, Lieutenant-Colonel Campbell exhibited no concern. True, the shots were behind him. But Campbell had much more on his mind. He was going for Fort Montgomery. As always is the case in any military operation, time races by.

Maintaining a rapid pace, Campbell marched around Bear Hill and entered the pass.

Likewise hearing the shots inside Fort Montgomery, Governor Clinton now knew that it would not be long. Sensing that the 60-man group which had departed with Newkirk, Fenno, and Lieutenant Machin might be understrength, the governor dispatched another 40 soldiers toward the group now positioned in the narrow valley between Bear Hill and The Torne. Mounting Lieutenant-Colonel Livingston's horse, Governor Clinton set off toward Newkirk. He wanted to take a closer look.

When Machin located a site quickly agreed upon by the other officers as suitable for defense, the brunt of their force was just starting to catch up. It had not been an easy task for the group, especially those hauling the cannon, to negotiate through the very rough terrain. This was especially true during the last approximately 500 yards where the path had narrowed and was exceptionally poor. In addition to the cannon being pushed and pulled along, everything else for operating the gun—the gunpowder barrels, cannon balls, grapeshot rounds, and the cannon's various artifacts—had to be hand carried as well. Some of the initial 60 soldiers were in place, but most were not. As for the 40 others, they had not yet caught up. Compounding the situation was that no time had been available to prepare a proper defense. When ordered to accompany the group, Machin proceeded to gather up some axes and shovels within Fort Montgomery to drop some trees and dig in. But because at that very moment no tools were available, the group departed without any tools. Deciding to advance slightly forward to take a better look Lieutenant Machin proceeded ahead but, as he would later recall—"Before I could reconnoiter the ground after posting my men, I found myself nearly surrounded."[77]

Appearing suddenly, Campbell's advance guard was spotted approaching through the trees and brush. Quickly wheeling the cannon around so that its barrel would point directly to the front and westward, Captain Fenno and his gunners fired a grapeshot round through the thick brush. Initially, Machin's intent had been to position the cannon on a higher piece of terrain but the lack of time prevented this from happening. Reloading rapidly, the gunners unleashed more rounds. As the cannon crewmen and defenders blazed away, they were quickly joined by the 40 soldiers dispatched to assist. A brisk firefight ensued.

As some of the British soldiers returned fire, others worked their way through the thick brush of the slopes to either flank or attack the Americans from the rear. Ably led and flanking the patriots, they began to fire down upon the defenders within the narrow pass. Another group of British soldiers succeeded in working their way behind the patriots. Now, the Americans were surrounded.

Yet, the surrounded patriots continued to resist ably. Rapidly reloading the cannon and their muskets, they blazed away. The massive boom of the cannon was heard far and wide. Grapeshot balls, along with accurate musket fire, took its toll of Campbell's force. Until somehow the patriots and their cannon crew would be dislodged or overrun, Campbell's advance for the moment was halted.

After moving rapidly into Doodletown, General Vaughan veered to the right. Prior to his arrival, the patriot force engaging the remnants of Campbell's force had retreated from the settlement. Vaughan's force was now about 2 miles from Fort Clinton. Noting that a sizable battle was now being waged on the other side of Bear Hill, Vaughan realized that if Fort Clinton should be overrun he would not only be in an excellent position to immediately attack Fort Montgomery but, likewise, would unhinge the entire patriot defense. Despite Sir Henry's order to slow the pace toward Fort Clinton, Vaughan decided otherwise. Now, his intent was to move forward as rapidly as possible. Vaughan ordered his soldiers to drop their heavy rucksacks and all unnecessary items.

Halfway out to where Newkirk's force was surrounded but still resisting, Governor Clinton, realizing that his sole appearance would not benefit anyone, turned the horse around and galloped back to Fort Montgomery where he quickly organized a force to cover Newkirk's group in the event Newkirk decided to retire back to the fort. Among those ordered for the covering force was an artillery lieutenant named Oliver Lawrence. Hauling a hefty, 12-pound naval cannon, this force quickly proceeded to a point not far from where the patriots were battling it out with Campbell's force. Readying the cannon, they positioned themselves for action.

Following their skirmish at Doodletown with the stragglers from Campbell's force, Bruyn and McLaughry quickly withdrew. But they did not withdraw very far. Behind a creek east of Doodletown the two lieutenant-colonels organized their first line of defense. Within minutes of the establishment of their defensive line, the patriots encountered Vaughan's quickly approaching leading element and proceeded to fire upon them. Totally disregarding the small arms fire being directed against them, the British pressed forward with fixed bayonets and forced the patriots to retire; however, though they withdrew, they fell back in order.

Previously, when en route to Doodletown, both Bruyn and McLaughry had noted an ideal position. Slightly beyond a quarter-of-a-mile from Fort Clinton lay a huge pond. Almost a mile in length with an average width of about a quarter-of-a-mile, the pond was known as the "One Mile Pond" or as "Lake Sinipink."[78] The pond, however, lay in a northerly to southerly direction and the terrain adjacent this body of water sloped downward.[79] From the edge of this pond eastward to the Hudson River, the distance is less than half-a-mile.

As mentioned previously, the road which forks to the right at Doodletown proceeds to the east and, after a short distance, turns sharply to the left and northward. As a traveler veers to the north (or left), this road exits directly into Fort Clinton. But a portion of this road is also tucked in between the pond and the Hudson River; furthermore, the terrain slopes upward as one proceeds farther northward and numerous trees, brush, rocks, and boulders characterize the lay of the land. So if a commander positioned a force to face southward between the pond and the cliffs of the Hudson River, he would effectively block the road and the avenue of approach for any force advancing northward. And that, exactly, is what both Bruyn and McLaughry had in mind.

Withdrawing in order, here and there along the way select riflemen were dropped off. Concealing themselves amid the trees, brush, and boulders, the task of these snipers was to hold up the British advance to buy time for Bruyn and McLaughry.

The snipers did not have to wait long. Well-placed shots, especially directed against British officers and sergeants, kept the British at bay. Though still advancing, Vaughan was slowed and he began to incur his first significant casualties.

1400 (2 P.M.)

In the narrow Popolopen Valley between Bear Hill and The Torne, Campbell's force began to overrun the small patriot force. Throughout the fighting, Captain Fenno and his crew had repeatedly turned, aimed, loaded, and fired their cannon with skill and precision. Knowing that they were running out of ammunition and if they remained in place they would be either killed or captured, they opted to break out. Mounting bayonets, they surged forward.

By now, the cannoneers were covered in sweat, grime, and burned powder; their eyes burned from the smoke and residue; their throats parched from the heat of the battle; their ears and heads rang from the constant massive booms of the cannon and the staccato of the uninterrupted small arms fire. Bullets and musket balls whizzed by, and on more than one occasion Captain Fenno wondered just how much more of this he could take. For the defenders it was, indeed, a very hellish affair.

"CHARGE!!!" With the shout of this one-word command, Captain Fenno's cannon boomed for one last time. Just moments before, the cannon had been turned to the east. Loaded with grapeshot, it was fired toward the enemy operating to the rear of the patriots. *Hopefully*, thought Fenno, *the blast had helped to create a hole.*

Leaping forward, the patriots charged into the British still momentarily stunned by the blast. Leading the way was Lieutenant Machin and Major Newkirk. Spiking the cannon, Captain Fenno and his crewmen also surged forward. The patriots were determined to break out.

Close-in combat ensued. Muskets were fired at point blank range and after, were swung like clubs. Knives, daggers, swords, and bayonets came out. Although the tomahawk in this part of the region was not so widely utilized as farther to the north, some of the men did possess this exotic weapon. Screaming like demons, they swung these lethal weapons and shattered bones and skulls. Every tomahawk was bloodied. Others killed with bare hands. Even rocks were picked up and hurled against opponents. "KEEP GOING! WE'RE ALMOST OUT OF THIS HELL-HOLE!!!" The name stuck. To this day, this particular piece of ground is known as the "Hell-Hole."

A short distance away, Lieutenant Lawrence and his men began to tense. The massive noise, along with the cloud of dust which rose hundreds of feet upward, began to near. Lawrence knew that his turn was rapidly approaching.

Southeast of the Hell-Hole, General Vaughan's soldiers, despite the deadly sniper fire, continued to advance. Encountering the hastily erected picket line established by Bruyn's and McLaughry's troops and unable to maneuver around it, Vaughan ordered a direct frontal assault.

Skillfully using the cover of the numerous trees, boulders, and rocks to their advantage, Vaughan's soldiers crawled, aimed, fired, reloaded, and leaped forward. For approximately the next two hours, until about 4 p.m., this type of fighting characterized the scene. Slowly but surely, the British were making progress. As they pressed closer, the patriots incurred more and more casualties. In an attempt to outflank the patriot defenders who were holding a position between the southeastern edge of the "One Mile Pond" and the Hudson River, the British decided to insert a sizable British force into the patriot rear. The British 63rd Foot was ordered to circle rapidly around the western and northern perimeter of the "One Mile Pond." Once repositioned, the 63rd Foot would cut off Bruyn's and McLaughry's troops from behind and assist in attacking Fort Clinton.

Looking beyond the ramparts overlooking the Hudson River Governor Clinton wondered for the 1,000th time why Putnam had not yet appeared. If he failed to appear, the governor was certain the two forts would fall.

By now, the battle was in full swing. Disregarding their casualties, the British continued to advance. Noting a critical situation, Sir Henry ordered Tryon to leave one battalion behind to protect Timp Pass and move the other battalions into Doodletown. Entering the settlement, Tryon noted that it had not yet been torched. Immediately, Tryon ordered that Doodletown be razed totally to the ground.

1600 (4 P.M.)

At approximately this time across the Hudson River in the vicinity of Peekskill, Governor Clinton's messenger, Sylvester Waterbury,[80] suddenly appeared at General Putnam's headquarters. Within minutes of his arrival, Livingston's servant also appeared. But it did not matter. Both messages were delivered too late. Because at this very moment General Putnam was farther downriver observing the events as best as he could from the Hudson's eastern bank, the messages were instead delivered to Colonel Samuel Wyllys.

Wyllys was shocked! The first message had been written at least eight hours before. Without waiting to notify General

Putnam on what course of action to take, Wyllys immediately took the initiative. Quickly gathering all of the continentals around him he placed them under the command of Colonel Jonathan Meigs and ordered the force to march as rapidly as possible to Robinson's Landing to cross the river and report immediately to Governor Clinton at Fort Montgomery.

As Colonel Meigs was rapidly marching to the river's crossing point, Major Newkirk and Lieutenant Machin, though fighting against superior odds, were breaking out. Shot in the chest, Machin disregarded his wound and continued to press forward. As the survivors who succeeded in breaking out ran down the road and surged past Lieutenant Lawrence's position, Lawrence readied his 20 men. Because the governor had personally stipulated to Lawrence that he was not to engage any incoming British forces but was only to cover Major Newkirk's force withdrawing into Fort Montgomery, Lawrence informed his men that his intent was to fire the cannon about two or three times along with a volley or two of musket fire prior to quickly retiring to the fort with the cannon.

As the remainder of the breakout force raced by, it was obvious that the patriot force had paid a heavy price for their epic stand in the ravine and during the breakout. Of the 100 or so who had initially entered the "Hell-Hole," at best only about 60 survivors emerged out of it. Amongst the non-returnees was Captain Fenno.

Along with Major Newkirk's battered remnants retreating back to Fort Montgomery, Lieutenant-Colonels Bruyn and McLaughry's troops were likewise retreating. Though their stand had served its purpose, they could no longer hold. Taking casualties, running out of ammunition and unlike the British who were continuously bringing up fresh manpower, Bruyn and McLaughry had no support other than Fort Clinton's sole cannon still hammering away.

Arriving at his headquarters, General Putnam was immediately informed by Colonel Samuel Wyllys on what had transpired. Fully agreeing and approving of the colonel's decision, General Putnam also ordered that Meigs' regiment be strengthened. A militia regiment of 500 strong was commanded to immediately follow and assist in the defense of the two forts.[81]

Retreating into Fort Clinton, Bruyn and McLaughry encountered General James Clinton who had just organized a force to rush out to support the two commanders. Knowing that his brother Governor George Clinton in adjacent Fort Montgomery was in need of extra troops, he now ordered Bruyn to reposition himself and his troops into Fort Montgomery while McLaughry was to occupy and defend a redoubt with its three small 6-pound cannons about 300 feet to the southwest of Fort Clinton.[82] Exiting Fort Clinton, Bruyn's force raced northward and down the bridge connecting the two forts; simultaneously, McLaughry quickly occupied the redoubt with his 80 troops[83] and immediately engaged the advancing enemy with small arms and cannon fire. In addition to taking fire from the redoubt, Vaughan's nearing troops were now also taking fire from Fort Clinton's riflemen and its remaining 12-pound cannon. But the British thrust could not be stopped. Augmented with grenadiers from the newly inserted 7th Foot and the German Hessians, Vaughan's force continued to surge forward.

Northwest of Fort Montgomery stood three small redoubts. Deciding to defend these as well, Governor Clinton ordered Colonel Lewis Dubois and Lieutenant-Colonels William Livingston and Samuel Logan to man each one of the redoubts. Approaching Fort Montgomery and noting its weak western wall, Lieutenant-Colonel Campbell ordered an attack against the three positions. The attackers were now no more than 80 yards in front of the redoubts.[84] Once overrun, Fort Montgomery would be immediately attacked.

Despite a strong assault, the redoubts held and the attackers were repulsed. Needing more troops, Campbell called for reinforcement. As he awaited them, from a short distance he continued to engage the redoubts and Fort Montgomery. In the meantime, small groups of British and loyalists began to infiltrate their way around the redoubts and into the area of the two forts. One such group reached the steep bank overlooking the river not far from the northern perimeter of Fort Montgomery. From here they edged closer to the fort and prepared to attack it from the edge of the cliff. Noting their movement from the deck of his ship the *Montgomery*, Captain John Hodges aimed the ship's 12-pound cannon in their direction and lobbed several cannon balls at them. Captain Hodges' action not only warned the defenders of the fort that an enemy force was sneaking in from behind but after exposing them to naval fire, forced the infiltrators to flee.

Needing more powder and ammunition, General James dispatched a detachment of men to run to Fort Montgomery to obtain the supplies. But as they proceeded down the bridge, they were forced to return. Through waist- and chest-high water and concealed by Popolopen Creek's thick brush, infiltrators succeeded in reaching the bridge. Concealing themselves around the narrow bridge, they opened fire upon the Americans heading to Fort Montgomery. After repulsing the patriots, the infiltrators proceeded to burn the bridge.

Chapter 7

The Highlands Fall to Sir Henry's Juggernaut!

Until the late afternoon of 6 October, the battle in the Highlands had solely been a land battle. But sometime between the hours of 4 and 5 p.m. it progressed into a river battle when the English Royal Navy intervened.

Noting that Sir Henry's troops would benefit from naval support Captain James Wallace, after circling around Salisbury Island (present day Iona Island), ordered his fleet to approach the closest they could to the western bank and the chain spanning the river. In itself, the chain was stretched across the Hudson River from the shoreline below Fort Montgomery to a land feature on the river's eastern edge which jutted outward into the Hudson River and was known as "Anthony's Nose."

Behind this chain were positioned four of Captain John Hodges' boats. The mission of Hodges' river fleet was to protect the chain, bar any enemy ships from traveling northward, assist the defenders of the forts adjacent the river banks, and transport men and material going back and forth across the river, as well as up and down the Hudson.

From the western bank to the eastern bank, Hodges' four patriot ships were positioned in a straight line. *Montgomery,* already engaging the enemy[1] was positioned closest to the western bank; next in line stood *Lady Washington* followed by the *Camden* and the *Shark*. *Lady Washington* and the *Camden* were positioned in the center while the *Shark* was positioned closest to the eastern bank. As for Captain Hodges, he remained on the *Montgomery*.

Captain Hodges' flotilla was, however, very weak. His four ships lacked crewmen and firepower. All were outgunned by the Royal Navy. When just one week previously before the captain of the *Congress*[2] had complained directly to Governor Clinton that he lacked a crew and only had "four men on board fit for duty!"[3] in response, the governor authorized the captain to impound some ferryboat operators.[4]

Nearing their targets, several of the British ships engaged the forts while the other ships sailed directly toward the patriot boats. The first to engage Sir Wallace's approaching ships was the *Lady Washington*. Possessing the fleet's one and only heavy 32-pound cannon, the patriot gunners attempted to halt Sir Wallace's efforts. Though *Lady Washington* was struck with a broadside, its captain continued to resist. Amid the Herculean noise of the cannons, the screams of "COMMENCE FIRE!" were repeatedly heralded.

It was bad enough for those fighting a savage and, now, close-in battle on the ground. But the intensity of the river's combat rose to a much higher tempo as cannoneers fired, reloaded rapidly, and fired over and over. Within minutes of the herculean thunder of the cannons, the entire river valley was filled with one massive cloud of thick smoke. Yet, gunners on both sides continued to blast away.

With darkness setting in, Sir Henry wanted to capture the two forts and put an end to the day's battle. It had been a long and exhaustive day. Almost all of his officers and soldiers had been up for nearly twenty-four hours and, as every commander knows, exhaustion in itself can destroy a force just as fast, if not even faster, than actual combat. Pressing for a final victory, Sir Henry ordered that Forts Clinton and Montgomery be attacked jointly.

Fort Clinton would be attacked from the west and south. The 63rd Foot Regiment, now approaching from the northwest after circling around the "One Mile Pond," would attack directly from the northwest as two flank companies from the 7th and 26th Foot Regiments and one company of Anspach grenadiers would attack from the south. The remaining companies of the 7th and 26th Foot, along with the dismounted dragoons from the 17th Light Dragoons and the one independent von Trumbach Hessian battalion, would stand by in reserve.

Fort Montgomery would be attacked directly from the west and northwest with five units positioned side-by-side: the 52nd and 57th Foot Regiments, the German Emmerich Chasseurs, the Loyal Americans, and the New York Volunteers.

1700 (5 P.M.)[5]

In an attempt to secure Fort Montgomery without any further bloodshed, Lieutenant-Colonel Campbell ordered that a white flag be hoisted. Both sides ceased to fire. An eerie silence prevailed over the entire area.

Within moments a very young drummer boy appeared. Beating his drum, the rattle of his drumming was heard far and wide. This beat, internationally known as "the parley" signifies that one commander wants to meet with the opposing commander. Emerging into the open, Lieutenant-Colonel Campbell stood proudly. Despite a long day, he looked immaculate in his full uniform. Campbell wanted to speak to the commander of Fort Montgomery.

Considering it improper for someone in the position and rank of a governor and general to negotiate with a lieutenant-colonel, Governor Clinton instead sent forward Lieutenant-Colonel Livingston who was equal in rank to Campbell. Accompanying Livingston was Lieutenant Machin who, despite his wound, was still fighting. Livingston was also a good choice because in his uniform and cape he portrayed the image of an aristocratic officer.

Approaching the English officer, Livingston and Machin were greeted with a cheerful friendliness. But then, Campbell got straight to the point. Citing that he wanted to prevent further bloodshed, he demanded the surrender of Fort Montgomery. The British commander was hoping that the psychological approach would work and the Americans would give in.

Livingston, however, not only rejected Campbell's request but, in a very polite manner, requested that Campbell surrender instead. Livingston assured Campbell that he and his men would be "well treated."[6] Rejecting Livingston's offer, Livingston responded "Very well then. You may renew the attack as soon as I shall return within the fort."[7] Turning around, the two patriot officers returned. The battle would resume.

Returning to his troops, Campbell issued the order to prepare for combat. Suddenly, no less than 800 to 900 soldiers[8] with fixed bayonets, stood up. From their throats a massive battle cry thundered far and wide and the combined English, German, and loyalist forces began to surge forward.

Campbell, however, would not live to see the soon-to-be victory. From the moment he had first ventured forward under a white flag until his return to his lines, Campbell had been kept under a constant and vigilant observation through the front and rear sights of a rifle. With a powerful eye and a finger upon the trigger, from the ramparts of Fort Montgomery, a rifleman was carefully tracking his target. Pulling the trigger, with tremendous force and speed, a bullet tore deep into Campbell's heart and lungs. Collapsing to the ground, the British officer never again stood up.

From where he stood Colonel Beverley Robinson witnessed the fall of Lieutenant-Colonel Campbell. With no other senior ranking British officer present, Robinson immediately assumed command. He was, however, a very competent and loyal officer. Determined to renew the attack, Robinson shouted one word: "CHARGE!!!"[9]

At this time, Fort Montgomery held 300 defenders; Fort Clinton had, at best, 200 plus.[10] Against Fort Clinton alone General Vaughan committed no less than 1,200 troops.[11] With ammunition running out and pressured by the enemy's land and river forces, the exhausted defenders began to collapse. With bayonets dripping blood, the enemy overran the three redoubts and surged toward the forts.

Despite their strong attack, it was no pushover for the attackers. Robinson and Vaughan suffered heavy casualties. Charging toward Fort Clinton, Count Grabowski was suddenly struck by gunfire. Collapsing to the ground, he never again would see his fine estate in faraway Poland. Reaching the walls, the attackers positioned their ladders and surged over, onto the ramparts; others, smashing open the main and rear gates of the fort, rushed in. Amid the massive noise of the battle, Governor Clinton knew that the end was now at hand. No more could be done. For those still alive inside and around Fort Clinton, the time to retreat was now.

But this in itself would be no easy matter. To begin with, there was no officially designated site to retreat to. As for those who had decided to escape, they would first have to break out. In close-in combat, this is never an easy affair. Despite the collapse of command and control, small groups of men, ably led by aggressive commanders, began to commence their breakouts. Mounting a bayonet to the tip of his musket, Issac Franks wondered if he would survive the night. A practicing Jew who joined the Northern Army, Franks mentally recited a Hebrew prayer. Charging forward, Franks and his compatriots bayoneted, slashed, and clubbed their way out of encirclement. So determined were they to break out that no one was willing to surrender. Amid the evening's darkness, noise, and crackle of burning buildings, and the terror and carnage of those still fighting and dying, Fort Clinton ceased to be a patriot stronghold.

1900 (7 P.M.)

Screaming like a demon and swinging the remains of a musket shattered moments before on a loyalist, Captain Hamtramck broke out. Attempting to reach his brother in Fort

Montgomery, General James Clinton first ran up the road and then proceeded cross-country through a field adjacent the shattered footbridge. As he ran, musket and rifle rounds whizzed by and he could not fail to note the numerous corpses lying around. Amid the darkness, confusion, numerous explosions, and gunfire flashes, the brutal and ugly night exhibited the awful look of a scene right out of Dante's Inferno. Racing as fast as he could, General James actually ran past a handful of British soldiers firing and reloading.

Suddenly, a British soldier lunged at him. A long bayonet blade sank deep into his thigh. But before the soldier could administer the coup-de-grace, General James got away. Despite his severe wound, he managed to hobble away quickly. Fortunately, the blade had not struck bone.

Reaching Fort Montgomery, General James noted that it was still somehow holding out. In an attempt to escape, some of the fort's defenders were going over the wall or exiting its rear. Once outside they fled into the direction of the steep bank overlooking the Hudson River. Entering the fort, General James found his brother.

When the three redoubts west of Fort Montgomery fell, its survivors retreated into the fort. Among them was Lieutenant-Colonel Dubois. Noting these individuals, General James urged Governor Clinton to flee while he still could. Amid the gunfire and noise, the governor proclaimed "I refuse to leave my men behind!"

Suddenly, another volley of patriot fire tore into the ranks of the New York Volunteers attacking Fort Montgomery directly from the north. A number of loyalists including Major Alexander Grant, the commanding officer of this loyalist force, were killed. Immediately Captain George Turnball, who served in the Loyal Americans Regiment, assumed command of the New York Volunteers.

Despite his initial reluctance to flee, Governor Clinton agreed to go. In actuality he had no choice for it was imperative that the governor not be killed or captured. Quickly assembling a handful of men for protection, the governor grabbed his suitcase with its important papers and scurried out of the fort heading directly to the cliff overlooking the Hudson. Amid the darkness and confusion the governor, his brother James, and some others succeeded in escaping by clambering over the side of the steep bank down to the river as others fled to the north.

Fortunately for the patriots, the British had not yet broken the chain. Though the four small patriot ships had taken hits, they were still floating. Noting the situation, their crewmen began to rescue those who had succeeded in clamboring down the steep cliff onto the river's bank but now, were stranded on it. Also assisting in the rescue effort were the men dispatched hours earlier to Robinson's Landing to pick up the soon-to-arrive reinforcements which, in the end, never appeared. For the next several hours they rowed back and forth across the river to transport those who had broken out. Because of the brave efforts of those such as Captain Hodges and the rowboaters, a number of the fleeing soldiers were successfully ferried from the Hudson River's western bank onto its eastern bank.

Boarding the *Montgomery,* Governor Clinton thanked Captain Hodges for his efforts. After conferring with Captain Hodges, he transferred himself onto a rowboat and the crew rowed him to a boat launching site on the Hudson's eastern bank. From there the governor quickly proceeded to Peekskill to meet with General Putnam. As for General James, after reaching the shoreline he and his escort immediately crossed the river upon the rafts floating side-by-side[12] holding up the heavy chain spanning the river. For the moment, General James and his followers were now safe on the other side.

2200 (10 P.M.)

Seeing that he could do no more, Captain Hodges ordered his small fleet to sail up the river to Constitution Island. But the night's darkness, along with heavy winds, tides, and much crew inexperience resulted in three of the ships running aground. Only the *Lady Washington* sailed away. On board she carried a number of the survivors. Unable to free themselves, the ship's crews had to abandon the boats. Not wanting the *Montgomery* to be captured, after ordering his men into the row boats, Captain Hodges torched his ship. In turn, the *Shark* and *Camden* followed suit. Along with the fires raging on the western side, three additional huge fires now engulfed the river. As flames reached the remaining powder and ammunition on board the ships, huge explosions heralded far and wide. Suddenly countless thousands of fiery sparks and pieces of burning wood rose hundreds of feet into the night sky. So intense were the flames that a viewer was actually able see a large portion of the river from a distance. From where he stood now miles away, Governor Clinton could hear the massive explosions and observe flames rising high into the dark sky. On the following day Charles Stedman, a loyalist historian who witnessed the death of the three patriot ships, wrote:

> "The flames suddenly broke forth; and, as every sail was set, the vessels soon became magnificent pyramids of fire. The reflection on the steep face of the opposite mountain [Anthony's Nose], and the long train of ruddy light that shone upon the water for a prodigious distance, had a wonderful effect; whilst the ear was awfully filled with the continued echoes from the rocky shores, as the flames gradually reached the cannon."[13]

Throughout the day, as Sir Henry's forces fought to capture Forts Clinton and Montgomery, Major Moffat's scouts continued with their scouting mission. Aggressively reconnoitering the entire region, in addition to monitoring the Hudson River they probed far and wide into various directions. In the vicinity of King's Ferry, four prisoners were nabbed. Bound and gagged, they were quickly taken to a site where several canoes were concealed under brush. In the late night dark hours of 6

October, the four were ferried across the Hudson. Soon, they appeared before Major Moffat.

SARATOGA

General Burgoyne completed a supply inventory. For the British commander, it was a grim matter. No forage existed. The horses were hungry. His food supply rations were low. At best, he could only feed his army for about another five days. True, he could again cut the food ration. But that had already been done. And a further cut would only prolong the inevitable end for just several more days. It no longer mattered. In a matter of days, his army would run out of food. Burgoyne desperately needed Sir Henry's help. Reaching for a pen, Burgoyne wrote out another quick dispatch for Sir Henry.

Miles away in Germantown, Pennsylvania, in late evening, British Army General William Howe received a note from General George Washington. Addressed directly to Howe, Washington's message was concise and straight to the point. The message stated:

NO. 40. NOTE TO SIR WILLIAM HOWE

General Washington's compliments to General Howe, does himself the pleasure to return to him a Dog, which accidentally fell into his [Washington's] hands, and by the inscription on the Collar, appears to belong to General Howe.
OCTOBER 6TH.1777

The issue was a bull dog canine. Somehow, two days earlier, as the Battle of Germantown had raged back and forth, Washington's soldiers picked up a dog within their lines with an inscription on the collar indicating that the canine belonged to Howe. Being a dog lover himself and, undoubtedly, Washington reasoned that a message from him to Howe would demonstrate that the American Army was still operating in the field; the dog was returned under a flag of truce.

TUESDAY, 7 OCTOBER. MIDNIGHT[14]

Forts Clinton and Montgomery were in British hands.

Shortly after midnight, Governor Clinton entered General Putnam's headquarters in Continental Village. [15] En route to Putnam's headquarters the governor encountered roads clogged with army stragglers and civilians fleeing northward, eastward, westward. Encountering Lieutenant-Colonel Meigs' regiment and the 500-men militia force heading to Robinson's Landing, from where they were to be ferried across the river to Forts Clinton and Montgomery, the governor was delighted to see that some units were still intact. Informing them that the forts had fallen, the governor ordered the troops to return to Peekskill to await new orders.

Upon meeting up with General Putnam, "Old Put" requested to be relieved of command. Knowing that Putnam had moved listlessly and ineffectively throughout that crucial day, Governor Clinton complied and immediately did so.[16]

0200 (2 A.M.)

Relinquishing his command to Governor Clinton,[17] Putnam disappeared into the darkness. Encountering Brigadier-General Samuel H. Parsons in Continental Village, Governor Clinton and Parsons quickly established some key decisions and orders began to be issued. It was going to be another sleepless night but with more capable leadership in charge, things began to improve.

Both agreed that Peekskill,[18] Continental Village, and the post at Sydnam's Bridge had to be abandoned. Although the chain spanning the river had not yet been breached, it was obvious that the unprotected chain would not hold for long. Convinced that Sir Henry's intent was to reach Burgoyne, the two commanders agreed that an immediate defensive effort would have to be made to initially halt, or at least slow, Sir Henry's push farther up river. To better counter the British thrust, it was agreed that the patriots would have to retreat farther northward into a newly designated assembly area in the higher terrain near the town of Fishkill. Once there, the survivors would be quickly reorganized and were reinforced with Colonel Samuel B. Webb's regiment. Afterward, the newly reconstituted force would re-cross the river onto its western side (in the vicinity of present day West Point) where earlier in 1777 a battery known as Machin's Battery had been positioned to protect Constitution Island. Here, a strong defensive position would be established with the newly inserted troops. It was anticipated that the chevaux-de-frise[19] constructed at Pollepel Island to the north of Constitution Island and across from New Windsor would likewise be effective in the defense. Yet, despite the planning, things quickly changed.

Governor Clinton and General Parsons, however, were not the only ones active that night. So, too, was Sir Henry.

After capturing the two forts, many things were happening: prisoners were being rounded up; the wounded and injured were being taken care of; the dead were being assembled for burial; and Sir Henry and his staff were planning another course of action to be undertaken immediately at daybreak. Throughout the night, intermittent gunfire was heard. As some of Sir Henry's soldiers searched the immediate countryside around the two forts for any patriot personnel still hiding out, they continuously encountered individuals still attempting to escape.

At daybreak, 265 patriot prisoners were counted.[20] Of these, almost half were from the 5th New York Continental Regiment.[21] The previous day the regiment carried 29 officers and 268 enlisted.[22] Colonel Allison, Lieutenant-Colonel's Bruyn, Livingston,[23] and McLaughry; Majors Stephen Lush, Samuel Logan, Hammill; Captains Henry Godwin and Fenno; Lieutenant Jackson and Quartermaster Nehemiah Carpenter, were just some of the officers captured. A sizable number of lieutenants and ensigns were also captured.[24] McLaughry, though bayoneted seven times, was still somehow surviving. As he lay on the ground with a fellow patriot attending his wounds, Sir Henry suddenly appeared and asked – "and where is my good friend George [Clinton]?" "Safe, thank God, and beyond the reach of your friendship!" was McLaughry's brisk response.[25]

For the British, it had not been an easy affair, though the Royal Navy had participated the brunt of the battle had been fought by the infantry. Because the trails were exceptionally rough and in many places narrow, and there simply was no time to clear and widen any approaches, no cannons or mortars were brought along. As an English participant later testified:

> "I never saw more gallantry and intrepidity shown on any occasion than on this. It is impossible to give an idea of the strength of the country we had to march through to this attack; well might they think it impregnable, for it certainly was so to any but British troops. But they took it even without cannon."[26]

Regarding casualties, the exact losses incurred by Sir Henry are not known. But they were high.[27]

In the aftermath of the capture of the Highlands, Sir Henry cited a loss of 7 officers, 3 sergeants, and 30 rank-and-file as being killed.[28] This included some of his top leaders such as Lieutenant-Colonel Campbell, Major Alexander Grant, Major Sill, and Count Grabowski. In addition to those killed, Sir Henry reported 11 officers, 4 sergeants, 1 drummer, and 130 grenadier soldiers were wounded.[29] According to one source, "in storming the forts, the British had about 150 men killed or wounded."[30] It is also not known if Sir Henry's casualty figures reflect the German and loyalist losses. But it is known that some of the wounded perished later outside of the area. Such was the case of Captain Von Erckert, a German grenadier. Wounded while storming Fort Montgomery, he succumbed to his wounds in New York City on 12 October.[31] And infantry grenadier Johann

Michael Krigbaum was among the Germans killed while attacking Fort Montgomery.[32] Despite Sir Henry's report, a German report dated 8 October cited a loss of 300 soldiers.[33] In consideration of all of this, it actually appears that Sir Henry's casualties were considerably higher than what he had initially alluded to.

0900 (9 A.M.)

By mid-morning, Governor Clinton had repositioned his headquarters in a building known as the Widow Falls House located in New Windsor Square.[34] From here, for the time being, the governor would direct the defense of the Highlands.

At the very moment that Governor Clinton was reestablishing his headquarters, the British were dismantling the chain barring the Hudson River. At first, Sir Hotham had attempted to float a boat, the *Dependence*, over the chain. Hotham felt that if enough weight and pressure from a sizable boat could be placed upon the chain, then perhaps the chain would be submerged deep enough to allow it and the other boats to pass over. Failing in this attempt, the British commodore knew that it would have to be shattered. The chain was simply too stiff and not flexible enough to be pushed under. "The construction of both [chain and boom] gives strong proofs of labour, industry, and skill"[35]—so stated Commodore Hotham in his praise of the river obstacle.[36] Since high-grade steel was also in demand, Hotham issued orders to those disassembling the chain to save as much of it as possible. How much was salvaged and how many chain linkages ended up in the river's bottom will never be known but it is known that a sizable number of its links were removed and transported down to New York City where steel was in demand.

As Commodore Hotham's naval personnel were struggling to dismantle the chain, a delegation of British military personnel, commanded by an officer, rowed up in a small boat toward Fort Constitution. The officer wanted to deliver a message from Sir Henry to the garrison's commander. Rowing toward the island fort under a huge white flag, the officer was never able to deliver the message because as they approached the island they came under musket fire. Quickly turning around, they rowed rapidly back down the river. Angered by this action, Sir Henry ordered that once the chain and boom obstacle was breached the island was to be immediately assaulted.

Throughout 6 October, as a furious battle raged for the two forts, the defenders of Fort Constitution knew that it was just a matter of time before they, too, would be embroiled in it. Previously, on 17 July 1777, a return of Major John Porter's troops at Fort Constitution revealed a total of 117 continentals and 86 militiamen for a total of 203 personnel.[37] On 24 July, a return of Major Porter's troops at Fort Constitution revealed a strength of 100 continental troops and 80 militiamen on duty for a total of 180.[38] Of the militiamen, 12 were in the artillery[39] commanded by Captain Gershom Mott. This figure, however, excluded the 33 continentals and 33 militiamen absent from duty.[40] The 24 July return also appears to be the last official return prior to Major Porter's position being assumed by Major Lewis Dubois[41] who commanded on 6 October.

Regardless of what the true strength had been, the July strength roster was no longer in effect on the day when Sir Henry attacked the Highlands. Well before 6 October, Fort Constitution's manpower strength had been depleted. When Sir Henry attacked, Major Dubois commanded approximately 100 "new levies and militia,"[42] about 30 rear-echelon supply troops,[43] and the artillery company still commanded by Captain Gershom Mott.[44]

What further complicated Major Dubois' situation was that Fort Constitution was not only weak in manpower but the fort itself was not yet completed. Excluding the uncompleted fort only one redoubt, some troop barracks, and one small underground ammunition storage bunker existed.[45] Furthermore, Fort Constitution was situated in a very precarious position. Directly across the river the terrain overlooked the island. From here even a small enemy force with just one cannon could easily devastate the island. Despite plans to construct a strong patriot position on the overlooking terrain, other than the one small established battery which on 6 and 7 October was not even occupied, these plans were never realized.

Unfortunately for Major Dubois, the events of 6 October proved to be hazardous. Commencing in the early evening hours but especially through the night of 6-7 October, numerous stragglers drifted in when fleeing northward. Some arrived by boat while others came on foot. Seeking either medical aid or something quick to eat prior to fleeing farther northward, they stopped at Fort Constitution. These individuals also brought news of the defeat and fall of Forts Clinton and Montgomery. As always is the case in such times stories will be exaggerated, rumors abound, and an air of defeatism sets in. The sight of the patriot ship *Congress* did not help matters either. Ordered northward to assist in the defense of the island, en route to the island but within sight of it, the *Congress* ran aground. Hopelessly stuck and unable to extradite itself, at daybreak the captain ordered the ship to be abandoned and burned. As the ship burned in full view and more stragglers appeared, the existing fears of the island's defenders were so heightened that a personnel count taken in late morning revealed that some of the island's defenders had deserted.

After breaking out, Colonels Lewis Dubois and John Lamb crossed the Hudson River to its eastern side. Retreating northward they, too, stopped at Fort Constitution. Prior to their departure they ordered Major Dubois and Captain Mott to abandon the island but to remove the supplies.[46] Another combatant who appeared was Lieutenant Machin whose wound by now had been treated and was stabilized. Deeply concerned about the cannons and munitions found on the island, he quickly secured some boatmen and made an attempt to move the items farther northward. But it was to no avail. With Governor Clinton in New Windsor and General Putnam no longer in command, and the two colonels gone, the situation in the Highlands became a free-for-all. Though Major Dubois and Captain Mott did have the time and enough boats to evacuate the island's cannons and supplies, neither of the two exhibited any firm leadership. In the following weeks Lieutenant Machin testified that he found Fort Constitution "in a mobbish condition!"[47] Abandoning the fort, someone torched the barracks and the island's personnel scattered far and wide.

From his headquarters in New Windsor, Governor Clinton dispatched a quick letter to the New York Council and its legislators.[48] In his opening lines the governor wrote:

"Gentlemen - the extreme fatigue I have undergone the three days past, and the want of rest for an equal number of nights, renders me unfit to write you on matters of so serious consequences to this State, as I have to communicate."

Yet, despite his tremendous exhaustion, the governor submitted a fairly accurate and detailed assessment of the fighting and on what had transpired so far. According to the governor the battle started at "about 10 o'clock A.M . . . . at Doodle Town." Governor Clinton cited an enemy strength "by appearance and accounts so far received, of 5,000." But he acknowledged that despite resistance "with great spirit, we were at length overpowered by numbers, and they gained the possession of both posts [Forts Clinton and Montgomery]." The governor also praised both the continental and militia troops. But though the governor added, "Our loss in slain can not be great," he did imply that the casualty rate could be high when he added "the number of missing I can not ascertain." Uncertain of his brother's fate, the governor wrote "My brother, Genr. Clinton, is wounded, and I believe made prisoner. This is the case with Major Logan."

Knowing that Fort Constitution had been evacuated, the governor added: "The ships are both burnt and Fort Constitution demolished, by our people, without my orders; but I can not, as yet, condemn the measure." Adding "Genl. [General] Putnam will retreat. . . [and] Genl. Putnam is to send Colo. Webb's regiment to join me" the governor also requested that "Genl. Gates be informed of the situation of this account." In conclusion, the governor expressed "regret [on] the loss of these posts; but I am consoled with the full persuasion that they [the enemy] have bought them dear, and that I have done the most in my power to save them."[49]

Throughout 7 October, Sir Henry's troops buried their remaining dead, took care of the wounded, and transported them along with the patriot prisoners downriver.[50] Knowing that his troops needed a rest, Sir Henry suspended further operations for the remainder of that day.

Unlike the British who for the moment were staying put, the patriots were in full retreat. Excluding the few units still ably led, by and large the retreat was an unorganized flight. The Northern Army's southern front was in shambles. No one was in firm control and no effort was even being made to gather up the stragglers. Of interest is that although General Putnam had resigned his command in the very early morning hours of 7 October, by the end of the day he had reestablished a headquarters in the town of Fishkill and began to dictate orders.

Chapter 8

Sir Henry Consolidates the Highlands But Quickly Retires

WEDNESDAY, 8 OCTOBER

A number of actions were undertaken by Sir Henry. Shortly before noon, his troops stormed Constitution Island. Expecting resistance, a strong force was dispatched to subdue the island and fort. But after landing it was evident that "the fort had been evacuated in the greatest confusion."[1] In addition to attacking Fort Constitution, other sites were also targeted. One force, commanded by General Tryon, rowed back across the river, secured the unmanned Fort Independence and destroyed it. No resistance of any sort was encountered. As for the 1,000-man force previously landed at Verplanck's Point, this force marched to Peekskill. Expecting resistance but encountering none, the raiders quickly secured their objective. Noting that no effort had been made to remove any of the military material and supplies positioned within Peekskill, the captured items were quickly removed and transported downriver to New York City. But whereas before, in March, the British raiders had not torched the entire town, the loyalists attached to this force acted differently. They not only burned Peekskill to the ground but virtually every home and farm in its vicinity. Peekskill ceased to exist.[2]

Another objective sought by Sir Henry was the patriot supply point dubbed as "Continental Village." Located slightly over 2 miles to the north/northwest of Peekskill on the Albany Post Road, Continental Village was also identified as being a main supply, housing, and communications center. Anticipating strong resistance, a two-pronged attack was ordered. One group, under General Tryon, marched northeastward from Fort Independence; simultaneously, a second group, composed of the same loyalists who earlier in the day had razed Peekskill, came in directly from Peekskill. The mission of these forces was to rendezvous at Continental Village, clear any patriot resistance in its vicinity and seize the village with its supplies.

But as previously at Peekskill, no patriot forces were encountered. Indeed, Continental Village was entirely empty. What also surprised the aggressors was that en route to this site none of the bridges had been destroyed nor had any trees been dropped or obstacles placed on the road.

Entering Continental Village, the raiders discovered a well-stocked supply depot. Storehouses were filled with supplies. Sizable troop buildings stood. Wagons, some loaded with supplies, stood in place. Even horses were found. Food supplies, cases of ammunition, gunpowder barrels, blankets, clothing, tents, rucksacks, and other items were piled high inside the buildings. Even the cannons stood parked in a row.

As just hours before in Peekskill, the raiders removed the cannons and supplies[3] and torched the rest. Not one building was spared. Despite the heavy rain, flames and smoke rose hundreds of feet upward. From across the river Sir Henry could see that his troops were conducting a successful operation. As the British and their loyalist allies retired back to the Hudson, behind them Continental Village was fully ablaze.

Yet, as oftentimes is the case with shattered units, many of its personnel initially written off as being either killed or captured began to reappear. Throughout the 7th and 8th and in the following days a sizable number of the soldiers who had been based at Forts Clinton, Montgomery, Independence, Constitution, Peekskill, and Continental Village resurfaced. Among the survivors were Colonel Dubois, Colonel Lamb, Captain Hamtramck, and the governor's wounded brother, General James Clinton. By the evening of the 8th over 200 survivors had trickled into New Windsor.[4]

Issac Franks was one such soldier. Not yet through with soldiering, in the aftermath of his breakout, the young Issac rallied a number of others around him and persuaded them to continue the fight. Peter Williams also reappeared. Colonel Lamb not only appeared but he also brought in an entire company of artillerymen to include its cannons. Small regional units never stationed in the Highlands made their presence known. Ably led and highly motivated, they reported into Poughkeepsie, Kingston, and the various other towns found throughout region. Though the patriots had suffered a defeat, many more had survived than was initially believed. As the patriot manpower grew by the hour, Governor Clinton's strength rose and the Northern Army's shattered southern sector was quickly being restored. Assisting the governor was Colonel Hughes. A native of the New England/New York region who knew the terrain very well, Hughes was a former British army staff officer with years of experience and one who had served in various continental and militia staff positions. Posted by Washington weeks earlier into the Northern Army, Hughes was a highly competent officer now serving as Governor Clinton's senior military advisor. Within days the army's southern front would not only be rebuilt but, actually, would be stronger than before.

Facing severe punishment or even execution, a young loyalist from the Loyal American Regiment decided that he had had enough. Shortly after midnight, he deserted. Unsure of what to do, he just roamed in the countryside.

Hearing the call of a crow, the deserter paid no attention to it. Never would he have imagined that the sounds he was hearing were not those of some birds but, rather, those of humans. Unknown to the deserter, he was being monitored by patriot scouts.

More crow sounds were exchanged. And then, it happened! So fast that the deserter never even knew what hit him! Two men, dressed in frontier-style clothing, swooped down upon him with drawn guns. The deserter was ordered to unshoulder his musket, place it on the ground, back up, turn around, and lie down. Realizing he had no choice, he complied. He was now a prisoner of war.

Both men were tall and had a ferocious look to them. Yet, they caused him no harm. Indeed, after checking him out and removing his knife and bayonet, they raised him up and offered him some water, rum, deer jerky, and cheese and crackers. Informing the deserter that they had been monitoring him for the last several miles, they added they knew that he was alone.

The deserter was now in the hands of Major Moffat's scouts. Unlike much of the scout warfare farther to the north where brutality and insanity were the norm, here on the southern front the scouts operated quite differently.

Repeatedly, Major Moffat had ordered his scouts not to shoot unless totally necessary. Prisoners were to be treated with respect and kindness. Wounded and injured personnel were to be afforded extra care. Information was always needed. "And dead men don't talk!" Moffat also banned scalping and the practice of pulling out an opponent's heart as he lay on the ground held down by others. In the vicious Wilderness War of 1777 Major Moffat was doing all that he could to at least instill some type of humanity into this struggle.

Within hours, the prisoner was delivered to Major Moffat. Noting that the loyalist possessed critical information, Moffat immediately dispatched him to New Windsor where he was interrogated. Governor Clinton also spoke with him. From this captive the patriots learned such:

"Their [Sir Henry's] force was 5000. Three thousand British Troops and Hessian Yagers [Jagers]. The Remainder New

Levies, Commanded by Brig'r Genl. Beverley Robinson
and colo. Fanning. Genl. Sir Henry Clinton commanded
in Person. Had three other Genl. Officers with him."

But the deserter also added "their Loss was great."[5]

That same day from his headquarters in Fishkill General Putnam
dispatched a letter to Governor Clinton. Copies of Putnam's
letter went to General Horatio Gates, the Commander of the
Northern Army, to General George Washington, and to the New
York Legislature. In his letter, Putnam informed the governor
that "Last night I arrived here . . . ." And the general wrote:

"Its my real and Sincere Opinion that Destroying the
Chain are by no means (at this juncture) their Chieff
Object, Its my firm Opinion that they will by every Pos-
sible Means Indeavor to Make Forced Marches Towards
Albany, and convey up the Baggage Stores in the small
Crafts. General Burgoyne is Certainly there first and
Chief Object[ive]."

In conclusion, General Putnam recommended:

"The moment our Baggage Stores are mov'd into some
secure Place, we aught to Proceed towards Albany and
act in Conjunction with Genl. Gates. I have wrote him
and shall hope to have his Opinion very soon, yours
upon the Subject I hope to be favored with Immediately
which will greatly Oblige."[6]

In short, General Putnam felt that it would be useless to
continue any further resistance in the Highlands. Major Moffat
also dispatched a quick letter from Ramapough Clove. The
major reported that the four prisoners previously captured near
King's Ferry were sent "this Day to Goshen with a warrant to

the Goal Keeper to received them, and see that they are properly Provided for." He also reported:

> "I have just now received a very straight and I believe authentic Account that on Saturday last Genl. Washington dislodged Mr. How [General Howe] from Advantageous Post near Germantown and destroyed a large part of his Army - that Genl. Washington had afterward received a reinforcement of five thousand Men from Virginia and three thousand from Maryland."

Major Moffat also wrote that the enemy had experienced shipping losses on the Delaware River. In conclusion, the major added "no Enemy have yet appeared in this [Ramapough Clove] Quarter."[7]

Determined to defeat the British in the Highlands or somewhere in its vicinity, Governor Clinton continued his activities as evidenced by his letter of 8 October to the state legislature.

In his report the governor reported that since his previous letter of 7 October, things had changed for the better. "The American loss is not so Heavy as at First apprehended." The governor wrote that his brother had survived and "his Wound does not appear to be any ways Dangerous." Continuing on, Governor Clinton added:

> "Many other of our officers have also arrived who we had Reason to believe [earlier] were made Prisoners. [Now] Not more than 11 officers of Colo. Dubois's [5th Continental] Regim't are mission. Two hundred of his Men, including Non-Commissioned have already Joined me at this Place [New Windsor]. Many more of them may be expected as we have heard of their Escape. Many of the two Companies of Artillery who were at those Posts have escaped and joined us. More of them hourly expected."

Though acknowledging that "Our Posts at Peeks Kill and Syndam's. . . have lost their Importance," the governor emphasized that "General Putnam had retreated to a very defensible pass in the Mountains about 3 Miles from Fishkill. In the meantime, militia from the east is rapidly to appear and I, to rally my Forces near this Place."

As for defending the Highlands, the governor emphasized "to defend the Cheveaux Defrize[8] in the Best manner I can and as long." In the event the Cheveaux Defrize located on the Hudson River's Pollepel Island to the north of Constitution Island was breached and the enemy should "pass the cheveaux Defrize, I will be forced march endeavour to gain Kingston and cover that town. . . and defeat the Enemy's Design in assisting their Northern [Burgoyne's] Canada Army."[9]

Governor Clinton, General Putnam, and Major Moffat were not the only ones communicating on 8 October. So, too, was Sir Henry. On this day, he dispatched a quick letter from Fort Montgomery to British General John Burgoyne. Sir Henry wrote:

> "Fort Montgomery, October 8, 1777.
>
> Nous y voici [Here we are], and nothing now between us but Gates. I sincerely hope this little success of ours may facilitate your operations. In answer to your letter of September 28th by C.C., I shall only say I cannot presume to order, or even to advise, for reasons obvious. I heartily wish you success.
>
> Faithfully yours, H. Clinton."[10]

In addition to his written letter, Sir Henry's messengers carried a verbal message. Burgoyne needed to know that Sir Henry was unable to advance all the way to Albany. His forces were simply too weak to undertake such a large-scale operation. To ensure that Burgoyne received the message, three messengers—Captain Campbell, Captain Scott,[11] and Lieutenant Daniel Taylor[12]—were utilized, and all three carried the same message. In consideration that they were experienced runners, Sir Henry was certain that at least one of them should get through.[13]

THURSDAY, 9 OCTOBER

Dressed in civilian attire and heading northward, in the vicinity of New Windsor, Lieutenant Taylor spotted several men dressed in British army uniforms. One of them was an officer. Believing them to be fellow Englishmen, Taylor approached them. Suspecting something odd about Taylor, the patriots placed him under guard and immediately took him to New Windsor where Governor Clinton had established his temporary headquarters and, at that very moment, was conducting a military briefing.

Within his long hair Taylor had concealed a silver-shaped oval capsule containing Sir Henry's message. This capsule, however, was quickly discovered by the patriots. But before it could be opened Taylor quickly grabbed it from his captors and swallowed it in front of them.

Immediately, Governor Clinton ordered that Dr. Moses Higby, a doctor serving in the Northern Army, be produced. Upon arrival the doctor administered an emetic of some sort which forced Taylor to vomit up the capsule. But the moment the capsule hit the floor Taylor instantly scooped it up and again, swallowed it.

Governor Clinton had had enough. Cursing and yelling at Taylor, the governor reached for a long hunting knife. Slamming Taylor against the wall, as several of the others held him firmly in place the governor brandished the knife directly to Taylor's face. Screaming at Taylor to produce the item or "By God, I'll cut you open right now!" it actually appeared as if the governor would carry out his threat.[14] For extra sensationalism

Governor Clinton screamed at Taylor "your partner, Captain Campbell, has already been captured and we have learned all we need to know from him!"[15] Bombarded with such news and fearing that the governor would actually cut him wide open, Taylor somehow regurgitated the bullet capsule. Under further interrogation, Taylor also revealed the message he was to verbally deliver to Burgoyne.[16] Denounced as a spy, Taylor was soon sentenced and executed.[17]

As this was occurring, down in the Highlands Sir Henry ordered that Fort Clinton would now be utilized as a base for future operations. In honor of General Vaughan who had captured the site, Clinton ordered that Fort Clinton be renamed as Fort Vaughan.[18] Orders were also issued for the fort to be expanded and improved upon. Within days additional soldiers and laborers were brought up from New York City to work on it. Wanting to inform Howe on what was occurring and seeking advice on what else to do, Sir Henry wrote:

> "How far I may co-operate with it or what commands you may have for the small corps under my orders, I am at a loss to determine what to do."[19]

Notified that Generals Alexander Leslie and James Robertson, his two senior ranking generals commanding New York City, were both ill and that Colonel Johann Ludwig Wilhelm Von Hanxleden had assumed command, Sir Henry feared for the worse. Despite his high-sounding Germanic name, Sir Henry had no faith in Colonel Johann. Perhaps this explains why the German colonel had been left behind.

Sir Henry, however, was not just worried about the city. He was also very concerned about the location of Washington's army. Fearing that if Washington's army or strong elements of it should march toward New York City to either secure the city or its area to the north, such a move would cut off and isolate Sir Henry in the Highlands. Trapped in the Highlands in an approaching winter, without sufficient supplies, Sir Henry's force would be annihilated.

To counter this threat, Sir Henry ordered such: General Vaughan, with 1,200 troops, would remain behind in Fort Vaughan to continue the work; Commodore Hotham and Captain Wallace would continue to probe up the river to destroy any patriot positions found on the lower Hudson River; and Sir Henry would return to New York City with the brunt of the forces on the following day. Movement orders were immediately issued to various units.

After calming down, Governor Clinton dispatched a quick letter to General Washington on what had transpired so far and to inform the Commander in Chief that the situation was not that critical as deemed at first. Clinton wrote:

> "Our loss, killed, wounded, and prisoners, is not so great as might have been expected, when the strength of the enemy and our weakness are properly considered. My brother was wounded with a bayonet. Many officers and men and myself. . . were fortunet as to effect our escape under cover of the night."[20]

Hoping to improve his position, Lieutenant Taylor agreed to write a confession. Late that afternoon, he submitted a report to the patriots. In his report, Taylor described what his mission was, what Sir Henry had ordered him (Taylor) to report to Burgoyne, and that "Genl. Howe was near Philadelphia and had defeated the Rebels and that the Frigates belonging to the Rebels in the river were both Burnt."

But in his confession, Taylor also admitted the British loss had been quite high. As Taylor conceded:

"Sir Henry stormed with small Arms the back of the
Fort which he carried with the loss of Lt.Col. Grant of
ye Volunt's, Major Campbell, Major Sela a number
of other officers and about 300 Rank and file."[21]

FRIDAY, 10 OCTOBER

The day was characterized by various letters and dispatches
between Governor Clinton and state militia commanders to
bring in as many militiamen as possible. The governor was also
informed by Colonel Hughes that he had received word from
Doctor Peter Tappen, a Northern Army surgeon who directed
a hospital, that his wife had been moved "Beyond the Reach
of the Enemy to Plisent [Pleasant] Valley about 8 miles back of
Poughkeepsie." Serving as a volunteer in a military hospital Mrs.
Clinton, along with the hospital's staff and all of the wounded
and ill such as Lieutenant Machin, were brought to Pleasant
Valley where a temporary medical center had been established
under Doctor Tappen. Suspecting that Kingston was a target,
Governor Clinton ordered A. B. Bancker, who supervised the
prisoners of war "To remove the Prisoners of War near Hudson's
River back toward Wausinck or any other safe Place. Those in
Goshen are taken care of."[22]

On this same day Sir Henry commenced his withdrawal to
New York City. Most of his troops were transported by boat
although some marched back on land. Carefully monitoring the enemy's movements were Major Moffat's scouts. By
midnight the governor was aware that excluding about 1,000
to 1,300 enemy personnel remaining behind in and around
the old Fort Clinton along with some some British bateaux
and ships positioned on the lower Hudson River, the brunt
of Sir Henry's force had returned to New York City. Though
Governor Clinton trusted Major Moffat's report, he could not
contemplate why such a large number of troops had suddenly
been diverted back southward.

SATURDAY, 11 OCTOBER

Assisted by better weather conditions, Captain Wallace quickly sailed up to Pollepel Island which lay directly to the east of New Windsor. His ship, the *Dilligent*, was in the lead followed by the *Spitfire, Crane,* and *Dependence*. Encountering no resistance and because the chevaux-de-frise obstacle was not protected by any land-based gunners on the river's edge or by any patriot gun boats, this obstacle was quickly breached. Though en route the naval armada had sailed past a gun battery constructed on Plum Point, its few cannons lacked any effective range. The one 24-pound cannon in position could have been a devastating piece but considering that no ammunition was available for it, it was totally useless. Continuing northward, Wallace sailed past the old German Palatine town of Newburgh and proceeded another 13 miles upriver to Poughkeepsie. There, he disembarked some of his naval and army personnel to burn docked boats, docks, and warehouses near the shoreline. Once accomplished, Wallace's flotilla turned around and sailed back downriver to Fort Vaughan. Wallace's mission, which was to breach the obstacle and conduct a reconnaissance upriver, had been successfully accomplished. In the meantime as this was happening, various patriot commanders were dispatching riders far and wide to warn the inhabitants of the countryside and messages were rushed back and forth, between Governor Clinton and the various military and political leaders, of this British activity. Efforts were continued by Governor Clinton to reinforce and rebuild the Northern Army's southern front. Other than some skirmishing, patrolling, and probing by both sides, for the time being there was a pause in the fighting. Though for the moment some calm had settled in, it would not be long before another fiery hell would soon be unleashed on the southern front of the Wilderness War of 1777.

Chapter 9

Sir Henry's Last Attack and the Conclusion of the Wilderness War of 1777

SATURDAY, 11 OCTOBER
British Army Headquarters, New York City.

Sir Henry called for a commander's meeting. As they conversed Lydia Darragh, a spy operating for the Northern Army, lay hidden on the floor above with her ear pressed firmly against the tiny crack in a floorboard. As she listened, she took notes in shorthand known only to her. By the end of the day, her information was being passed along to the Northern Army's headquarters in the Highlands.[1]

Reconsidering his position, Sir Henry decided to once again assist Burgoyne. Possibly, he might even *reach* Burgoyne. Orders were issued to General Vaughan to advance northward to assist Burgoyne in any possible way and, if the opportunity arose, Vaughan was to link up with Burgoyne.[2] In support, Sir Henry also dispatched the 45th Foot Regiment[3] commanded by Major William Gardiner; the Anspach-Bayreuth Regiment commanded by Colonel August Voit von Salzburg; and the 4th Hessian Grenadier Battalion commanded by Lieutenant-Colonel Johann von Koehler. New York's Royal Governor Tryon would also accommodate this force and he would command Colonel Beverley Robinson's loyalist force left behind in the Highlands. Verplanck's Point was designated as being the jumping off point for the northward thrust. As for the 45th Foot, it was Sir Henry's pride and joy because it was his personal regiment. Wanting to position himself closer to the area of operations, Sir Henry accompanied the troops back to the Highlands. Realizing that Vaughan would require a strong naval presence, an 11–warship English fleet was assembled. This fleet was organized around the *Cerberus, Tartar, Preston, Thomas,* 2 brigs (one named *Dependence*), 3 galleys, 1 sloop, and a command vessel ironically named *Friendship*; additionally, a number of transports, tenders, and supply horse ships were added.[4] Along with the British troops positioned in the Highlands, no less than 1,600 British soldiers were to participate.[5] Of interest is that this force carried enough provisions to last 5,000 troops for six months.

SUNDAY, 12 OCTOBER

Continuing efforts to gather up the many soldiers and militiamen scattered all over the countryside proved productive. Via the city's spies and Major Moffat's scouts, Governor Clinton was informed that General Vaughan was the senior commanding officer in the Highlands, that Sir Henry had returned to New York City but was now returning to the Highlands with additional forces, and that the Highlands were to be utilized as a jumping off point for a renewed attack all the way up to, if possible, Saratoga.[6] Convinced that Kingston was an objective, Governor Clinton issued orders for its troops to defend the place. Governor Clinton reported how "an armed Schooner, two Row Gallies and a small Brigg passed the Cheveaux Defrize and are ought of Sight up the River this Morning" and from the main Northern Army Headquarters in Albany the governor requested more mounted horse soldiers to ride on both sides of the Hudson River up and down to monitor British movements on the river. Although a "small [horse] Company under

a Captain Woodhull" did exist, more mounted troops were
needed. Ammunition needs were also addressed.[7]

MONDAY – TUESDAY, 13–14 OCTOBER

Arriving at Fort Vaughan on 13 October, Sir Henry briefed
General Vaughan and the assembled army and navy commanders
on what they were expected to do in the event they would go.
On the following day, 14 October, Captain Wallace returned
from his raiding and briefed Sir Henry. Wallace reported that
no river obstacles were barring the way and that he had only
encountered light sporadic resistance. Based on this information
and sensing no immediate threat from the patriots, Sir
Henry issued the order to commence an advance northward.
Vaughan was specifically instructed "to feel your way to
General Burgoyne."[8]

From his headquarters Governor Clinton dispatched a quick
letter to General Gates, the commanding officer of the Northern
Army. The governor cited that heavy fighting was continuing in
the Highlands and the patriots were continuously engaging and
monitoring enemy movements up the river.[9]

This day, General Putnam's wife passed away in the Robinson
home. Shortly before her death she was seen by Colonel Beverley
Robinson who, since the recapture of the Highlands, had moved
back into his home and was using it as his headquarters. Colonel
Robinson, however, allowed the ill woman to stay. Following
her death, Colonel Robinson dispatched a delegation under a
white flag northward. They were to seek out General Putnam
and inquire from the patriot general on what was to be done in
regard to the deceased woman.[10]

WEDNESDAY, 15 OCTOBER

With 2,000 British, German, and loyalist troops, a strong
naval escort, and accompanied with General Tryon who still
retained the title as Colonial Governor of the Colony of New
York, General Vaughan set forth.[11] Positioning himself on the

Friendship, the British general was to attack as far northward as possible. Designating Kingston as his first objective, Kingston lay almost 40 miles directly (straight line distance) to the north of Fort Vaughan on the western side of the Hudson River. General Vaughan also reasoned that if Kingston was captured, a major psychological blow would be inflicted against the patriots.

En route to Kingston, Sir Henry's force at first encountered virtually no resistance. Along the way they burned every boat, dock, and farm they encountered. Though here and there from some shore bank cannon and small arms fire was directed against the flotilla, the patriots were unable to formulate a solid defense. Soon the cries of "The British Are Coming!" were ringing far and wide as Vaughan's fleet proceeded farther and farther upriver. For Vaughan and Tryon, it actually appeared as if they would succeed. By evening, General Vaughan was positioned just to the south of Kingston in the vicinity of Esopus.

SARATOGA

Receiving Governor Clinton's letter of 13 October at his field headquarters, General Gates immediately responded to it. Noting that the governor was very concerned about the events farther to the south of Albany, the commander of the Northern Army agreed on the military actions being taken by the governor. Gates wrote:[12]

> "Dear Sir, I have just received your letter of the 13th Inst. It is certainly right, to collect your whole Force, and push up the East Side of the [Hudson] River, after the Enemy .... Yesterday General Burgoyne proposed to surrender upon the inclosed Terms, the Capitulation will, I believe, be settled today, when I shall have Nothing but [British] General [Sir Henry] Clinton to think of. But if you keep Pace, with him on one Side, the Governor on the other and I in his Front, I cannot see how he is to get home again."

General Gates assured the governor that once Burgoyne's force had surrendered and the enemy threat from the north is eliminated, Gates would immediately engage Sir Henry's forces. Wanting to keep the governor well informed on how the surrender negotiations were under way, General Gates submitted copies of each and every letter written to and from Burgoyne.

THURSDAY, 16 OCTOBER. 2400–0900 (MIDNIGHT–9 A.M.)

During the night hours a small patriot force, commanded by Colonel Levi Pawling, moved into the mouth of the Esopus Creek.[13] Armed with five cannons, they quickly erected two positions and in the opening daylight hours engaged Vaughan's fleet with cannon fire.[14]

Concluding that these positions posed a threat to his fleet, communications, and rear, General Vaughan ordered a force to land and take out the guns. Landing almost directly to the front of the defenders and charging rapidly forward with fixed bayonets, the patriot resistance was easily overcome. Despite a show of bravery, the patriots could not stop the redcoats. In large measure this was attributable to the fact that most of the defenders were teenagers, some as young as 14. Overwhelming the defenders, after spiking the guns and destroying the powder kegs, the soldiers re-boarded their ships.[15] Sailing farther on, at the mouth of Roundout Creek the patriot ship *Lady Washington* was encountered and immediately, skilled British gunners engaged the ship. Struck several times, *Lady Washington* disengaged herself from the fight and retired farther upriver. The road to Kingston was now open.

0900 (9 A.M.)

Departing New Windsor with some hastily assembled continentals and militiamen, Governor Clinton commenced a forced foot march northward to Kingston in hopes of reaching the town in time. In the meantime, reinforcements from various parts of New York State were also en route to Kingston. Among those marching to Kingston was Captain Hamtramck.

1200–1600 (12 P.M.– 4 P.M.)

Shortly after 12 p.m.,[16] General Vaughan proceeded to attack Kingston. Just hours before, the state's government officials had first fled to nearby Marbletown and, from there, to Hurley. Expecting resistance, General Vaughan ordered that the town be approached from two directions. The main body, accompanied with Vaughan, landed in a cove right above Columbus Point; the other force landed in the mouth of Rondout Creek from where, just shortly before, the *Lady Washington* had retired.

Seizing a black man, the British forced him to lead them to Kingston. After occupying a hill not far from the town, Vaughan linked up with the other incoming force. Encountering no resistance, the combined force marched into Kingston.

Inside the town, the troops were divided into small groups; in turn, each group was accompanied by two or three loyalists. Proceeding through the town, they began to burn the homes and buildings of known patriots. Accompanying the arsonists was General Tryon. As days before in the Highlands, Tryon was delighted to see a patriot's home, farm, or business go up in flames. Overcome with hate, as Tryon ran from one site to another being torched, his cries of "BURN IT! GODDAMN IT! BURN IT!" were heard far and wide.

And suddenly, it happened! What initially started as a controlled burning of only certain selected sites now quickly became a free-for-all. All control was lost. Doors were smashed in, occupants forcefully evicted and looting became the norm. Citizens were robbed and beaten and some of the younger women were repeatedly raped. Murder even occurred. Amid the crackle of the flames, no mercy was shown. Excluding just the old Van Steenbergh House which belonged to a well-known loyalist, nothing else was spared.

From where he now stood just miles away, Governor Clinton could actually see smoke rising hundreds of feet upward.

Kingston, the capital of the newly established New York State, had ceased to exist.[17]

As Kingston was being razed, another British force was landing on the eastern bank of the Hudson River. Marching slightly inland, this force proceeded toward the town of Rhinebeck.

But unlike at Kingston where the British and loyalists marched inland without encountering any resistance, here the opposite occurred. Militia members, bolstered by many armed citizens to include even women fighters with guns, put up a battle. From upper storied buildings, rooftops; from behind trees, stone walls and buildings; patriots blazed away with muskets and rifles. Well-concealed snipers, some perched high up in thickly-leaved trees, specifically targeted officers, sergeants, and loyalists. With each passing moment, the strength of the raiders diminished significantly.

Though taking casualties, the raiders finally fought their way into Rhinebeck. Angered about their losses, they prepared to burn the entire town. But with darkness setting in and the resistance only intensifying, the raiders quickly withdrew to the safety of their fleet. Yet it was no easy withdrawal. Patriot fire continued to decimate them. Though the raiders withdrew to the safety of their boats, they returned with no goods. The patriots not only saved Rhinebeck and its outlying area but also inflicted upon the raiders their very first defeat. In the following days, Rhinebeck's citizenry would be very busy burying the numerous dead left behind by the raiders.

Noting the resistance, General Vaughan decided to remain in place through the night. But it would not be an easy night. Through the remaining evening and night hours of 16–17 October, heavy sniper fire continuously raked the ships and transports from both sides of the river.

FRIDAY, 17 OCTOBER

Proceeding upriver at the crack of dawn, along the way General Vaughan continued to destroy every boat, dock, and settlement. Disembarking a mixed force of loyalists and British troops on the east bank, they marched into the settlement of Clermont and burned it to the ground.

Not far from Clermont stood the Livingston estate. A huge—and beautiful—manor house adorned the estate. From this mansion one could not only see across the Hudson River but actually the distant mountains of the eastern Catskills. Noting the incoming danger Margaret Livingston, the wife of Colonel Robert Livingston, quickly gathered up her servants and a few possessions and fled with everyone into the nearby woods.

Occupying the estate, Tryon ordered that it be burned. Along with the mansion, all of the barns and support buildings were also torched. Some of the food products were removed but most of the stored crops were destroyed. Cows, goats, pigs, and sheep were shot, bayoneted, or herded into the barns and burned alive. From where Margaret hid, she could see flames rising far upward. Amid the crackle of the burning barns and buildings, the screams of the animals could be heard. Needless to say, this action did not terrorize Margaret into submission; rather, it only reinforced her will to resist. Nor did it stop the eleven Livingstons from serving in the Northern Army.[18]

After destroying Clermont and the Livingston estate, the flotilla continued its journey upriver. Along the way, more farms adjacent and near the river were looted and burned. Another estate torched was the one owned by the Van Cortlandts. Informing the mother of Colonel Philip Van Cortlandt that her home is to be burned because her son is serving in the Northern Army, in defiance and anger Mrs. Van Cortlandt supposedly shouted: "Officer, my deepest regret is that I have but only one son in that army! And not many more! Burn it! I still have the satisfaction to know that in the end, you bastards will lose!"[19]

1100–1500 (11 A.M.– 3 P.M.)

As Vaughan's troops were laying waste to the Hudson River Valley, miles farther to the north on the edge of the great wilderness, General Burgoyne surrendered the remnants of what, just months before, had been a proud army. The Battle of Saratoga had ended. At long last the Wilderness War of 1777 was finally winding down. "Burgoyne has surrendered!" Like a lightning bolt shooting out of the sky, these words quickly vibrated far and wide through entire regions, towns, and cities.

Following the destruction of Clermont, General Vaughan did not travel very far up-river. Though his intent was to continue to probe further, Vaughan's civilian river pilots,[20] fearing the intensifying patriot resistance, began to insist that the river was too narrow and shallow. Though in fact the river was still negotiable, the increasing patriot resistance was unnerving them and casualties were on the rise. Army troops and loyalists were not the only ones suffering. Navy Lieutenant Clarke, an officer on the *Dependence* along with several other sailors, was killed on this day. The almost constant small arms fire began to take its toll—both physically and psychologically. More and more cannons appeared, and mounted patriot cavalrymen were spotted for the first time along the shorelines. What at first had been a sporadic, unorganized patriot resistance was now quickly developing into that of a more professional and formidable characteristic.

Despite Vaughan's arguments and pleas to press on, it was to no avail. The river pilots refused to venture any farther.[21] Acknowledging that perhaps the river pilots had a point and sensing that he could do no more, Vaughan halted in place and dispatched a message to Sir Henry. Citing that "it is a most uncomfortable situation not to be able to go on ...,"[22] Vaughan estimated a patriot troop strength of at least 5,000 on the eastern side with at least another 1,500 on the western side.[23] And this strength, added Vaughan, was growing.[24]

But the most distressing news reaching Vaughan on this day was that Burgoyne had surrendered. Uncertain on what to do, Vaughan requested further guidance from Sir Henry.

That evening, Captain Jason Wallace submitted a detailed report to his superior, Commodore Hotham. In his report, Captain Wallace described the actions which had taken place both on and adjacent the river, and cited the "loss of Lieutenant Clarke with two or three others." But in a separate sentence (as if to especially emphasize the point) and at the bottom of his report (clearly to make sure it was seen) the captain wrote: "By all our information I am afraid that Gen. Burgoyne is retreated, if not worse."[25]

Late that evening in Fort Vaughan, Sir Henry received news that Burgoyne had surrendered. Pondering on whether this was true or not, a messenger suddenly appeared from Howe. Initially sent to New York City, the message was immediately forwarded to the Highlands. Opening it, Sir Henry read that Howe was requesting more troops for Philadelphia. Howe wrote: "4,000 troops to be sent at the earliest possible moment."[26] But the news would only get worse. Later that evening, Vaughan's messenger arrived with Vaughan's message citing that the river pilots had refused to proceed any farther upriver, the rebels were offering stiff resistance, their strength was rapidly growing, and it was rumored that General Burgoyne had surrendered earlier in the morning.

SARATOGA, 2000 (8 P.M.)

Informing his commanders that the struggle is not yet over, General Gates emphasized that the Northern Army was still engaging sizable British forces to the south of Albany. To counter the enemy push northward, certain army units were ordered to immediately march southward. As for the remainder of the army, Gates placed it on standby with orders to march on a moment's notice.

SATURDAY, 18 OCTOBER

Taken to the gallows not far from Kingston, a town in ruins and still smoldering, Lieutenant Taylor was hung. Unfortunately for the lieutenant, the hanging was poorly executed and Taylor was dropped three or four times. Finally, weighed down with heavy sand bags tied to his lower legs and ankles to ensure that his neck would snap, when the lieutenant was dropped the rope's tension was so taut that his head actually snapped off. In such a way ended the career of a spy.

On this day General Gates, the commander of the Northern Army, began to shift additional continental and militia units southward to Governor Clinton; simultaneously, from Waywayanda, a settlement in New York State directly across the New Jersey border, General William Winds, a regional New Jersey militia commander, dispatched a quick message to Governor Clinton. General Winds wrote:

> "I am now at this place on My way to New Windsor, with 300 Men, the front of My Brigade of New Jersey Militia, In aid of General Putnam. The remainder are In March by this Time. When joined by the Whole, Believe I shall have from 800 to 1,000 Men."[27]

The patriot strength was rapidly growing. From all corners— New Jersey, Connecticut, Vermont, New Hampshire, New York, and Massachusetts—volunteers were pouring in. By now Kingston, Clermont, and Rhinebeck were household names.

SUNDAY, 19 OCTOBER

Disgusted with the way things had worked out, unsure of whether Burgoyne had surrendered or not but suspecting that the news was probably true, angry with Howe, distraught about his losses, and suffering from stomach pains and a constant head- ache, Sir Henry decided to return to New York City. In actuality, he had no choice.

Prior to leaving, Sir Henry issued two orders: the first was that work on Fort Vaughan was to continue and that General

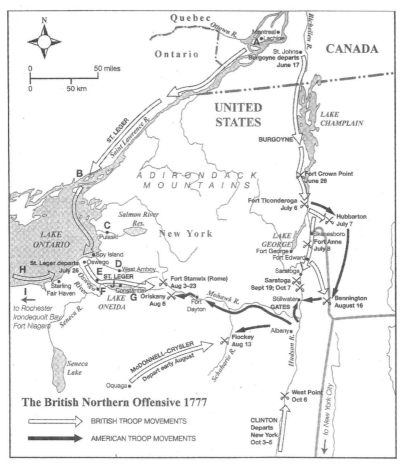

The British Northern Offensive 1777 (*author's collection*)

A. St. Leger departs Montreal/Lachine 28 June–2 July, approx.
B. Carleton Island
C. Salmon River
D. Little Salmon River/South Branch (*Proposed Route*)
E. Old Block House (*Fort Brewerton*)
F. Three Rivers (*Seneca, Oneida, Oswego*)
G. Wood Creek
H. Walter Butler
I. Irondequoit Bay, Fort Niagara
J. Constantia

George Clinton: Governor & General (credit: Benson Lossing - *The Pictorial Field-Book of the [American] Revolution*)

General James Clinton (credit: *The Pictorial Field-Book of the [American] Revolution*)

Colonel Beverley Robinson (credit: *The Pictorial Field-Book of the [American] Revolution*)

This stately manor, owned by Loyalist Beverly Robinson, was located near West Point, and served as headquarter for both the British and Washington. (credit: *The Pictorial Field-Book of the [American] Revolution*)

Twin Forts – Clinton & Montgomery – protecting the Hudson (painting by Mead, credit: Fort Montgomery collection)

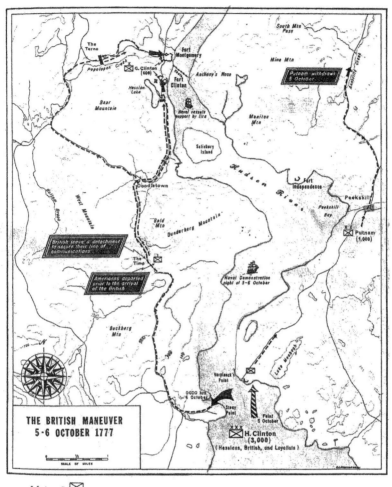

The British maneuver, 5-6 October, 1777 (courtesy: West Point Association of Graduates)

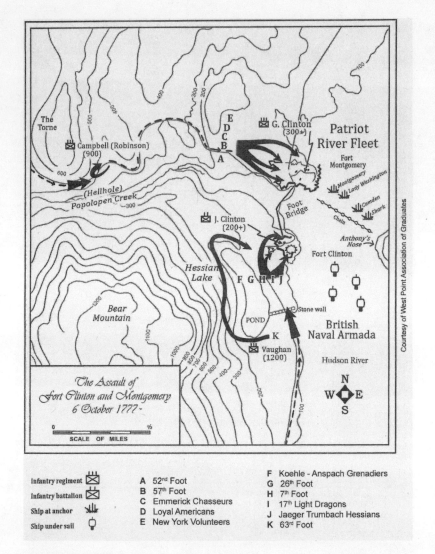

The Assault of Fort Clinton and Montgomery, 6 October, 1777 (courtesy: West Point Association of Graduates)

Redoubt attack (painting by Mead, credit: Fort Montgomery collection)

Parley scene, at which Livingston and Campbell confer (painting by Mead, credit: Fort Montgomery collection)

Burning ships in the Hudson harbor (painting by Mead, credit: Fort Montgomery collection)

Sir Henry (credit: The Anne S. K. Brown collection)

General Howe (credit: The Anne S. K. Brown collection)

Vaughan and Commodore Hotham were to continue, for several more days, "river operations." That order, however, was not very explicit as to what, exactly, was meant by "river operations."

That afternoon a boat, flying a large white flag, was observed floating downriver toward the British fleet. Aboard was Lord Petersham. Captured several days earlier in Saratoga, Lord Petersham was dispatched by the patriots to personally inform Sir Henry that Burgoyne had actually surrendered. But Petersham was also carrying a letter for General Vaughan.

When informed about the destruction of Kingston, Clermont, Peekskill, Continental Village, the Livingston and Van Cortlandt Estates, and the destruction of numerous private homes, farms, and settlements within the Hudson River Valley, General Gates wrote a strong letter of protest directly to General Vaughan. Titled "Northern Army Headquarters, Albany" and dated 19 October 1777, General Gates denounced the widespread destruction undertaken by the British raiders and he demanded an immediate end to it. General Gates also added that if this practice should continue, the perpetrators would be held accountable for this uncivilized activity in the near future. Straight to the point it was, indeed, a very strong warning from Gates.[28]

MONDAY, 20 OCTOBER – TUESDAY, 28 OCTOBER

Since his civilian river pilots refused to proceed any farther upriver and Sir Henry's orders were not specific, Vaughan was unable to accomplish much more. He now stood about 45 miles to the south of Albany and about 85 miles from Saratoga.[29] In military logic, Vaughan was still very far from Saratoga. Had Burgoyne continued to resist, it would not have mattered because no one would have been able to reach him.

Though in the following days Vaughan continued to conduct some raids, none of them occurred farther upriver and they were limited in size and scope. From the vicinity of Kingston back down to the Highlands, the British struck everything which previously had been bypassed or somehow missed. Because the patriots were rapidly growing in strength, the British did not dare to venture far from their boats. Regardless, for the civilians residing on or near the river, it was an exceptionally difficult time. One of the places raided during this time was the estate of Governor Clinton. It, too, was burned.

During this time, Commodore Hotham was likewise experiencing exceptional difficulties. He had to protect Vaughan's rear, keep a line of communications open to him, and thwart any patriot attempts in reinserting any obstacles into the river. In order to accomplish his mission Hotham positioned his ships in four locations. From the south to the north the *Cerebus* covered Stony Point; the *Preston* floated by Peekskill; the *Tartar* floated near Fort Montgomery; and the *Mercury* covered the river from Constitution Island to Pollepel Island.[30] North of Pollepel Island, Vaughan was supported and protected by Captain Wallace's small river fleet.

WEDNESDAY, 22 OCTOBER

Sir Henry ordered General Vaughan and Captain Wallace to retire to the Lower Highlands. In disgust, a young German officer recorded such in his diary:

> "Another year's campaigning is finished and all that we have accomplished, with the loss of a great many men, is the taking of Philadelphia, as according to all reports we have taken nothing else. In balance, the conquest of this single city without considering the many people lost during the expedition and those lost at Saratoga and made prisoners by the truce, makes the scale tip in favor of the enemy."[31]

THURSDAY, 23 OCTOBER

General Vaughan and Captain Wallace proceeded to retire down the Hudson River. As they sailed southward past

Poughkeepsie, Plum Point, the Crow's Nest,[32] and various other locations, their fleet frequently came under heavy cannon, rifle, and musket fire. In response and to protect the withdrawing troop transports, Captain Wallace's ships repeatedly engaged the patriot forces with broadsides of cannon fire.

SATURDAY, 25 OCTOBER
British Army Headquarters, New York City.

Meeting with Sir Petersham, Sir Henry was personally informed that Burgoyne's army had, in fact, surrendered and that Burgoyne was a prisoner. Disgusted with the news and the way the entire British campaign had been handled, Sir Henry ordered the remaining troops and navy personnel to immediately retire totally out of the Highlands back to New York City. As for Fort Vaughan, it was to be abandoned and destroyed. For the time being, the Highlands were to remain unoccupied.[33]

For the rank and file who withdrew, it was just another event. But for the many loyalists who supported the Crown the withdrawal was, in fact, a very painful experience. Packing a few of his belongings, Colonel Robinson stepped out of his stately home. He wondered when he would next return. Suddenly, an ugly feeling of "I'll never see this place again" overcame him. And so it would be. His property was confiscated by the patriots.[34]

Robinson, however, was by no means an exception. In the aftermath of the British defeat and retreat from the Highlands, the loyalists who remained behind were immediately targeted. As previously had been the fate of the patriots, in the days and weeks that followed, loyalists experienced much cruelty. Terrorized and seeking protection, they fled to New York City in large numbers. In a city already overcrowded, they only complicated matters.

SUNDAY, 26 OCTOBER
Convinced that England would now lose the war, Sir Henry submitted his letter of resignation. Along with Howe, Burgoyne,

St. Leger, Carleton, Tryon, and numerous others, the Wilderness War of 1777 had thoroughly ruined many careers.

MONDAY, 27 OCTOBER

Major Moffat's scouts reported that excluding the soldiers left behind to destroy the fort and what could not be removed, the brunt of the British forces had withdrawn from the Highlands; simultaneously, patriot spies operating in New York City reported that Sir Henry and General Vaughan were back in the city with most of their troops.

TUESDAY, 28 OCTOBER

The *Spitfire* and *Crane* sailed back into New York City. Aboard its decks stood the last of the rear guard. Late that evening Major Moffat verified that not one British, loyalist, or foreign soldier remained in the Highlands or, for that matter, in the area between the Highlands and New York City.

WEDNESDAY, 29 OCTOBER

On this day, General James Clinton wrote a letter to his governor brother. General James recommended that each regiment "Discharge one half or two-thirds [of its strength]."[35] Agreeing with his brother, Governor George Clinton issued the discharge order. With this action, the brutal fighting in the Highlands and the Hudson Valley's southern front had finally come to its conclusion. As for the Wilderness War of 1777, it was now history.

Chapter 10

African Americans in the Wilderness War of 1777

One group of people who, in 1777, found themselves at the crossroads in the Colonies of New York, Vermont, New Hampshire and, in general throughout the New England region, were the black people of African descent.[1]

The high percentage—if not the majority—of the black people who resided in the New World when the Revolutionary War erupted were of slave ancestry. Excluding the black people who arrived as skilled workers or domestic servants, a much higher number were brought over forcefully. Slavery ran hand-in-hand with the exploration and early settlement of the New World. Among the Dutch who played an instrumental role in the early settlement of the northeast, there were those who earned their living as slavers. Dutch rule was not very stringent in regard to the control and ownership of blacks. This explains why, in due time, a number of the slaves became free. Under Dutch rule, free blacks could own property, a home, or business; free blacks also trapped, sold fur pelts, could own a gun, join a Dutch militia unit, and marry within or outside their race and even within a church. Free blacks could also recruit an indentured servant from Europe or hire men and women for labor—whether black or white. And some of the more affluent blacks actually possessed a black slave(s).[2]

In 1664, England put an end to the Dutch rule in the New World. New Netherlands ceased to exist. Until 1783, England would rule in the New World. Unlike the very liberal Dutch system, English rule proved to be not only very harsh but, in fact, was racist especially to those of African and Indian descent. Now, blacks were no longer permitted to own land, a business, employ people, own guns, join an English militia unit, marry outside their race and inside a church. Heavy taxes were imposed upon those who owned property and this, in turn, forced them to lose their homes, farms, and businesses. The numerous laws, rules and regulations imposed upon all of the colonists residing in the New World by England's authorities likewise affected many of the black people in a negative and harsh manner. The Appalachian Act of 1763 did not just affect white settlers and trappers, it restricted the activity of black settlers and trappers as well. In the event of any kind of anti-British infraction, black people (as well as white colonists) could be publicly whipped or executed.[3]

With the eruption of the American Revolutionary War in April 1775, black people found themselves in an awkward situation. Many—if not most—did not fully understand what the new nation was all about. In itself, the American Continental Congress was not always clear and explicit on how it viewed the black issue; nor was it clear on what the status of black people would be in the aftermath of the establishment of the new nation. Would slavery, for example, be totally banned? Would the "All Men Are Created Equal" idealism of the Declaration of Independence ensure both freedom and a higher quality of life for black people? What further confused and, indeed, complicated the issue was that various states and regions—with their newly organized governments—addressed black issues in different ways. And some of the founders of the new nation and signers of the Declaration of Independence had previously been slave owners or were actually still maintaining slaves.

When the Revolutionary War erupted, slightly less than four million inhabitants resided in what would soon be declared, on

4 July 1776, the United States of America. Of these, about 20 percent were black people.[4]

Regardless of what the true figure was, the events of 1775/76 soon culminated into the Wilderness War of 1777. With the eruption of a war within and adjacent to the endless forests of the northeast, the black people who resided in these regions found themselves fully involved in this conflict.

Though prior to the events of 1777 many colonists condemned slavery, in actuality very little was done about it. It would finally be during the American Revolutionary War, but especially during the Wilderness War of 1777, where the nation's anti-slavery sentiment would finally be fully realized and nurtured.[5]

From the outset of the war, a number of English military commanders and Royal Governors began to elicit the support of black people. Though not fully eliminating slavery, they encouraged black people to resist the newly established American nation. Various reasons were cited for this. Part of this stemmed from a major plan to induce as many blacks—along with whites and Indians—to support the Crown and, thus, weaken the newly created and revolting nation; simultaneously, it would draw additional manpower for the British army and navy. Though a number of blacks did join the British military, by and large, England's effort to recruit black support for their war effort was not very successful.[6]

How many blacks served within England's Royal Army and Navy is not known and figures are difficult to establish. But it is known that in the period of 1775–1783, many thousands of Americans of African descent, in fact no less than 5,000, served in the new nation's various Continental Armies.[7]

Many of the African Americans who resided in the northeast, but especially those within and around the wilderness, supported the patriot cause in 1777 because within the land of the endless forests, they had carved for themselves a way of life. England's restrictions hampered their lifestyle as it also hampered the whites and Native American Indians; therefore, by 1775, a large proportion of the black populace had developed a strong resentment of England's rule. With the eruption of the war, by 1777 many soldiers who hailed from Massachusetts, Connecticut, Vermont, New Hampshire, New York, and the wilderness region serving in the ranks of the Northern Army were black. So the question remains: why did so many people of African descent become ardent patriots of the American cause? What motivated them to join the Northern Army? And what compelled them to serve so loyally in the Wilderness War of 1777 when, in fact, they themselves were not totally certain as to what, perhaps, might be their final fate? In order to better understand the factors behind these questions it is important to first examine what occurred on the northern front in 1777, as well as British views and policy pertaining to slavery on the North American continent, how various British commanders viewed the people of African descent, and the political and military events which circulated within and around the Wilderness War of 1777.

On 15 January 1777, Vermont declared its independence. Shortly after on 8 July 1777, Vermont's legislation not only proclaimed full and equal rights to all of its citizens but, on that very same day, totally abolished slavery.[8] Any slaves residing in Vermont were immediately set free. This included those who, though not residents of Vermont, just happened to be in Vermont on the day of the proclamation. By the conclusion of the war, Massachusetts and New Hampshire joined Vermont in totally abolishing slavery.[9]

Fearing a British invasion, New Hampshire's Committee of Safety urged in April 1776, that all males over 21 years of age sign a declaration pledging themselves to resist any British incursions into New Hampshire. Exemptions, however, were imposed. Lunatics, known criminals, and those deemed as being incompetent were excluded from military service. Six months later, in October 1776, the exemption was also extended to New Hampshire's Indians and blacks.[10]

Yet, despite its previous rulings, New Hampshire quickly reversed in 1777 its position denying minority men access to military service. Whether the ruling was influenced by Vermont's actions or the threat of a British invasion from Canada may only be surmised. Regardless, New Hampshire began to recruit black soldiers—both free and slave.[11] In the wilderness battles of 1777, New Hampshire's regiments were fully integrated. New Hampshire's black soldiers served honorably and demonstrated true loyalty and bravery in combat. So moved was the state's populace by their performance that in the aftermath of 1777 very strict restrictions were imposed against slavery. In 1775, 470 slaves were registered in New Hampshire.[12] By the early 1800's, slavery was likewise totally banned in New Hampshire.[13]

On 28 July 1777, from his field headquarters in Saratoga, General Philip Schuyler, the Commander of the Northern Army, dispatched a letter to General William Heath, a Massachusetts commander. In his letter Schuyler cited low troop strengths, that he was not receiving many soldiers, and of those received "one-third are boys, old men and Negroes."[14] General Schuyler's criticism, however, was not based on any ill feelings toward black people or, for that matter, against boys and older men. Rather, the patriot general's criticism was based solely on military concerns and needs because in actuality, many of the arrivals—whether black or white—were untrained, unarmed, and poorly equipped.

By mid-1777, sizable numbers of African American soldiers were serving within the various patriot regiments and battalions organized in the northeast. One unit, raised in Rhode Island, was solely a black unit with a strength of 125 black soldiers. But in actuality, such units were rare.[15] Most of the black soldiers and militiamen were integrated and they served side-by-side with their white compatriots in the various regular army continental regiments, independent battalions, and militia units. In 1777, in central Massachusetts an observer noted that each regiment had "a lot of Negroes."[16] Simultaneously, as black soldiers enlisted into the various units organized in Massachusetts its citizens, noting the patriotism of its black soldiers, began to appeal and petition the Massachusetts legislature to abolish slavery.

In response, in June 1777 Massachusetts drafted a bill banning slavery. Unfortunately, critical and rapidly moving events precluded, for the moment, the passage of the bill. Regardless, in 1780, the Massachusetts legislature, remembering the role that its black citizen soldiers played especially during the critical year of 1777 and adhering to the notion "that all men are equal," totally eliminated slavery from the state.

In 1777, the residents of the newly created New York State voted in its first gubernatorial election. General George Clinton was elected the state's first governor. In this free election, free blacks—to include those serving in the Northern Army—were permitted to vote. Of historical significance was that this was the very first time that blacks ever voted in the newly established state and, for that matter, nation.

Personally, Governor Clinton had always opposed slavery. Sympathetic to the black plight, he supported measures to curb and eliminate slavery within the state. (Various other New York State legislators and prominent officials, such as Alexander Hamilton, also opposed slavery.) Clinton also supported the usage of black manpower for the state's continental and militia units and by the time the Revolutionary War concluded, black servicemen had been utilized extensively by the newly established state.

Despite England's 1763 ban ending slavery within England proper, England's authorities not only continued to tolerate slavery in its colonies but, in fact, even promoted it. In reality, England had no intention of turning the Revolutionary War into any kind of crusade against slavery. England did not care in the least for the black people residing in the colonies. British rule was established solely to exploit the inhabitants and the natural resources of the North American continent. If a black person needed to be exploited to further England's needs, then so be it. The British also quickly dropped their early promises of freedom to any black runaways. British officials not only maintained a close and harmonious relationship with loyalist plantation owners who owned sizable numbers of slaves but, also, some British officials themselves owned a slave or two. Various English officials were even involved in the slave trade. As for any slaves belonging to the loyalists, upon escaping but in the event of recapture, the runaway slaves were frequently returned to their loyalist owners by the regional British authority.[17] A prime example is that of William Henry Mills, a powerful loyalist in Cheraw, South Carolina. In 1780, militia patriots raided his plantation and freed 57 of his slaves. Shortly after, Major James Wemyss, the regional British commander who also commanded the 63rd Foot Regiment, delivered exactly 100 chained slaves to the Mills plantation as compensation for those previously lost by Mills.[18]

Frequently, blacks became booty for resale into other British colonies, such as into the West Indies. Just alone Lord John Murray Dunmore, the Royal Governor of Virginia, took almost 1,000 black men and women out of Virginia to be sold in the Caribbean region. And Francis Rawdon-Hastings, a British army officer and official (also well known for certain ruthless activities such as advocating and condoning the crime of rape while serving in America during the Revolutionary War), also partook in the slave trade. During the Camden campaign, while withdrawing from the advancing patriot forces commanded by General Nathanael Greene, Rawdon departed Camden, South Carolina, with over 400 slaves for the port city of Charleston, South Carolina, and a British bastion. En route to Charleston, he gathered up more blacks. In December 1782, when the British evacuated Charleston prior to its occupation by patriot forces, no less than 5,000 Americans of African descent were forcibly deported during this evacuation alone.[19] If one included those dispatched to the slave trade prior to the evacuation of late 1782, the human slave figure would be significantly higher.

In New York City, William Cunningham, who served as the city's Provost Marshal, was a racist who despised blacks. Cunningham also knew (as did the entire British high command), that certain British officers and officials were even running a secret slave trade from the city. Criminals and thugs were hired to go out in the late night hours to grab young blacks. Once kidnapped the chained or tied up black male or female was taken to a dock, sold, and placed on a boat. Their next stop would be some slave plantation in the Caribbean region. In turn, the money was passed along to the corrupt individuals involved in the city's underground slave trade. And this practice did not just exist in British-occupied New York City. Corrupt British officers and officials ran vibrant underground slave trades from other port cities such as Boston, Charlestown, and Savannah.[20]

Terrorized at the thought of being kidnapped, many blacks fled into an area within New York City known as "Canvas City." Here, they found some protection among themselves. Others, however, fled totally out of the city. Because the area to the immediate north of New York City was referred to as the "No-Man's Land" and various gangs operated freely within this area, the black people fleeing from harm continued to flee farther northward. Ending up in patriot administered zones, a number of the black people, but especially the young men, finally found safety and haven for the time being in the Northern Army, an army which never barred blacks from joining and itself was a fully integrated army.[21]

In late June 1777, General John Burgoyne's Canadian–based English army commenced its operations. Burgoyne's mission was to shatter the Northern Army, overrun the critical fortification system of Fort Ticonderoga, and capture the city of Albany, which was his main objective. En route to Albany, he was also to recruit the "numerous loyalists awaiting the King's arrival" into his army.

From the moment Burgoyne commenced his operations, he issued a number of appeals and declarations to citizens residing in and around the wilderness. In these declarations, Burgoyne urged everyone to oppose the newly established patriot government and nation, and to support the British war effort. Various promises were also made to those who would support the Crown.

Yet, an examination of Burgoyne's numerous appeals and proclamations reveals that not one was ever addressed to the black inhabitants. Surely, Burgoyne knew that many black people existed within the wilderness region. And yet, no strong effort was ever made by Burgoyne to illicit their support.

Burgoyne's views pertaining to slavery, especially in the year of 1777, are not well known. Though it appears that on a personal level he opposed slavery, it is known that amid his circle of commanders, loyalist supporters, and advisors a sizable number were in fact slave owners and/or dealt in the slave trade.

Chevalier St. Luc de la Corne and Charles de Langlade, two French Canadian mercenary leaders accompanying Burgoyne, supported slavery. Prior to 1777, both of these individuals were also well known throughout the entire wilderness and New England region as deliverers of death and destruction. In fact, they were regarded as "devils."[22] Though born into a wealthy family, Chevalier St. Luc was a businessman. He profited from the fur trade and ran dubious security operations. But he was also a middleman in the slave trade who bought and resold slaves.And the only reason why St. Luc and de Langlade accompanied Burgoyne was to plunder the countryside. Regarding black people, their orders to their men were explicit: all blacks, whether free or slave, were to be seized.

One of the most powerful loyalist leaders accompanying Burgoyne was Philip Skene. Originally a native of England, Skene was very wealthy, owning tens of thousands of acres of land in the vicinity of southern Lake Ticonderoga. An entire town was even named for him. Known as Skenesborough, it lay at the base of Lake Ticonderoga.

In 1776, Skene fled to Canada. Patriot activities had forced him to flee. Shortly after, Skene sailed to England. While there he learned about the upcoming British campaign. Returning to Canada, Skene immediately volunteered for British service. Approaching Burgoyne, Skene informed the British commander that he could be of tremendous service to him because he (Skene) was a very influential person with the region's inhabitants, and he also knew the lay of the land. Convinced that Skene would be an asset to him, Burgoyne even endorsed an officer's rank for Skene and placed him on his staff. Skene, who was very loyal to the Crown, also harbored the idea that perhaps, after the collapse of the American republic, the king would even appoint him to be the next Royal Governor of New York.

One of the reasons—if not the main reason—why Skene wanted to come along was to recover his property and wealth. Months earlier, Skene's estate had been seized by the patriots. In the aftermath of the Revolutionary War, Skene demanded from the British ministry a payment for his loss. Among the losses cited by Skene were "eight healthy Negro men." Skene was, after all, a slave owner.[23]

General Burgoyne's superior officer was General Guy Carleton. In addition to holding the rank of general, Carleton was also the British appointed governor of the entire colony of Canada. Throughout his tenure, Governor-General Carleton never opposed slavery or the slave trade within Canada.

To support Burgoyne, a secondary offensive was also undertaken. The idea of a secondary offensive was actually conceived in the early planning phases of the British campaign of 1777. The plan was that a smaller but nevertheless sizable military force would land in Oswego sometime in June or July of 1777. Its initial mission was to proceed eastward through the wilderness to capture Fort Stanwix. Afterwards, this force was to overrun the Mohawk Valley and somewhere in the vicinity of Albany link up with Burgoyne's army advancing southward.

The commander of this force would be General Barry St. Leger. Personally, St. Leger neither endorsed nor opposed slavery. But he was surrounded by a host of men who not only supported slavery but also possessed slaves right up until 1775–1776. Among them stood out Sir John Johnson, the son of Sir William Johnson. Until his death in July 1774, Sir William had been the Superintendent of Indian Affairs for the English king. At the time of his death he was residing at his sizable estate in the Mohawk Valley worked also by a number of slaves. "Sir William (Johnson) kept from 12 to 15 slaves on his farm under the direction of the Bouw-master, a farm manager named Flood, an Irishman. These slaves, some of whom had families, lived in small dwellings erected for them across the creek from the hall."[24] This figure, however, did not include the other slaves who also worked the smaller manor house owned by the Johnsons at Sacandaga. (These, too, escaped at the beginning of the Revolutionary War.) Following Sir William Johnson's sudden death shortly before the American Revolution his son, John, and a nephew named Guy Johnson, now inherited his authority, position, and wealth. Supportive of slavery, the two maintained the slaves.

In 1775, Sir John was forced to flee. He fled to Canada. For the moment, patriot activities had put an end to his reign. Among the losses he soon cited were the slaves he had inherited on the main estate.[25] Even where Sir William had his summer house "a trusty pair of the baronet's slaves who were there to keep everything in order for his comfort" maintained the place year-round.[26] As early as 1742, purchase records reveal that "negroe Handcuffs" were among the items he purchased.[26] Along with Sir John, Sir Guy also fled to Canada.

As for Sir Guy, until 1775 he, too, had possessed slaves. While in Canada, they also raised a sizable loyalist regiment for the King's forces. Blacks, however, were not permitted to join the "King's Royal Green Regiment of New York."

Whenever patriot militiamen raided a loyalist plantation or estate, they immediately freed any slaves found on the property. After confiscating Sir Johnson's property, his slaves were freed. Angered by their losses and determined to restore English authority back to the Mohawk Valley region and, in the process, regain their properties to include their lost slaves, the Johnsons strongly supported the British campaign of 1777.

Along with the Johnsons there also existed Colonel John Butler and his son, Captain Walter Butler. As in the case of the Johnsons, the Butlers also fled to Canada. Very supportive of slavery, both father and son endorsed it. While in Canada, the elder Butler raised a unit titled as "Butler's Rangers." Of importance to note is that neither within Butler's unit nor within Johnson's "King's Royal Green Regiment" were any black soldiers found serving. In fact, though St. Leger's entire army was a multinational force comprised of English, German, Canadian, and loyalist soldiers along with numerous Indians from various American and Canadian tribes, not one individual serving with St. Leger was of African descent.

All of this, of course, was known to those of African heritage. While it was also common knowledge that General George Washington himself possessed some slaves, it was known that prior to the Revolutionary War, Washington had freed a number of them. During the war Washington was so moved by black loyalty, support, and devotion to the cause that by the time conflict ended he totally opposed slavery. Prior to his death in 1799, he made provisions to free his slaves.

Before the Revolutionary War and the monumental events of 1777, the commander of the Northern Army, General Philip Schuyler, had possessed several domestic slave servants. Concluding that slavery was inhumane, prior to the conclusion of the war his servants were officially freed and allowed to stay on as paid domestic servants. Schuyler was, by no means, an exception. Among America's patriotic elite, residing in the northeast adjacent the wilderness regions were those such as the Van Cortlandts and Livingstons. These families, who supported the patriot cause and fought in the Wilderness War of 1777, had always opposed slavery. None were ever slave owners. Black people were known to work their estates but they were paid for their services and were even housed and fed if employed for an extended period of time.

Excluding a few such as Herkimer, the brunt of the Northern Army's top leadership did not possess slaves and they favored an end to slavery. This was, of course, very different from the sentiment found within the British and loyalist command.

The performance of the men and women of African descent who served in the ranks of the Northern Army was superb. From Fort Ticonderoga into the Catskill Highlands and from the Vermont/New England region to Oswego, across an immense area encompassing many tens of thousands of square miles— wherever the fighting raged, black soldiers, militia personnel, and support personnel where found.

The newly established nation's black military personnel never faltered. No matter how bleak a situation appeared to be, they always gave their fullest. Seldom did African Americans complain or display an attitude of defeat. From the beginning, they were always confident that a final victory would yet be achieved. They proved that an army could be integrated and that soldiers of various races could serve jointly. They also won the trust of the new nation and its army. Their service opened the door to a military establishment which offered opportunities and a way of life for future generations of African Americans.

In conclusion, it must be noted that the promises made by the recruiters of the Northern Army to those of African descent were kept. When discharged, black soldiers received their land grants. Worldwide, ownership of land was perceived as a major step toward economic freedom and a better way of life. Upon returning home, many brought along equipment, horses, weapons, and material no longer needed by the army. In the army some also learned how to read and write and all progressed socially and culturally. Along with white soldiers they were paid for their services and, in future years, likewise received benefits and pensions. Those who also entered the army as slaves departed as freemen. Perhaps Frederick Douglass summed it up best when he acknowledged that it was during the Revolutionary War that the true emancipation of black people commenced.[27]

Chapter 11

Women Fighters in the Wilderness War of 1777

One of the principal reasons the Northern Army survived and succeeded in 1777 is because of the immense support females rendered to that army. Exactly how many women served or supported the Northern Army in some capacity in 1777 is not known. However, if one included all of the female agents, spies, couriers, messenger runners, repairers, doctors, nurses, cooks, bakers, guides, wagon drivers, and propagandists, then surely the figure would be in the thousands.[1]

Well before 1775, women began to voice disillusionment and frustration with England. Such was the case regarding the Appalachian Act of 1763 which banned those residing in the British Colony of New York from ever settling beyond the Catskill and Adirondack Mountains.[2] Furthermore, those who desired to trade with the Iroquois could now only do so with permission granted by England's administrators. If granted, the traders also had to buy a special license and permit.[3] As acknowledged by Schwarz and Goldberg, this proclamation made the colonists very unhappy, especially the fur trappers and traders. Among the many unhappy colonists were the dissatisfied women settlers and traders.[4]

Another factor which turned many women, including loyalist women, into Pro-American patriots, was New York City's crime, but especially the ugly crime of rape. By the spring of 1777 hundreds—if not thousands—of women had been raped and/or victimized in some way since the British had captured the city.[5] Indeed, the problem was so rampant that it was dangerous "to walk the streets at night or be in a crowd in the day."[6] Even various British officials and officers acknowledged that rape was rampant.[7] Although no formal or accurate records exist on how much crime existed in New York City during the British occupational period of 1776–1783, it is known that under their occupation crime was out of control not only throughout the city but, as well, on Staten Island and its nearby environs. Theft, common street crime, extortion, drug dealing and usage (especially among certain British officials and officers), and the running of an illegal and sizable slave trade into the Bahamas (also organized and directed by various British officials and officers), was the norm. And it remained so until "one day, in 1783, General George Washington and Governor George Clinton marched into New York City with elements of the Continental Army and restored law and order."[8] Regarding the crime of rape, "clearly, many hundreds of women were raped under British rule. Young women and girls were even terrified of stepping outside."[9] This was largely attributable to the inefficient, inept, and brutal rule of the Colonial Governor of New York, Lord Tryon who, since 1775, had been residing in New York City and to Lord Cunningham, the city's British Provost Marshal. Needless to say such awful crimes, along with the inability by the British occupiers to deal effecttively with the city's crime, drove many women—and even men—into the ranks of the patriots.[10]

Early authors, such as Jeptha R. Simms, also acknowledged that Governor Tryon was a brutal ruler, especially in the year 1777 when critical events were under way.[11] "The problem of preserving order was, indeed, no easy one. The town [New York City] was crowded with people who sought the protection of the crown, many of whom did not know the meaning of law and order, or when removed from their home communities, were quite irresponsible."[12]

Angered, frustrated, humiliated, and physically/emotionally battered, the women of New York City began to lash out. And when they lashed out, they struck hard![13]

British soldiers were found stabbed to death. Others were shot at point blank range or had their heads bashed in. Because in 1775 and 1776 few weapons were found in New York City, it was hard to resist. But as the Wilderness War of 1777 worked itself into the city, smuggled weapons made their appearance. As weapons appeared, women began to use them. By now the city's patriot women were augmented by a sizable number of ex-neutral women turned revolutionary. Even some of the loyalist women, disgusted by the conduct of England's appointed officials or themselves victimized in some way, joined the ranks of the women patriots.

Soldiers were not just targeted. British and loyalist officials were also assassinated. Not even their families were spared. Women targeted the wives and daughters of known loyalists. Terrified, the loyalists screamed for protection, constantly harassing the English commanders for help. Burdened with their demands, New York City's commanders and officials began to increasingly despise their loyalist allies. Indeed, life became very difficult and miserable for those who sided with the Crown. Along with the loyalists the city's civilian criminals, but especially the rapists, were specifically sought out.

Mysterious fires rose in number. Arson became the norm. Sabotage rose. Anti-British leaflets and propaganda pamphlets filled the city. Graffiti slogans WASHINGTON LIVES! KILL TRYON! DEATH TO CUNNINGHAM! KILL LOYALISTS! LONG LIVE 1777! plastered the walls. Stepping out of a club on Murray Street late one night, Cunningham was suddenly approached by a woman. In his intoxicated state he never saw the short broomstick swinging toward his face. Shattering his face and lips, Cunningham fell to the street. As he attempted to stand up, the woman struck him several more times about the head. As quickly as she appeared, she fled. And Lord Tryon, the Royal Governor of New York, after narrowly escaping a bombing assassination attempt by two females, was so terrified of being killed that he actually moved himself onto the British warship the *Dutchess of Gordon* berthed in the harbor. For extra personal protection, Tryon even surrounded himself with an entire company of Royal Marines, having called them in because he no longer had any faith in the army. Wherever he went, marines accompanied him.

In a letter to Lord Germain dated 23 September 1776, General Howe wrote: "A most horrid attempt was made by a number of wretches to burn the town of New York, in which they succeeded to well, having set it on fire in several places with matches and combustibles that had been prepared with great art and ingenuity."[14]

The city's women became agents, spies, and couriers. How many women served in that capacity has never been determined but it is known that many female agents and spies thrived in the city. The horrible prison conditions that the sadistic provost marshal Cunningham created also drove many women into the ranks.[15] As eyewitnesses noted: "When Cunningham was drunk, he would roar through the prison corridors, cursing and kicking over pots of soup the women had brought."[16] Packed into crowded jails or prison ships such as the *Jersey*, approximately 11,500 patriots perished in these hell-holes by the conclusion of the Revolutionary War. "No one knows how many perished on board the *Jersey* and her sister ships, but plausible estimates exceed ten thousand."[17] Another huge hell-hole was the former New York City Sugarhouse converted into a prisoner-of-war camp. Here, prisoners also died in mass numbers from deliberate starvation.[18]

To assist the imprisoned, women were also involved in organizing escape attempts. Deborah Franklin, for example, was especially involved in helping prisoners to escape from New York City.[19] Of interest is that in the aftermath of the Revolutionary War when Cunningham returned to England, he began to swindle government money. Charged with the offense and found guilty, Cunningham was hung on the gallows in 1791. Just before his execution, he confessed to killing over 2,000 New York prisoners.[20]

Whatever was the motive(s) behind their support, it must be noted that a number of the women who joined a Continental Army did so because they, too, were swayed by the promises of army recruiters. Recruiters promised adventure, training, lifetime medical care, benefits, pensions, land grants, pay and, at the conclusion of service some of the items issued to a soldier would be theirs to keep. Many colonial women looked upon this as a good start in life.[21] In fact, no less than 20,000 women served the armies in some capacity during the Revolutionary War.[22] "Enthusiasm" and "expectation of bounties" motivated some women to join a patriot army[23] though "some [women], no doubt, came for a taste of adventure."[24]

Many women agents were also recruited. Among them was the famous Agent 355. These agents operated for Major Benjamin Tallmadge, a Continental Army officer who, by 1778, was running a fairly effective intelligence service for Washington. That year, Major Tallmadge established the so-called "Culper" Spy Ring which also operated out of New York City. Tallmadge's spy ring became well noted for obtaining much critically needed information.[25]

The Northern Army's women soldiers who served and fought in or around the wilderness regions or waged war in an urban environment were, in due time, afforded pensions, land grants, compensations, and medical benefits for life. Even the alcohol allotment initially denied to them was in due time extended to the pensioned women soldiers. Benefits were even extended to the women who served as spies, couriers, guides, medical and support personnel, and to the militia women who served in some militia unit which fell under the Northern Army. Until the end of their lives Generals Schuyler, Gates and, even, Washington always held the brave women of 1777 in exceptional high esteem and ensured that their needs were taken care of.[26]

Chapter 12

New York State's Political Election During the Wilderness War of 1777

As the massive Wilderness War of 1777 raged through and adjacent the forested regions, another conflict was also under way. Though it did not involve any guns and tomahawks, the struggle was just as fiery and important as the one being waged violently amidst the endless forests around the Hudson.

From the outset, America's Continental Congress urged the various states to organize their own internal governments. The state governments were to be established upon the democratic principles as written and proclaimed in the Declaration of Independence. By also establishing state governments, it would be easier for the Continental Congress to control the states and assist them with their needs.

Shortly after the Declaration of Independence was announced, the General Assembly of New York, known as the "Provincial Congress of the Colony," was born. In mid-1776, the General Assembly changed its title to the "Convention of the Representatives of the State of New York."

Initially, New York State's congressional representatives planned to meet in New York City on 8 July 1776. But the two Howe brothers, one an admiral in the British navy and the other an army general, suddenly appeared. Therefore, the representatives met on 9 July in the town of White Plains, located in Westchester County approximately 25 miles directly to the north of New York City. Upon gathering, its representatives received news that just days before the Congressional Congress had adopted the Declaration of Independence. In support of this critical declaration, New York's delegates immediately approved it with a unanimous vote.

On 1 August 1776, the New York delegates established a committee to draw up a Constitution for the soon to be created New York State. Thirty-year-old John Jay, who represented New York in the Continental Congress and was one of the framers of the Declaration of Independence, was nominated to be the Chairman of this committee. Other members included John Sloss Hobart, William Smith, William Duer, Gouverneur Morris, Robert R. Livingston, John Broome, John Morris Scott, Abraham Yates, Jr., Henry Wisner, Samuel Townsend, Charles DeWitt, Robert Yates and James Duane. As for John Jay, he was the key player in drafting the first state constitution.[1]

During the remainder of 1776 and early 1777, military events frequently disrupted the newly established committee's efforts in constructing a Constitution for the state. New York City, along with areas adjacent to it, was also under firm British control. Therefore, the state committee was forced to relocate from place to place. Cases even occurred where its members were forced to flee in the advance of either a British or loyalist force. In fact, so real was the danger that some members of the committee bore personal arms. White Plains and the town of Fishkill in Dutchess County were just some of the places utilized by committee members. But in February, 1777, the entire committee selected the town of Kingston to be its official site.

Initially, Kingston was an old Dutch town established about 1616. At first it was known as Wiltwych, from the Dutch, meaning "Wild Witch." The town was also known as Esopus, the name deriving from the Esopus Indian tribe which once resided in the area. Regardless, by 1777, it was commonly referred to as

Kingston and by this time "Kingston had developed into a pretty, thriving village situated on a plain a short distance west of the [Hudson] river."[2] For the time being, Kingston would officially be the capital of New York State. The committee's members met in the home of Mr. James W. Baldwin, an attorney sympathetic to the patriot cause. Located on the corner of Maiden Lane and Fair Street, it was a beautiful two-storied home of blue limestone known as "the Constitution House."

In October 1777, excluding just one or two homes, the entire village was burned down by British and loyalist troops. Prior to this, vital political activities had been undertaken in Kingston as evidenced on 12 March 1777 when, following a month of discussions, the committee reported that a draft of the state constitution had been developed.[3] Shortly after, on 20 April, it was officially adopted and ratified.[4] According to future American historians "New York established a constitution that, in the largeness of its humane liberally, excelled them all."[5] Soon after, on 13 May, the committee announced that free elections were to be held. The elections were scheduled for June 1777.

The New York Committee which met during the period of 9 July 1776 until 13 May 1777 not only framed and developed New York's first constitution but, just as importantly, advocated and organized a free election. The symbolic meaning behind the free election was of special importance. Free elections would not only demonstrate that a true state democracy existed but, just as importantly, that the state existed in accordance with the ideals of the newly established American nation. Along with the birth of the New York Constitution in April 1777, a free election was also planned for the same year. This election would demonstrate that the patriots were governing a free state.

During this time the commander of the Northern Army, General Philip Schuyler, was urged by some to run for governor. Favorable to the idea, Schuyler became a candidate.

Before adjourning in May 1777, the New York committee designated a so-called "Council of Safety" to govern the state until the elections would form the new state government. This organization was only to exist until shortly after the election was held. Selected were such men for such positions: John Jay served as the state's chief justice (the title of "governor" was reserved until after the election); Robert R. Livingston was appointed as chancellor; John Sloss Hobart and Robert Yates served as judges; and Egbert Benson was appointed as attorney general. The committee voted on these appointments and confirmed all in place. Elections were also set for mid-June 1777.

Prior to the June election the Convention also created, in May 1777, a so-called Vigilance Committee.[6] The function of this committee was to "inquire into and detecting and defeating all conspiracies that may be formed in the State against the liberties of America."[7] John Jay was appointed its chairman.[8] The mission of the Vigilance Committee was to protect important persons; safeguard critical papers; suppress any insurrection; apprehend, secure, or remove any persons deemed as being dangerous to the newly forming state; safeguard the new money treasury; and ensure that members of the Vigilance Committee, along with any individuals employed by the committee, would be afforded protection and secrecy.[9] Various militias were utilized by the Vigilance Committee during this period.

Voting commenced in mid-June. Excluding the regions of New York City, Long Island, Staten Island, and some of the other areas under British occupation, ballots were freely cast. In consideration of the distances involved, the voting lasted until the end of the month. No political speeches, candidate campaigning, or rallies were held. But word of mouth, along with numerous posters, newsletters, leaflets, pamphlets, and announcements in newspapers, proclaimed the elections to one and all. Any free citizen could vote.

Six candidates ran for governor: General Philip Schuyler, General George Clinton, John Morin Scott, John Jay, Robert R. Livingston, and Philip Livingston.[10]

In the meantime, to ensure that some form of government existed, the Convention selected fifteen members to assist the Council of Safety in governing the state until the election.[11]

Unfortunately for the state's future historians, the results of the New York election of 1777 were never fully documented. It will never be known how many people actually voted; however, strong efforts were made to secure each and every vote. By the end of June, the first tallied voter returns from Albany, Cumberland, Dutchess, Tryon (in the aftermath of the Revolutionary War, Tryon County, initially named after Royal British Governor William Tryon was renamed as Montgomery County, in honor of General Richard Montgomery, an American general killed during the Revolutionary War), Ulster, and Westchester Counties had arrived. The candidates received such votes:[12]

Schuyler – 1,012;
Clinton – 865;
Scott – 386;
Jay – 367;
R. R. Livingston – 7;
Philip Livingston – 5.

But the count was not yet over. Two critical areas had not yet been tallied: the votes from Orange County and the soldiers' votes. From among these votes, Clinton received 963 votes; Schuyler only 187.[13] Thus, in the end, Schuyler's total was 1,199 while Clinton's rose to 1,828.[14] According to Lossing, "the [voting] returns were made to the Council early in July. Governor George Clinton was chosen as governor, and Pierre Van Cortlandt lieutenant-governor."[15] General George Clinton won the election.

On 3 July, it was officially declared that General George Clinton was elected as the governor of New York State. Clinton became the very first of many governors to be freely elected. Pierre Van Cortlandt became the state's lieutenant-governor.[16] On 30 July 1777, the two men were sworn in at Kingston.

Because the newly-sworn-in governor was still a soldier, Clinton returned to a militia unit following the ceremony. Credit must be given to Governor Clinton that despite the large Wilderness War raging around him, he still managed to perform many state duties and responsibilities throughout 1777. Though it was not an easy matter, he did successfully juggle both military and political affairs under very difficult conditions. Fortunately, Clinton's right-hand man, Pierre Van Cortlandt, was a strong leader who worked long hours to ensure that the system worked. Through the efforts of leaders such as Governor Clinton and Lieutenant-Governor Van Cortlandt, a strong state foundation was established which remains in place to this day. As for the Council of Safety, as previously agreed upon, this council soon ceased to exist and it never arose again.

Needless to say, south of Kingston, in New York City, England's Royal Governor William Tryon immediately denounced the patriot free election of 1777 as an illegal event. Denouncing Governor Clinton as a "bandit," Tryon reiterated his position that he was the only true governor. As for the newly created state, Tryon condemned it and formally proclaimed that New York is still an English colony. To counter the political events of 1777, Tryon ordered the disbandment of the newly established state government and the arrest of Governor Clinton and his lieutenant-governor.

Acknowledgments

For many decades, indeed centuries, the old ruins of Fort Montgomery, Fort Clinton, Doodletown, Fort Constitution, Fort Independence, the batteries overlooking the barracks of present day West Point and America's military academy, along with the various other historic sites which stood along the banks of the Hudson River northward to Saratoga where one of history's most decisive military surrenders occurred, stood in silence and, by and large, lay underneath a thick canopy of brush, trees, vines, thick pricker bushes, and poison ivy and oak plants.

Until recent times, few had any interest in these historical sites and the events centered around the Wilderness War of 1777. Aside from some occasional author who expressed some interest in America's Revolutionary War history, for the most part the region was not widely read about or studied. Even when I was stationed at West Point with the 57th Military Police (MP) Company (redesignated in 1982 as the United States Military Academy (USMA) Company) between the years of 1981–1984, very little was ever stated or presented about the origins of West Point or, in general, about the American Revolutionary War of 1775–1783. Amongst my fellow MP's, the academy's cadets, and visitors to West Point, much more was related about the American Civil War, the conflict of World War II, the Korean War (two conflicts in which the 57th played a role), Vietnam, and the ongoing global wars of the 1980's. Heavy discussions also arose about the World War II German Army, Rommel's Afrika

Korps, the Waffen-SS, German and Allied Airborne forces, and the Eastern (Russian) Front of 1941–1945. Members of the MP company collected medals, made models of military aircraft, tanks, armored vehicles or whatever, and purchased memorabilia from different armies and American and foreign police forces. But little was ever expressed about our nation's very first conflict.

On October 6, 2002, in a public opening ceremony officiated by New York State then-Governor George E. Pataki, Fort Montgomery finally opened its grounds to the public. Various factors helped to create this: America's public began to express a strong interest in America's early history to include its Revolutionary War period; personal efforts by those such as Governor Pataki, the former mayor of Peekskill, New York, and a local history buff with an immense interest in early American history, and the emergence of a very strong environmental awareness. Through the combined efforts of such enthusiasts, historians, young politicians and corporate/business leaders, strides were made and monies secured to restore and rehabilitate that historic part of New York State. Needless to say, it was well worth the effort.

As my dear Army friend, Lieutenant-Colonel Dennis Pinigis, a graduate of West Point Class of '84 (whose son Alex would graduate Class of 2013) and I, sometime in the spring of 2012, approached Trophy Point, which overlooks Constitution Island, where the Hudson River takes its 90-degree turn, I noted to Dennis, "Smell the river? It's a clean smell!" Perhaps, for readers, this comment might appear to be meaningless if not even ridiculous. But I still vividly recall that hot day, more than 30 years earlier, in July 1981, when I first arrived to West Point situated in the Highlands region about 50 miles to the north of New York City to commence my Army tour. On that day, the river not only smelled like a giant sewer but where it bends at the base of Trophy Point it was a carpet of cluttered junk to include 55-gallon oil drums, rubber tires, water-logged crates, shattered lumber boards, half-floating rotting mattresses, numerous refrigerators/old ice-boxes . . . you name it, and it was out there. Indeed, so thick was the mess that one probably would have been able to walk out upon it.

With the clean-up of this historic river along with the revival of past early American history, tourism began to flourish. Along with the efforts made by those already cited, credit must also be given to John D. Rockefeller, Jr., who financed the research and effort to recover the historic Fort Montgomery site; Mr. Jack Mead, who conducted extensive archaeological investigations that actually revealed the surprisingly intact ruins of the fort; the recently organized Fort Montgomery Battle Site Association; the Hudson River Valley Greenway organization which promotes the cleaning and greening of both the river and its valley; the New York State National Historic Landmark and State Historic Site along with the Palisades Interstate Commission, and the New York State Office of Parks, Recreation and Historic Preservation.

In this work *With Musket & Tomahawk, Volume III: The West Point – Hudson Valley Campaign in the Wilderness War of 1777,* I credit the above for their deeds which helped in producing this work. In addition to these individuals and organizations, the military academy's museum, library, and archives department located at both West Point and on the grounds of the old Lady Cliff College proved to be of tremendous value. Here, I had the pleasure to confer with Alan C. Aimone, the Senior Archivist and Special Collections Librarian at USMA. With his and the kind assistance of other Academy staff personnel, I was able to better understand what truly occurred at West Point and its region before, during, and in the aftermath of the critical year of 1777. Prior to the publication of this volume, Mr. Aimone carefully read my work and made a number of fruitful corrections, additions, and suggestions. To Mr. Aimone and the wonderful USMA staff, I extend my gratitude and thanks.

Mr. Grant E. Miller, Fort Montgomery's Historic Site Manager, was also of exceptional help. Via his tour, the information he provided as well as a number of enlightening phone conversations, from all of this I learned more about the crucial month of October 1777, in the Lower Highlands and its impact on the events occurring all the way northward to Saratoga. I thank Mr. Miller and his staff.

The Palisades Interstate Parks Commission, and their willingness to share archival materials such as the interesting wood graphics painted by a former local resident artist, Mr. Mead, assisted me tremendously. Such graphic re-creations, for example, make it easier for readers to understand what it took to construct the defenses of the Highlands as well as to understand the terrain and combat activities occurring in the fall of 1777 in West Point and its vicinity. Mead's works will forever stand out as true works of art.

Gratitude is also expressed to Ms. Kim McDermott, West Point Class of '87 and the West Point Association of Graduates for permission to use maps from a work previously published by Dave Palmer, a retired general and former Superintendent of West Point.

Once again down in New York City, William "Bill" Nasi proved his value. Very informative on what life was like in New York City during the British occupation, Mr. Nasi gave me the facts. For the city's inhabitants, whether military or civilian, life within and around New York City during the American Revolutionary War but especially in 1777–1778 was, indeed, a very difficult period. In these pages readers truly learn about the hardships and tragedies one can only experience during a time of war while under foreign occupation. Thanks, Bill.

Again, information found for this book was obtained in Washington, D.C., from the former Charles Sumner School Museum. An African American Institute, its floors were filled with much information relating to African American history. Ms. Harriet Lesser, former curator and director of this institute, along with her staff, were very supportive of my efforts to reveal the events to include many of the little known events that African

American soldiers and black support personnel performed in helping the newly established American nation secure a victory in the northeast wilderness. To this former archival center, I likewise extend my thanks and gratitude.

The local hometown libraries of Fair Haven and Hannibal, as well as the libraries located in Oswego, Fulton, and Utica, New York, reveal a good amount of information on the American Revolutionary War. Simply by just studying the old land grants provided to soldiers in the aftermath of the American Revolution reveals much. In each library, I always encountered supportive staff and librarians and to them, I also extend my thanks and gratitude.

And to the memory of my dear uncle Bohdan "Dan" Fedorowycz who, in the aftermath of World War II and in the rank of Sergeant First Class (SFC), served in the U.S. Army on the border line in Germany separating Soviet Pact forces versus the American-NATO forces. During the time we resided in upper New York State in the Town of Sterling, on many occasions my uncle would visit and with his family we would hunt, fish, camp, and enjoy life on the very same land that in 1777 was traversed by so many individuals from so many different combat units and irregular forces serving either in the Northern Army or some European force.

Last but not least, this book is dedicated to those who have served or are presently serving in our nation's armed forces.

C'est la Guerre!

NOTES

Chapter 1. The Military Situation on the Southern Front, Late 1777

[1]Because at this time various Clintons existed both on the American and British side, for purposes of clarity British Army General Sir Henry Clinton will be referred to throughout this book solely as Sir Henry.

[2]See William B. Willcox, *Portrait of a General. Sir Henry Clinton in the War of Independence* (N.Y.: Alfred A. Knopf, 1962), pp. 143-144. (Hereafter cited as *Portrait of a General Sir Henry*). According to Willcox, "The two parts of the campaign, the invasion from Canada and the move against Pennsylvania, were planned separately by generals who were as far apart in their thinking as they were in distance." (p. 143). Willcox also cites that Lord George Germain, the Secretary of State for the American Colonies, was also at fault for not being clear as to what the various commanders were to do. According to Willcox, "Germain failed to discharge his responsibilities. He knew by early March [1777], when Burgoyne was preparing to leave London [England] to take command of the [British] Canadian army, that the objective assigned to it was to cooperate with Howe; he also knew that Howe's eyes were on Pennsylvania." See also Willcox, *Portrait of a General Sir Henry*, pp. 153-154. (At this time, General George Washington's Main Continental Army was in Pennsylvania. For a brief period of time in 1775-76, this army was also known as the Central Army).

Willcox cites that prior to Sir Henry's arrival to New York City in early July, he firmly believed that Howe would be advancing northward and had no knowledge of Howe's true intent. See pp. 153-154, 155-160. And Thomas Fleming, *Liberty! The American Revolution* (N.Y.: Viking-Penguin Group, 1997), p. 237, cites "Lord George Germain, the man in charge of overall planning, approved both campaigns." Germain sincerely believed that once Howe captured Philadelphia, Howe would march his army to Albany to meet with Burgoyne. (Ibid., p. 237). (Hereafter cited as *Liberty!*).

Perhaps Sir John Fortescue, a British army historian, summed it up best: "Never was there a finer example of the art of organizing a disaster." (Ibid.).

[3]Though to this day many historians cite that Howe had assured Sir Henry that he would return in time, no evidence exists that Howe's intent was to return once General Washington had been defeated and Philadelphia was captured, or as soon as Howe realized that nothing positive was being gained by being in Pennsylvania.

[4]General Barry St. Leger, who commanded a western force which encompassed a mixed British, German, Indian, and loyalist force augmented with Canadian mercenaries, was to march eastward from Oswego to Albany. (At this time St. Leger also believed that Howe was going to advance northward to Albany). See R. Ernest Dupuy and Colonel Trevor N. Dupuy, *The Encyclopedia of Military History From 3500 B.C. to the Present* (N.Y.: Harper and Row Publishers, 1977, Revised Edition), p. 714. (Hereafter cited as *Encyclopedia of Military History*). Simultaneously, in conjunction with St. Leger's eastward thrust from Oswego another force from Oquaga (Oquaga lay just to the east of present day Binghamton, New York), containing a mixed Indian-loyalist force with British advisors, was to proceed northeastward into the Schoharie Valley. After accomplishing its mission, this group was to link up with St. Leger somewhere to the west of Albany and together, the combined force was to march eastward to link up with both Burgoyne and Howe in Albany.

[5]For details on this portion of the campaign see Michael O. Logusz, *With Musket & Tomahawk - The Mohawk Valley Campaign In the Wilderness War of 1777* (PA.: Casemate Publishers, 2012), and Gavin K. Watt and James F. Morrison, *The British Campaign in 1777. Volume One, the St. Leger Expedition, the force of the Crown and Congress* (Canada: Global Heritage Press, 2003).

[6] John Luzader, *The Saratoga Campaign of 1777* (Washington, D.C.: National Park Service Publications, 1975), p. 16. (Hereafter cited as *The Saratoga Campaign*); Trevor Dupuy, *Encyclopedia of Military History*, p. 715. Robert Leckie, *The Wars of America (Updated Edition)* (N.Y.: HarperCollins Publishers, 1992), p. 164, cites "Howe sailed for the mouth of the Delaware River with 260 ships and about 15,000 soldiers." Undoubtedly, the 3,000 or so loyalists were not included in this figure of 15,000. (Hereafter cited as *Wars of America*).

[7] Luzader, p. 16; Willcox, *Portrait of a General Sir Henry,* pp. 153-154. According to Willcox "He [Howe] intended to leave with [Sir Henry] Clinton at New York a mere forty-seven hundred regulars and a few thousand provincials, far too weak a complement for the task he sketched." See p. 152.

[8] Sir Henry's health was, in fact, quite poor. And New York City's sad state of affairs only complicated and worsened matters for him. For an excellent study of the difficulties experienced in New York City during the Revolutionary War, see Oscar Theodore Barck, *New York City During the War For Independence* (N.Y.: Columbia University Press, 1931). (Reprinted: N.Y.: Ira J. Friedman, Inc., 1966). (Hereafter cited as *New York City During the War).* According to Barck, "The problem of preserving order was, indeed, no easy one. The town [New York City] was crowded with people who sought the protection of the Crown, many of whom did not know the meaning of law and order, or when removed from their home communities, were quite irresponsible (See p. 57). See especially "Keeping the Peace in the War-Time City," Chapter III, pp. 49-73. According to author Thomas Jones, ". . . frustrations were already demonstrated in September, 1776, when a group of unruly soldiers even broke into City Hall and stole and wrecked furniture, tore paintings; beat and robbed those within and around the building, and created much disorder. Even the officers within the premises could not stop them." See Thomas Jones, *History of New York During the Revolutionary War* (N.Y.) 1879, Vol. I, pp. 136-137. See also Barck, p. 57. For additional information regarding problems and hardships see Robert M. Calhoon, *The Loyalists in Revolutionary America, 1760-1781.* (N.Y.: Harcourt Brace Jovanovich, Inc., 1973). (Hereaf-

ter cited as *Loyalists in America*). Another interesting study of the city during the Revolutionary War is Barnet Schecter, *The Battle for New York. The City at the Heart of the American Revolution* (N.Y.: Walker & Company, 2002). Hereafter cited as *Battle for New York*.

[9]Along with the numerous female spies operating for the patriots in New York City there was also a spy named James Rivington. A native of London, England, with close ties to England's ruling class, in 1760 Rivington had emigrated to the colonies. Initially settling in Philadelphia, Rivington established a bookstore business. The following year, in 1761, he opened a bookstore in lower Manhattan near Wall Street. Shortly after the British occupation of New York City, Rivington established, in 1777, a loyalist newspaper titled "Rivington's New York Loyal Gazette." On 13 December 1777, the paper's name was changed to "The Royal Gazette." Though publicly he harbored a pro-British sentiment, in actuality Rivington was one of Washington's best spies.

Throughout the Revolutionary War, Rivington's newspaper was the official newspaper of the loyalists. Indeed, so critical was the paper of Washington, the Congress, and the patriots that Ethan Allen of Vermont publicly stated that "I will lick Rivington at the very first opportunity I have!" (Lossing, Vol. 1, p. 508.) More than likely, when Ethan Allen used the word "lick," Allen meant that he would someday cause Rivington physical harm, such as killing him. Knowing that Ethan Allen enjoyed a good drink, in response to Allen's comment Rivington published a very funny pictorial on what actually would happen in the event the two should ever meet. Centered around a bottle of Madeira, a Spanish wine very prized by Rivington, the publisher cited how the two would finish off two such bottles and part as very good friends. (Ibid.). (See also "The Press and Public Opinion" in Theodore Barck's, *New York City During the War For Independence*).

In the aftermath of the war in 1783, Rivington did not depart the city. Upon entering the city, that very same day General Washington looked up the publisher. Instructing his aides and security to wait outside, Washington entered himself. In his hands, he held a small pouch containing gold coins. Rivington never returned to England. Remaining in the city in July, 1802, at the age of 78, he passed away.

By now, it was rumored both in England and America that Rivington had been Washington's personal spy.

Factually speaking, this was the case. In addition to publishing a newspaper, Rivington also published books. Within certain pages known only to Washington, Rivington inserted secret words, numbers and codes. These words and figures were assembled in such a way as for only Washington to understand. Any books bound for Washington were placed into special drop-off points with unknown couriers ensuring that Washington himself received the books.

[10]According to Willcox, *Portrait of General Sir Henry*, pp.144 and 146, "Between March 3 and April 19 Germain wrote him [Sir Henry] no less than eight letters none of which contained a reference to Burgoyne." Willcox also cites how Sir William Howe complained to Sir Henry that Germain "did not understand what the invasion was to accomplish." (Ibid., p. 146). It appears that Germain was so confident that his army commanders could take care of themselves that Germain failed to inform them on what, exactly, their missions were to be and he failed to properly coordinate their activities. (Ibid.).

[11]16 August 1777 is the date Howe later claimed he received the letter. See also Willcox, p. 171, fn.4. Shortly before, on 18 May 1777, Germain again responded favorably to Howe's intent. However, though "he approved Sir William [Howe's] plans . . . " Germain insisted "that it should be completed in time for cooperation with the [British Canada] northern army." Ibid., p. 151. See also pp. 152-153.

[12]Ibid. Possibly, Howe might have considered on returning. But because he was so determined to take Philadelphia and Germain's guidance was not explicit on returning, Howe might have reasoned that if he could finish off Washington in Philadelphia's vicinity, he would still have ample time to return to New York City to conduct a second thrust northward toward Albany.

Chapter 2. West Point
[1]Other tributary rivers include the Schroon, Sacandaga, Batten Kill, Champlain, Hoosic, Roeliff, Fish Kill, Wappinger, and Popolopen Rivers and creeks.

[2]In honor of a soldier and statesman named Prince Maurice Mauritius.

[3]For a simple but quite detailed study of the Hudson River and its role in America's history see Mary McNeer, *The Hudson, River of History* (Illinois: Garrard Publishing Co., 1962).

[4]Dave Richard Palmer, *The River and the Rock. The History of Fortress West Point, 1775-1783* (N.Y.: Greenwood Publishing Co., 1969), p. 23. (Hereafter cited as *History of Fortress West Point, 1775-1783*). At the time of his book's publication, Palmer was in the rank of Lieutenant-Colonel. He would retire as a Lieutenant-General and have the distinction to serve as one of West Point's Superintendents.

[5]Ibid.

[6]Charles E. Miller, Jr., Donald V. Lockey, and Joseph Visconti, Jr., *Highland Fortress: The Fortification of West Point During the American Revolution, 1775-1783*. (Unpublished text at the United States Military Academy (USMA) Library, West Point), p. 12. (Hereafter referred to as *Highland Fortress*).

[7]LTG Dave Palmer, *History of Fortress West Point, 1774-1783*, p. 15.

[8]To cite an example: some of the so-called "Irish potato crop famines" were not attributable to natural disasters. Rather, British officials imposed deliberate hunger campaigns by confiscating and destroying food items, crops and livestock animals.

[9]Charles Miller, Jr., *Highland Fortress*, p. 13. This included the various textile mills, small iron works, and foundries which made an appearance before 1775.

[10]Ibid. For an excellent study of the three most critical factors for patriot concerns see especially pp. 11-14.

[11]Miller, *Highland Fortress*, p. 27; John E. Wilmot, ed., *Journals of the Provincial Congress of New York* (Albany, 1842), Vol. I, p. 723.

[12]Miller, *Highland Fortress*, pp. 12-13. According to Colonel Kevin W. Farrell in "The Geology Driving the Battle" in 'The [American] Revolution's Boldest Venture' in *Army Magazine* (VA: July, 2014), p. 65, though the British had occupied New York City since August, 1776, "the [American] Continental possession of the Hudson Highlands prevented British use of the Hudson River as a convenient and

reliable means of communication and transport from New York City
to Canada" and "the Hudson was the most important river in the 13
Colonies." See also pp. 64-67.

[13]Born in the Netherlands, Bernard Romans studied engineering in England. In the early 1700s he emigrated to the colonies and
settled in Spanish Florida.

Romans was a highly talented artist and mapmaker. While in
Florida he drew sketches of its varied plants, animals, and reptiles, and
portraits of native Floridian Indians. He was hired by Spanish authorities to produce maps of uncharted Florida regions. Based on some
information he obtained in 1775 on ten Spanish treasure ships which
sank off Florida's coast sixty years previously during a violent storm in
1715 Romans, in early 1775 plotted on a map (also produced by him)
the exact location of these sunken ships. For nearly the next two centuries this treasure map lay in various Florida museums and archives.
Later, the map made its way to the National Archives in Washington,
D.C. In the early 1960's a skin diver and treasure hunter came across
the map and Romans' information. So accurate was Romans in his
plotting that upon arrival to the site, the remains of these ships were
discovered. Amongst the hulks, much treasure was recovered.

In the very true sense, Romans was Florida's first environmentalist.
Nearly two centuries before the advent of any kind of environmental
concerns he advocated preserving Florida's rich, diverse, and delicate
flora and fauna. After writing a work about Florida's animal and plant
life, he traveled to Boston, Massachusetts, in 1776 to have his manuscript published into a book. There, he heard about the newly forming
Northern Army. Though about 56 years of age, he still craved adventure. Purchasing a musket, some gear, and a tomahawk, he located a
recruiting office and joined the Northern Army. Stationed in Fort
Ticonderoga, he underwent military training and assisted its garrison
in constructing a defensive system.

Despite his enthusiasm, Romans was neither a skilled military
engineer nor a good contractor. Even his civilian engineering
skills were questionable. When on leave from Fort Ticonderoga, he
appeared in Philadelphia to the Continental Congress seeking a pro-

motion to the rank and full pay of a colonel in the engineers. Since his abilities and educational level were questionable, he was denied the rank. Romans was, however, transferred to West Point and despite no formal military rank, was entrusted to construct a fortifications system there. Romans' efforts quickly proved to be unproductive and in time he was dismissed. Appointed to the rank of captain in the artillery, he served in a Pennsylvania artillery unit. Toward the close of the Revolutionary War, Romans returned to Florida where he resided until his death at about the age of 100. (For more information on the role Romans undertook at West Point see Palmer, *History of Fortress West Point, 1775-1783*, pp. 32-40).

[14]Records reveal it was owned by a Mr. Bunn.

[15]Also known as Martler's Rock and Martyr's Cliff, the name derived from a French family by the name of Martelaire who either resided on it or by it in approximately 1720. See Captain Edward C. Boynton, *History of West Point, and Its Military Importance During the American Revolution; and the Origin and Progress of the United States Military Academy* (Freeport, N.Y.: Book for Libraries Press, 1863. Reprinted 1970), p. 21. For an interesting study of West Point's early history prior to and at the commencement of the Revolutionary war, see pp. 1-38. (Hereafter cited as *History of West Point*).

It is not known what happened to the Martelaire family. But of interest is that on 19 September 1775, the New York Committee of Safety, by order of the Continental Congress, wrote a letter to Mr. Beverley Robinson who, they believed, was the legal owner of Martelaer's (as the name was now spelled) Rock Island. In their letter, the committee explained "the Provincial Congress of this Colony has undertaken to erect a fortification on your land, opposite West Point, in the Highlands. As the Provincial Congress by no means intend to invade private property, this Committee, in their recess, have thought proper to request you to put as reasonable price upon the whole point of dry land, or island, called Martelaer's Rock Island; which price, if they approve of it, they are ready to pay you for it. We are, Sir, your humble serVants." (See Captain Boynton, *History of West Point,* p. 23. For the entire short letter, see pp. 22-23).

On 2 October 1775, Mr. Robinson responded: "Sir... I must inform you that the point of land on which the fort is erecting does not belong to me, but is the property of Mrs. Ogilvie and her children. Was it mine, the public should be extremely welcome to it. The building a fort there can be no disadvantage to the small quantity of arable land on the island. I have a proportion of the meadow land, that lays on the east side of the island. I am, Sir, your most humble servant, Bev. Robinson." (See p. 23 for the entire letter).

In actuality, Mrs. Ogilvie owned half of the island. (Who owned the other half is not known. Possibly, Mr. Bunn, whose abandoned house was used on occasion, was the other owner).

Despite Robinson's sincere words, unknown to the committee members was that he was a loyalist. Possibly, during this time, Robinson was one of those providing the British army down in New York City information on patriot activities. When in October, 1777, Sir Henry launched an expedition against the Highlands, Robinson, in the rank of colonel and the commander of a loyalist regiment, participated in the attack. According to Mr. Alan C. Aimone, Senior Special Collections Librarian and a curator at West Point's USMA Library, "Robinson planned the attack. He knew the rear trail to Forts Clinton and Montgomery." (Personal discussion with Aimone).

[16]Martalaer's Rock was renamed Constitution Island. Because three of its sides jut into the Hudson River and its rear is surrounded by a swampy marsh averaging about one-to-three feet of water for much of the year, for this reason the site is officially classified as an "island." But the marsh can actually dry up during a hot summer. When this happens, a jeep or four-wheel type of vehicle can actually be driven onto the rear of the island or, a person can just simply walk onto it.

From July 1981–May 1984, the author of this book served with the 57th Military Police Company (designated in 1982 as the USMA - United States Military Academy Company) at West Point. Although Constitution Island was not patrolled routinely (one of the reasons being because it was directly across the old Military Police station and barracks and was easily observed at all times), on rare occasions it was necessary to dispatch a patrol onto the island. In the event this happened an MP patrol would first proceed down Route 9W South to the Bear Mountain Bridge. Crossing the bridge over to the eastern side of the Hudson River, the MP patrol would then proceed northward on 9D North for about 3 miles to the village of Cold Spring. Here, amid some homes, is an alley street which connects into the marsh. Once a motorist drives over the dry marsh and onto the rear of the island, the rest of the island may easily be covered on foot. Another way to cross onto the island (as cited by Mr. Alan C. Aimone, historical curator at West Point) is by foot via an old railroad bridge.

[17]As for the name Constitution, Bernard Romans and his three colleagues actually coined this name. The name evolved from a discussion Romans and the others had one evening about the English constitution. Since it had been agreed that a fort needed to be constructed upon the island, everyone agreed to name the island with its new fort as Constitution. The name stuck and Constitution Island, along with Fort Constitution, was accepted. See also Palmer, *History of Fortress West Point, 1775-1783*, p. 33.

[18] Palmer, *History of Fortress West Point*, p. 34.

[19]Ibid.

[20]Ibid.

[21]Ibid.

[22]Palmer, p. 34. For additional information see Lieutenant-Colonel James M. Johnson, "Staff Rides and the Flawed Works of Fort Constitution" in *Engineer. The Professional Bulletin for Army Engineers* (October, 1990), p. 10. LTC Johnson cites Romans began to construct the "Grand Bastion" (soon dubbed as Fort Constitution) on 29 August 1775. (p. 10).

[23]In the end, Romans neither obtained the rank he sought nor constructed a proper site.

[24]One can see the importance of securing and fortifying the Highlands by a series of letters found in George Clinton's *The Public Papers of George Clinton* (N.Y.: Albany, 1904). (Hereafter cited as *The Public Papers of George Clinton*). In Volume I see "Vouchers for Work Done in the Highlands," Letter of December 27, 1776 and signed by Thomas Machin, pp. 499-500; the four short letters signed by Colonel Jonathan Hasbrouck on 1 August 1777 pertaining to Fort

Montgomery, p. 500; "Draft of Agreement with Carpenters to Prepare Obstructions in the Hudson," letter just dated 1777; General George Clinton's report to the State Convention "Obstructing the Hudson," report dated 13 February 1777, pp. 592-594; "One Item of Two Thousand Pounds for Obstructing the Hudson," letter dated 23 February 1777, signed by William Bedlow, p. 617; General George Clinton's "General Clinton Confident the Hudson River Obstructions Will be Effective," letter of 23 February 1777, signed by General Clinton, pp. 618-620; "The State Convention Urges Completion of Obstructions in the Hudson without Delay," letter dated March 18, 1777, during a Convention of New York Representatives in Kingston, N.Y. Letter signed by Abraham Ten Broeck, p. 671; letter submitted to the New York State Convention, "By Interference with His Work on the Defenses and by a Resolution of the State Convention," letter dated 23 March 1777, signed by George Clinton, Brigadier General, pp. 675-677; "Ropes and Cables for the Great Chain," letter of 19 April 1777, signed by August Lawrence, p. 722; "Gen. McDougall Suspects that the High-land's are the objective point of the British," letter dated 21 April 1777, signed by Alexander McDougall, pp. 724-725; "General James Clinton Voices the General Sentiment - that the Enemy's Objective is the Highlands," letter dated April 22, 1777, from James Clinton, Brigadier General to (his brother) General George Clinton, pp. 825-827 and 831-835. And pp. 842-848 reveal the strength figures for Forts Constitution, Clinton, Montgomery, and Independence. For additional letters and dispatches on the importance of securing and effectively fortifying the Highlands see also Volume II.

[25]Palmer, *History of Fortress West Point,* p. 42. The three were such: Robert R. Livingston, who hailed from a prominent New York family and from the beginning was highly involved with fortifying the Hudson River; John Langdon, a wealthy merchant from New Hampshire and politician; and Robert T. Paine, a lawyer who prosecuted the British army captain who gave the order to fire on the night of 2 March 1770 in Boston, thus creating the forever known "Boston Massacre."

[26]Palmer, p. 42.

[27]Ibid.

[28]In 1760, Robert T. Paine served briefly as a chaplain on a military expedition to Crown Point. But that was the extent of his military service.

[29]Palmer, p. 42.

[30]Ibid.

[31]Various other military and non-military men had already concluded that Romans' work was useless.

[32]In a letter written from Fort Constitution as early as 25 September 1775, several New York Commissioners, writing to the State Committee of Safety, warned that Romans' defense plan was not only insufficient against an invading force but actually, was totally ineffective. See Captain Boynton, *History of West Point*, p. 23.

[33]Palmer, p. 44; Boynton, p. 27.

[34]Personal discussion with Mr. Aimone. Of interest is that on 11 December 1776, Brigadier-General James Clinton, in a letter to the New York Provincial Congress, acknowledged that the situation in Fort Montgomery was quite dire when the general wrote: "I have but a small garrison here at present . . . and many of them without shoes and other clothes. Without shoes and some clothing we will not be able to keep up our guards and get firewood, and do the other necessary duty of a garrison." (Cited in a letter displayed at Fort Clinton, Highland Falls, NY).

Chapter 3. The First Battles of the Wilderness War of 1777

[1]In 1777, New York State was arranged differently than today. At that time, New York State consisted of fourteen counties. (See Benson J. Lossing, *The Empire State. A Compendious History of the Commonwealth of New York*, p. 256. (Hereafter cited as *The Empire State*). At this time, Westchester and Orange Counties were among the fourteen. In 1777, both counties were larger in size than what they currently are. Eventually, a portion of northern Westchester County would be incorporated into Putnam County and southeastern Orange County became Rockland County.

[2]This was the very first Fort Independence to be constructed by the patriots. It was built in what is now known as the Bronx in the northern borough of New York City. This fort should not be confused

with the soon-to-be constructed Fort Independence about 30 miles farther upriver in the vicinity of Peekskill; nor with the Fort Independence found in the Fort Ticonderoga defensive system overlooking Lake Champlain, located north of Albany outside of the new American nation in the wilderness region of the north country.

[3]Mark M. Boatner, *Landmarks of the American Revolution. People and Places Vital to the Quest for Independence* (Harrisburg, Pa.: Stackpole Books, 1992), p. 285. (Hereafter cited *as Landmarks of American Revolution*).

[4]After 1776, Fort Independence would never be utilized by the Americans.

[5]Currently known as the Valentine-Varian House. The house still stands at Bainbridge Avenue and east 208th St. not far from the King's Bridge in the Bronx. Owned at that time by Issac Valentine, the son of Peter Valentine, Issac sided with the patriots. Along with his entire family he fled northward when General George Washington was forced to retreat from New York City in 1776. In 1791 Issac Varian (whose son was elected mayor of New York City in 1839) purchased the house from the Issac Valentine family. Hence the Valentine-Varian House name. Today, it is a public museum.

[6]Mark V. Kwasny, *Washington's Partisan War, 1775-1783* (Ohio: Kent State University Press, 1996), p. 118. (Hereafter cited as *Washington's Partisan War*).

[7]Kwasny, *Washington's Partisan War,* p. 118.

[8]From the West Point Special Collections and Archives Division, USMA Library. *Unpublished text of Highland commanders.* Prior to McDougall, Major General William Heath commanded the Highland Region from 12 November 1776 until 12 March 1777.

[9]Kwasny, p. 118. As for Drum Hill, it was named for the beat of the military drums. Presently, Drum Hill is a residential neighborhood just to the south of the main town of Peekskill.

[10]McDougall also wanted them to be reinforced with some local militiamen prior to engaging the incoming enemy force. According to Colonel Robert L. Tonsetic, *Special Operations During the American Revolution* (PA: Casemate Publishers, 2013), p. 146, on 23 March 1777,

Howe landed a force of 500 men and four artillery pieces near Peekskill to destroy the large American supply depot filled with military supplies, barracks, and mills within Peekskill. According to Tonsetic, General McDougall received advance warning of the British raid. (Tonsetic does not cite the source of this warning but undoubtedly, it came from the spies operating in New York City). After securing positions on Drum Hill, the British opened fire both on Peekskill and an American position named Fort Hill which, in actuality, was more like a redoubt than a fort. (Today, Fort Hill is a park in the center of Peekskill). Realizing his forces were understrength, McDougall ordered that the supplies be removed but a lack of time prevented this. After removing some of the supplies, a retreat was ordered and the remaining supplies, barracks, and storehouses were torched. McDougall also dispatched messages to a regional militia unit as well as to the 3rd New York Continental Regiment (temporarily commanded by Lieutenant-Colonel Willett and positioned at Constitution Island) to immediately appear. In the meantime, as McDougall awaited his reinforcement, the British raiders occupied Peekskill and destroyed the remaining supplies, storehouses, and military material. (Tonsetic, pp. 146-147. Hereafter cited as *Special Operations*).

[11]On 24 March 1777, General George Clinton dispatched two short letters regarding the events of 23 March. Both letters were written from Fort Montgomery. One was addressed to Colonel A. Hawkes Hay and the other to Colonel Levi Pawling. In Clinton's letter to Hay, Clinton described how "a considerable Body of Troops (generally supported about 1000) landed at Peek's Kill yesterday about 12 o'Clock." He further described what occurred and how he had called up reinforcements (undoubtedly militia) but acknowledged that "Til the above Regiments arrive we can't possibly spare any Men from this, as it [Fort Montgomery] is a Post of the utmost Consequence." Clinton did, however, cite "we will give you every Aid and Protection in our power the Moment a Reinforcement arrives." Clinton also ordered Hay to attack the enemy in the rear in the event they should attack Fort Montgomery. "If their Designs are against this Post you will fall on the Enemy's Rear which may be done with grreat

advantage should they Land below us." Clinton also informed Hay
that Colonel Pawling would reinforce his (Hay's) force.

In General Clinton's letter to Colonel Pawling, Clinton approved
the retreat conducted by Pawling. One day previously, Clinton also
informed Pawling that reinforcement is enroute and added "Should
the Enemy attempt any thing against the Post it will be by landing
below us and marching up in which Case you will be able to fall on
their Rear with part of your Troops." See *The Public Papers of George
Clinton,* Vol. I, pp. 679–681.

[12]Willett was correct that the British attacked on a Sunday. But he
slightly erred when he cited 22 March as the date. All sources reveal
that Sunday's date was 23 March and not 22 March. See William M.
Willett, *A Narrative of the Military Actions of Colonel Mari-nus Willett,
Taken Chiefly From His Own Manuscript* (N.Y.: G.&C.&H. Carvill,
1831), p. 40. (Hereafter cited as *Military Actions of Colonel Willett*). For
Willett's entire role during this attack see pp. 39–42.

[13]Kwasny, p. 119. The Americans took 7 casualties. (Ibid.). Tonsetic,
Special Operations, cites Willett's counterattack killed 9 British soldiers
and wounded 4 with Willett reporting a loss of 2 dead and 5 wounded.
(P. 147). Overall, the British lost 13 killed and 4 wounded. (Ibid.).
Tonsetic also cites the raid occurred throughout 23–24 March 1777.

[14]*Military Actions of Colonel Willett,* p. 40. In his writings Willett
does not cite the name of Captain Abraham Swarthout. But in the
aftermath of the Revolutionary War, for his services Captain Swarthout was provided land in what currently is the Town of Sterling in
New York State. (As for Sterling, it was named after Major-General
"Lord" Alexander William Stirling, a general in Washington's main
army who also received a large acreage site in the same place for his
services. Of interest is how one day a state records official incorrectly
recorded the name of Sterling with an "e" instead of an "i" and, to this
day, the mistake has stuck). As for the property owned by Swarthout,
it remained in his family until the 1950's. Presently, a portion of the
Swarthout land is owned by the author and his family.

[15]Some allege that it was at Fort Stanwix that the American flag
was first flown in the face of an enemy. Whether this was actually the

case is not known but it is known that material from the previously secured blue cape was used for the making of the flag flown at Stanwix. As for the flag, it was actually quickly sewed by Fort Stanwix's females who, caught up in its encirclement, performed various heroic tasks.

[16]Lieutenant-Colonel William L. Otten, Jr., *Colonel J. F. Hamtramck. His Life and Times (Volume One, 1756-1783) Captain of the Revolution* (Texas: Otten Publishing, 1997), p. 81. According to Otten, in addition to seizing supplies, the British also burned a schooner and "plundered everything in sight." (Ibid.). (Hereafter cited as *Colonel J. F. Hamtramck*, with appropriate Volume).

[17]From 1775 until 1778, the patriots simply did not have enough troops to effectively occupy and control this entire and sizable region. Had they attempted to do so, they would have also positioned themselves too close to the British and this could have resulted in the destruction of any patriot personnel placed almost adjacent to any British forces. And in 1776/early 1777, the patriots could not risk this. Therefore, until their strength rose, the patriots had to remain in the higher terrain of the Highlands, located approximately 40 miles to the north of New York City.

Simultaneously, the British were not in a position to man this entire region either. And with Howe off to Pennsylvania to pursue Washington and capture Philadelphia, the capital of the newly established nation, the British forces left behind to garrison New York City and its environs now lacked the manpower to effectively occupy this region. Therefore, the British attempted to rule this so-called "Neutral Ground" or "No-Man's Land" with proxy forces from outlaw gangs such as the "Cowboy's," "Skinners," and the Delancey regiment. (Because it was largely referred to as "No-Man's Land" hereafter, "No-Man's Land" will solely be cited. See also Mark V. Kwasny, *Washington's Partisan War,* p. 119, and Tonsetic, *Special Operations,* p. 147).

As for the Delancey unit, it was also known as "Delancey's Refugees" and "the West Chester Refugees." Officially, this unit was raised in New York City in the fall of 1776. Initially stationed in Westchester County, after October 1777 and the defeat of the British in the Wilderness War of 1777, the unit retired to New York City.

Until 1783, it was utilized for conducting raids out of the city into New Jersey and lower New York State. In 1783, the unit was transferred to Canada where, that same year, it was disbanded. In 1777, a green colored coat uniform with white and brown cloth leggings was issued to its personnel. Though a Major Barmore is identified as being the unit's commander in 1776–1777, it is known that James Delancey was a key player in organizing this loyalist outfit. From 1777 until 1783 James Delancey, now in the rank of Lieutenant-Colonel, is cited as being its formal commander. Tonsetic, p. 147, spells Delancey as DeLancey.

[18]In the letter of 7 April 1777 to General Clinton, the commissioners cited "the Tories our Inveterate foes have been busy for the space of a fortnight in driving off Cattle and horses; last Friday night a drove of 40 fatt Cattle were driven thro' Rye." (See *The Public Papers of George Clinton*, Vol. I, p. 704). "We doubt not during the above mentioned space of time 500 Cattle and horses have been driven to the Enemy; ourselves and good friends are much exposed to the Cruel and merciless outrages of the Enemy." (Ibid.). The commissioners also warned: "We doubt not that many of a week [weak] Resolution have Deserted to the Enemy from the weakness of our forces that would otherwise have been of service to our Cause." (Ibid.).

According to Kwasny, *Washington's Partisan War,* p. 119, "By May 1777, no one was safe in Westchester." In actuality, no one was safe well before May 1777. This fact was acknowledged in a letter dated 7 April 1777 by Mr. Richard Hatfield, a New York State Secretary to Brigadier General George Clinton who soon would be elected as the first governor of New York State. (See also pp. 124–125).

In his letter titled "Complaints of the Commissioners that Westchester County is in a Dismal Condition and the Continental Cause has Suffered in Consequence," Hatfield wrote how the commissioners acknowledged that "Our [Westchester] County is in a Dismal situation." (See *The Public Papers of George Clinton*, Vol. I, pp. 703–704). The commissioners also cited that neighboring Orange and Dutchess Counties are weakly manned with troops and "we beg leave to Inform you, that from the weekness [weakness] of the forces in this County, they are unable to Execute the trust reposed in them." (Ibid., p. 703).

[19]Ibid. Indeed, the rustling and thievery was so widespread and rampant that cattle and other animals were rustled from regions as far away as western Connecticut and the western regions of the Catskills. Kwasny, p. 119, cites the Cowboys and Skinners also caught deserters from the British army and whenever a deserter was delivered back to the British, a ransom was paid by the British. (See also Kwasny, pp. 116-125). According to Wrong, *Canada and the American Revolution. The Disruption of the First British Empire* (N.Y.: Cooper Square Publishers, Inc., 1968), p. 382, "Guerrilla warfare made the country of New York, Long Island, Northern New Jersey and Connecticut a No-Man's Land where life was unsafe." (Hereafter cited as *Canada and the American Revolution*).

[20]The figure of 2,000 was cited in a letter written by Congressional Congressman John Adams in the aftermath of the raid. Henry B. Carrington, *Battles of the American Revolution, 1775-1781. Historical and Military Criticism, with Topographical Illustration* (N.Y.: A.S. Barnes and Company, 1877), p. 297. See also Kwasny, *Washington's Partisan War*, p. 125. Mark Mayo Boatner, *Encyclopedia of the American Revolution* (N.Y.: David McKay Co., Inc., 1966), cites also a strength of 2,000 along with what units and commanders were utilized. See Boatner's "Danbury Raid," pp. 315-316. Boatner also cites that this force landed between Fairfield and Norwalk, present day Westport. According to Wendy Van Wie, *The Homestead At 188 Cross Highway In Its Historical Context* (Westport, CT: 2014), the British raiders commenced their debarkation at 5 p.m. on 25 April and occupied Compo Hill and what was known as Bennet's Rocks. At 11:30 p.m., they began a night march to Danbury. (See map, p. 6). (Hereafter cited as *The Homestead*).

[21]Kwasny, *Washington's Partisan War*, pp. 121-122.

[22]Boatner, *Encyclopedia of the American Revolution*, pp. 315-316.

[23]Around Bethel the townships of Redding, Brookfield, and Newtown stood.

[24]In American history, Sybil Ludington is known as the "female Paul Revere." She also served as a messenger rider for the Northern Army and carried dispatches.

[25]Kwasny, Ibid., p. 124.

[26]Ibid., p. 122.

[27]Ibid. See also Carrington, *Battles of the American Revolution, 1775-1781,* p. 297. Boatner, *Encyclopedia of the American Revolution,* p. 315 cites 1,700 tents destroyed along with many provisions and clothing items.

[28]Kwasny, p. 123.

[29]Ibid.

[30]According to Carrington, p. 297, by the time the British retired totally, General Arnold had two horses shot from under him.

[31]The Connecticut River, which originates in the vicinity of Canada, is the main river which flows through Connecticut southward into the Long Island Sound. It divides Connecticut in half.

[32]Kwasny, p. 122.

[33]Kwasny, p. 124. Efforts were also made to rescue private citizens abducted by the raiders. Such was the case with Benjamin Meeker and his brother Daniel. In addition to driving off the Meekers' cattle, the British arrested the two brothers and removed them to New York City were they were incarcerated for a period of 18 months in the so-called "Sugar House Period." The brothers were arrested because of their pro-patriot sentiments and because their sister, Molly Meeker, was serving in the Continental Army. (Van Wie, *The Homestead,* p. 6).

[34]According to Plumb, the British did succeed in getting away. (p. 62). Plumb, who went through the Town of Danbury in pursuit of the raiders, had "an ample opportunity to see the devastation caused there by the British." (Ibid., p. 63). "The town had been laid in ashes, a number of the inhabitants murdered and cast into their burning houses . . . " (Ibid.). Plumb, however, stayed only a short time in Danbury. His unit "then marched to Peekskill, on the Hudson River, and encamped in the edge of the Highlands, at a place called old Orchard." (Ibid.).

In the following days and weeks, various charges and countercharges arose out of the Danbury Raid. Totally disgusted with the events of the raid and what he perceived as being poor resistance on the part of the American forces, Congressman John Adams wrote:

"We have a fine Piece of News this Morning of the March of 2000 of the Enemy, and destroying a fine [supply] Magazine there – and the stupid sordid cowardly torified County People let them pass Without Opposition.

"All New England is petrified with astonishment, Horror, and Despair, I believe in my Conscience. They behave worse than any Part of the Continent. Even in N. [orth] Jersey Men [British-loyalist raiders] could not have marched so far."

By and large, the Congressional Congress agreed with Adams' assessment.

Yet, a careful review of Adams' criticism reveals that perhaps he, too, was hasty. In actuality, a considerable amount of resistance had been offered. Though sporadic and to an extent poorly directed and executed, undoubtedly, this was largely attributable to (as cited by General Arnold) a lack of daring and boldness on several occasions. Arnold presented how when at Ridgefield, General Wooster fell, the militiamen ceased to attack and left; on the following day, at Compo Hill, they refused to attack to cut off the raiders.

To analyze the entire situation would take pages. But a review of the actions of the continental and militia units which fell under the Northern Army's jurisdiction actually reveals a number of positive actions, such as the quick reaction to the British threat. And various continental and militia units marched many miles rapidly into the battle area to assist one another. Furthermore, the British raid was not a total success. Their losses were significant and most of the captured livestock was lost en route during their retreat. In the pursuit of the British, Wooster captured about 40 enemy personnel. (Boatner, p. 316). In all, 154 British soldiers were killed and wounded. (Ibid.). Patriot casualties were about 20 dead including General Wooster and 80 wounded. (Ibid.). But most important was that the Northern Army demonstrated a willingness to resist and that it could hold its own in combat. In the aftermath of the raid, this likewise was noted by various British officials.

[35]Undoubtedly, the letter of 7 April 1777 regarding the commissioners' concerns played an important role in dispatching troops to quell the gangs and restore order. As the commissioners requested in their letter: "We, therefore, hope and earnestly Intreat, the favour of your affording us and the well affected inhabitants, Relief, by ordering down Immediately [from West Point and the Northern Army] a sufficient Number of Forces to Enable us to do our duty, and to Cutt off all Communication from the Enemy." (See *The Public Papers of George Clinton*, Vol. I, p. 704. For the entire letter see pp. 703-704).

[36]John A. Pope, Jr., ed., *Strange Stories, Amazing Facts of America's Past* (Reader's Digest Publishers, 1989), p. 364.

[37]William Stewart would later serve in Washington's main army to include Valley Forge.

[38]Indeed, with the failure of the British to secure the meat, another hardship hit the city.

By the conclusion of 1777 meat, all food products, firewood, and just about everything else needed for living was in tremendous shortage. Prices rose significantly. Items quadrupled and, in time, rose even higher. Hunger set in. Desperate to assist those in need and to raise morale, the city's occupiers staged the first "Great Public Charity Event" on Christmas Eve in 1777. (See Oscar T. Barck, *New York City During the War For Independence*, p. 91). Though noble, in actuality England's officials could not alleviate the suffering. And on p. 104, Barck cites "the winter of 1777 caused much suffering among the inhabitants." Barck acknowledged that in addition to employment and housing shortages, "add to these circumstances the high cost of the necessities of life caused by scarcity and war-time conditions, and it is easy to understand why there were so many poor persons in the city during the British occupation." (Ibid., pp. 90-91). Barck also correctly cited that "The most difficult problem facing the [British] army and the civilian population was that of supplying the city with food." (Ibid., p. 98). Though Barck mentioned that food and other shortages were already prevalent before 1777, Barck strongly emphasized "As the year 1777 advanced, however, prices continued to rise in spite of military regulation; nor did the food gain in quality; one diarist called it 'poison.'" (Ibid., p. 102).

For further studies of the hardships experienced in New York City during 1777 but especially in the aftermath of the Wilderness War of 1777 see especially Chapter 4, "Physical Welfare of War-Time Population" and Chapter 5, "Food and Fuel." And Thomas Jones, *History of New York During the Revolutionary War* (N.Y.: 1879), Vol. I, cites on various pages (such as pp. 136-137) how in addition to the city's food shortages, lawlessness also plagued the city. Another work depicting the harshness experienced in the city during this time is Barnet Schecter's *The Battle for New York. The City at the Heart of the American Revolution* (N.Y.: Walker & Co., 2002).

³⁹For an in-depth study of this conflict *see The Encyclopedia Americana. International Edition. U.S. Constitution Bicentennial Commemorative Edition* (CT: Grolier Incorporated, 1988), Vol. 21, pp. 637-638. See also Dupuy, *Encyclopedia of Military History*, p. 708. Dupuy cites that though by 1782 the issue was largely resolved by America's Congress, the war formally ended in 1807. *Encyclopedia Americana* cites 1799.

⁴⁰At that time, the Wyoming Valley encompassed a sizable region stretching from Pennsylvania deep into the wilderness area of New York.

⁴¹All of these treaties were concluded in Fort Stanwix.

⁴²Significant actions occurred in late 1774 and into 1775 such as when Pennsylvania dispatched a large armed force of no less then 700 commanded by Colonel William Plunkett. Marching into the Wyoming Valley to enforce Pennsylvania's demands, though neither side wanted a battle, sadly one occurred and before the gunfire ended, men perished on both sides. Taking casualties, Plunkett retreated. Shortly after, in April 1775, the American Revolutionary War erupted.

One of the last actions of the Yankee-Pennamite War occurred on 28 September 1775. But with the eruption of hostilities against England, both sides in general supported the American effort. As for Zebulon Butler (1731-1795), he served as a continental officer in the Northern Army's 3rd Connecticut Continental Regiment in the rank of lieutenant-colonel. In 1778, while on leave and at home in the Wyoming Valley, he engaged and fought a sizable loyalist force commanded by Colonel John Butler (of no relation to Zebulon) at Forty Fort, PA. Though defeated by John Butler, Zebulon's actions forced the loyalist raiders to retire. Continuing his service, he remained in the 3rd Connecticut but also advised the Wyoming Valley's militia forces. In the aftermath of the Revolutionary War he expressed no further interest in the previous dispute and personally ensured that a peaceful settlement be undertaken by America's Congress.

[43]Of interest to note is that despite the fears of America's Continental Congress that the British would exploit this conflict to their advantage, this never occurred. Indeed, it appears that the British either had no knowledge of this or, if they did, they simply overlooked a situation which, if properly exploited, could have been very favorable to them.

Chapter 4. June–July–August–September, 1777

[1]The 1st New York Regiment of 1777 (not to be confused with the 1st New York Regiment of 1776 which, in late 1776, needed to be massively reorganized) was organized between November 1776 and early October 1777. From its inception in November 1776 until its disbandment on 3 November 1783, it was commanded by Colonel Goose Van Shaik. This regiment served throughout New York State during the Revolutionary War. The 1st New York Regiment, however, was not in the Highlands when Sir Henry attacked in October, 1777.

[2]The 2nd New York Regiment of 1775 was initially organized as a battalion in 1775. On 8 March 1776, the American Continental Congress elected field officers for four new battalions (soon to be upgraded into regiments) from New York. The units were to serve with the newly forming Continental Army. Although raised, all of the regiments lost most of their personnel when enlistments expired in late 1776. In late 1776/early 1777, a new 2nd New York Regiment, designated as the New York Regiment of 1777, was organized. In 1776 and 1777, it served in the Highlands.

[3]The 4th New York Regiment of 1775 and the 4th New York Regiment of 1776 had a history similar to the 2nd New York Regiment of 1775 and 1776.

[4]The 5th New York Regiment was organized on 26 June 1776. On this day, Colonel Lewis Dubois was appointed by the Continental

Congress to raise a Continental regiment. Utilizing Lieutenant-Colonel Nicholson's New York battalion as a cadre, around Nicholson's unit Colonel Dubois built a regiment. On 21 November 1776, the regiment was officially designated as the 5th Regiment of the New York line and it was assigned to the Northern Army. Posted into the Highlands and Fort Montgomery, the 5th New York Regiment was not in full strength when British General Henry Clinton attacked the Highlands. On 6 October 1777, the regiment was overrun at Fort Montgomery. By the end of the year, it had ceased to exist. Of interest, however, is that as late as 22 December 1779, Colonel Lewis Dubois was still, officially listed as being regimental commander. See also Fred Berg, *Encyclopedia of Continental Army Units,* p. 85.

[5]Congress itself designated the Highlands as a defense area to be fortified by 1777.

[6]The 1st New York Continental Brigade was organized in late 1776. Five New York Continental regiments, the 1st to the 5th, fell into the 1st Continental Brigade.

[7]Commanded by Colonel Peter Gansevoort, the 3rd New York Regiment was ordered by the Northern Army high command to deploy in May, 1777, from the Highlands to Fort Stanwix to assist in the defense of the western frontier. An elite unit in near regimental strength, the 3rd New York successfully defended the western region in 1777. For an in-depth study of the 3rd New York from 1776/1777 see Michael O. Logusz, *With Musket & Tomahawk: The Mohawk Valley Campaign In the Wilderness War of 1777* (PA: Casemate Publishers, 2012).

[8]Primarily the Oneidas and Tuscaroras.

[9]Primarily the Mohawks, Onondagas, Cayugas, and Senecas. However, members of each of these tribes did side with the patriots although by and large these tribes sided with the English Crown.

[10]Palmer. *History of Fortress West Point,* p. 93.

[11]Ibid.

[12]For activities pertaining to June, 1777, see *The Public Papers of George Clinton,* Vol. 1, pp. 842-857 and vol. II, pp. 3-60. See also letter of General George Clinton to Captain Hodges dated 6 June 1777

from Fort Montgomery and letter of General Clinton to General Washington "Cables Placed in the River, Fort Montgomery July 11, 1777." For the letters dated 6 June and July 11, 1777, these are also in the museum/archives at Fort Clinton.

[13]Otten, *Colonel J.F. Hamtramck*, p. 85. General Israel "Old Put" Putnam was born 7 January 1718 in Salem Village (now known as Danvers), Massachusetts. During the French and Indian War he served in Rogers' Rangers and rose to the rank of major. Captured by the Indians, he was tied to a stake to be burned alive but his life was suddenly saved when raiders struck the camp. A fiery patriot, he served at Lexington, Bunker Hill, Long Island, and assisted Washington with operations in the late 1776/early 1777 winter offensive against Trenton and Princeton in New Jersey.

[14]Because General Schuyler was very concerned about the defense of the Highlands and concluded that the blocking of the Hudson River was imperative for halting all enemy movement northward, he offered various proposals and suggestions on how this could be done. Believing that in the vicinity of Fort Montgomery where the Hudson River bends the water was very shallow, Schuyler even proposed that a sizable boat or "Sloops filled with Stone" be sunk or "Two Cassoons or Vessels one upon the other would answer the purpose." Realizing the importance of maintaining a passage for patriot watercraft, Schuyler proposed "A passage might be kept open in the shallowest part, and one or more Vessels ready for sinking at Hand." Schuyler also advised keeping "... a Body of Troops well Intrenched above Fort Montgomery ..." thus creating a situation where " ... the Enemy would find it Extremely Difficult to Force a Passage thro. The Highlands." For Schuyler's concerns and his discussions see Lincoln Diamant, *Chaining the Hudson. The Fight For the River In the American Revolution,"* (N.Y.: Carol Publishing Group, 1989), pp. 94–96. (Hereafter cited *Chaining the Hudson*). The book also explains the various weights of the chain, its construction, the depths of the river and the difficulties of spanning a chain across the Hudson River.

[15]Otten, pp. 85–86.

[16]Lieutenant-Colonel William L. Otten, Jr., (Ret'd) *Colonel J.F. Hamtramck. His Life and Times Volume One (1756-1783) Captain of*

the Revolution (Port Aranas, Texas: 1997), pp. 85-86. (Hereafter cited as *Colonel Hamtramck*). Hereafter General George Clinton will be referred to as Governor Clinton.

In the annals of America's history but especially in the history of New York State, the free election of 1777 - though conducted under very adverse and difficult circumstances - was a huge success. Throughout the entire state and the newly formed nation, the election demonstrated the resolve of those willing to establish a new state within a new nation. Needless to say independence, free elections, and freedom are not synonymous with peace, liberty, justice, and happiness. Nor is it guaranteed. A long road still lay ahead and the final outcome to determine if the state would indeed survive was still being waged within the savagery of the Wilderness War of 1777.

[17]On 1 January 1777, Glover's 21st Continental (Sailor) Regiment had received the numerical designation of 14th Massachusetts.

[18]The 1st New York Continental Brigade comprising the five continental regiments was not the sole patriot military unit found at this time in the Highlands. Various militia units also served in the Highlands; however, unlike the continentals who served for a prescribed period of time, many of the militia personnel rotated in and out. Though the greater number of the militia units were understrength, some of the militia units were in full strength when mobilized. Such was the case with General Nixon's militia regiment which contained a strength of over 600 personnel. A well-led and effective unit, General Washington ordered Nixon's unit to assist the patriots in the northern sector in resisting the enemy advance following the patriot retreat from Fort Ticonderoga. Dispatched northward, Nixon's unit remained in the Albany-Saratoga sector until mid-October, 1777. Following General Burgoyne's surrender, Nixon's unit was rushed back down into the Northern Army's southern sector to engage the British attack into and beyond the Highlands. It appears, however, that Nixon's militiamen saw no further action in late 1777.

General Glover's crack 14th Massachusetts Regiment (previously titled as the 21st Massachusetts (Sailor) Regiment) was a part of

General Washington's Main Continental Army. Dispatched to the Northern Army, the 14th was stationed briefly in the Highlands prior to receiving its order to move (along with Nixon's regiment) further northward. Whereas Nixon's regiment was formally headquartered in the Highlands, Glover's regiment never was.

[19]Willcox, *Portrait of a General. Sir Henry Clinton*, p. 164.

[20]Popolopen Creek flows into the Hudson River. On the day the governor was viewing the countryside, Fort Montgomery stood to the north of Popolopen Creek.

[21]A reading would later reveal that the hilly knoll upon which Clinton stood was 123 feet in height. This is 23 feet higher than the other. Though the height difference is not that much more significant, it did overlook the other nearby hilltop positions to include the one upon which Fort Montgomery was being constructed. In the event someone placed just one or two cannons upon this hill, Fort Montgomery would be in grave danger.

[22]Otten, *Colonel Hamtramck*, p. 75. The new fort, named as Fort Clinton, was constructed to the south of the Popolopen Creek. (See map in Otten, p. 76). After receiving the letter, Washington immediately ordered Lieutenant Thomas Machin, an engineering officer serving in Washington's Main Continental Army, to immediately report to the Highlands to supervise the construction of the fort to be constructed on Popolopen's southern side.

[23]*The Public Papers of George Clinton,* Vol. II, pp. 124–127.

[24]For Sir Henry's concerns see Willcox, pp. 169–172. According to Colonel Dupuy, *The Encyclopedia of Military History,* p. 174, Howe took "some 18,000 men in transports." Dupuy clearly implies that Howe's move left Sir Henry, Burgoyne, and the British campaign of 1777 in grave danger. Lossing, *The Empire State*, p. 286, also cites a strength of 18,000 embarked.

[25]Thomas Machin was born in England. By profession he was an engineer. Emigrating to the colonies when the Revolutionary War erupted, though Machin was English in blood, he quickly sided with the patriots. He helped to construct the fortifications on Bunker (actually Breed's) Hill overlooking Boston. Wounded as British

forces attacked and overran the hill, he still managed to escape. Shortly after, he was commissioned as an officer in General Knox's artillery. In 1777, he was transferred to the Northern Army and was posted into the Highlands. Returning to Washington's main army after the Wilderness War of 1777, until the conclusion of the Revolutionary War Machin served with distinction. In October 1781, he witnessed the British surrender at Yorktown.

[26]For the entire letter, see *The Public Papers of George Clinton,* Vol. I, pp. 275-277. See also Otten, *Colonel Hamtramck,* p. 75. (For a map depicting the positions of the two forts see p. 76). Of importance to note is how rapidly the various letters moved between Highland's command and General Washington.

[27]Palmer, p. 97, cites two brigades were deployed. Palmer, however, does not reveal a strength figure.

[28]Christopher Ward, *The War of the Revolution* (N.Y.:The MacMillan Co., 1952) (Volumes I-II),Vol. II, p. 513. (Hereafter cited as *War of the Revolution*). See also Willcox, *Sir Henry,* p. 171.

[29]Letter of General Washington to George Clinton, 1 August 1777. See *The Public Papers of George Clinton,*Vol. II, p. 185.

[30]Otten, p. 90. Although not a significant figure, the transfer of 180 men was felt.

[31]These command positions were never permanent. Leadership changes always occurred. To cite an example: according to "Return of Troops at Forts Montgomery, Constitution, and Independence" (dated July 11, 1777 and July 25, 1777), Governor and Brigadier General George Clinton was identified as being the commander of these three forts. (See *The Public Papers of George Clinton,*Vol. II, pp. 98 and 135). But on 19 August, Fort Clinton was commanded by Colonel Levi Pawling.

[32]See "George Clinton Orders Brig.-Gen. Ten Broeck to Increase His Levies in Order to Reinforce the Northern Army," in *The Public Papers of George Clinton,* Vol. II, p. 163.

General Ten Broeck was New York State's top commanding militia commander who commanded a total force of no less than 20,000 to about 25,000 militia men and women organized around the fighters

and support personnel. He had three higher commands over him –
Governor Clinton, commander and headquarters Northern Army,
and General Washington himself. A participant of the Battle of Saratoga, there Ten Broeck commanded 12,000-13,000 militia personnel.

[33]Richard M. Ketchum, *Saratoga. Turning Point of America's Revolutionary War* (N.Y.: Henry Holt and Company, 1977), pp. 282-283.
(Hereafter cited as *Saratoga, Turning Point*).

[34]According to Ketchum, *Saratoga, Turning Point*, p. 283, on that
day (3 August 1777), Howe and his army "were south of the Delaware
River." As for Washington, possibly he speculated that Howe's advance
into the Delaware was solely a diversion to keep patriot forces pinned
down in Pennsylvania and New Jersey while the real attack would be
launched against the Highlands.

[35]In general, the patriots in the northeast had a very good
communications system in motion well before 5 August; however, on
5 August, the communications system was further improved upon. See
also *The Public Papers of George Clinton,* Vol. II, pp. 140, 183-187, 195-197.

[36]This was the message delivered to Sir Henry: "Edmund Palmer,
an officer in the enemy's service, was taken as a spy lurking within our
lines; he has been tried as a spy, condemned as a spy, shall be executed
as a spy, and the flag is ordered to depart immediately.

P.S. He has been accordingly executed!"

(See also Palmer, p. 98).

Chapter 5. West Point Prepares for War

[1]Hopkins' force of 55 officers and militiamen were detached from
Colonel Morris Graham's militia regiment. (Otten, p. 79).

[2]Otten, *Colonel Hamtramck*, p. 79. In *The Public Papers of George
Clinton,* Vol. II, p. 26, the strength return for Fort Constitution on
12 June 1777 cites a Lieutenant-Colonel Jotham Loring as being its
commander. There is no mention of a Major Pleas or Captain Mott.
But on p. 42, the strength return for Fort Constitution on 19 June
1777 reveals Major Mauris Pleas, a militia commander from "Dutchis"
(Dutchess) County, as the commanding officer of Fort Constitution.
Yet, the 26 June 1777 strength return again reveals Loring as being

in command. (See p. 54). Therefore, Lieutenant-Colonel Loring was either transferred to another site for just a short while or, possibly, he was away on leave for the time being.

[3]Otten, p. 79.

[4]Ibid.

[5]Ibid.

[6]Ibid.

[7]Otten, p. 92.

[8]Ibid.

[9]Ibid.

[10]One can see the urgency of halting Burgoyne by a series of letters written by and to the Council of Safety of New York State in the period of mid-August 1777. See *The Public Papers of George Clinton,* Vol. II, pp. 215-236.

[11]Undoubtedly, this explains why the 5th New York Continental Regiment was never deployed.

[12]Otten, p. 78.

[13]At that time, Trier was actually a part of the Austrian-Hungarian Empire.

[14]Otten, p. 26.

[15]Ibid.

[16]Unfortunately for Hamtramck, when the Articles of Exchange (signed 6 p.m. on 27 May 1776) led to the exchange of the prisoners held by both sides, Captain Hamtramck was one of the few not released. Possibly, this occurred because the British regarded him as a Canadian/British national. In hand and leg irons, Hamtramck and a number of other prisoners were taken to Oswegatchie (near present day Ogdensburg, New York), where a British garrison commanded by a Captain Fraser existed and where another 497 patriot prisoners of war were being held. (Otten. P. 44). Of these, 483 were released under the exchange. (Ibid.). Hamtramck, however, was one of the fourteen not released. At this time, the British garrison was also ordered to withdraw back across the St. Lawrence River into Canada proper. After loading up his bateaux with his troops, their gear, equipment, cannons, powder, ammunition, personal items and various other material, there

simply was no room left for the prisoners. Because Captain Fraser had no firm orders on what to do with the prisoners, as they rowed away, Hamtramck and the others were just left stranded on the river's bank. With no more than the clothes on their backs they decided to head to Montreal, a city about 100 away miles in hopes of linking up with some patriot force. During their very difficult trek the group made contact with an American force commanded by General Benedict Arnold and retiring back into the colonies. This is how Hamtramck entered the colonies. Soon, he rejoined the Continental Northern Army and was posted into its southern sector at West Point.

Captain Hamtramck, however, was not an exception. When the Americans withdrew from Canada a sizable number of French Canadian citizens fell back with the patriots. Some had served with the Americans as soldiers; others, as civilians, had assisted the patriot cause in some support capacity and others, initially brought as prisoners to New York prior to the American withdrawal from Canada and released under the agreements, did not care to return to Canada because they feared that upon return England's Canada–based authorities would classify them as "collaborators" and, possibly, would punish them. Though still loyal to the English Crown, like those who fled voluntarily, they remained in the colonies and resided for the time being as refugees in the Albany and Kingston areas. The Northern Army's Relief Bureau provided them with food, clothing, and shelter.

[17]In 1777, Kingston was designated as the capital of New York State.

[18]Otten, pp. 61–62.

[19]Ibid., p. 80. *In the Public Papers of George Clinton,* Vol. II, p. 23, a troop strength return for the 5th New York Continental Regiment is presented. This strength table was submitted on 12 June 1777. According to the return, "267 privates are present for duty." 1 Colonel (Colonel Dubois), 1 lieutenant-colonel, 5 captains, 6 first lieutenants, and 3 second lieutenants for a total of 16 officers is cited. 32 non-commissioned officers are cited. 1 sergeant-major, 1 quarter master sergeant, 2 drum and fife majors, and 28 sergeants. 3 ensigns, 1 staff adjutant, 1 staff quarter master and 13 drums and fifes

are listed as well. Lacking were also a major, a chaplain, a surgeon, and a surgeon's mate. Among the identified five captains, Captain Hamtramck is listed.

[20]Otten, p. 80.

[21] "St. Leger Attacks in 1777 . . .," in *Oswego Palladium Times,* November 20, 1945, pp. 10-11.

[22]Palmer, p. 100; Robert Calhoon, *The Loyalists in Revolutionary America, 1760-1781* (N.Y.: Harcourt Brace Jovanovich, Inc., 1973), p. 428; Crisfield Johnson, *History of Oswego County, New York, 1739-1877* (N.Y.: 1878), p. 40.

[23]Michael Pearson, *Those Damned Rebels. The American Revolution as Seen Through British Eyes* (N.Y.: G.P. Putnam's Sons, 1972), p. 267. (Hereafter cited as *Those Damned Rebels*).

[24]Palmer, p. 99.

[25]Otten, p. 92.

[26]Willcox, *Portrait of General Sir Henry,* p. 179; Palmer, p. 101; and Pearson, *Those Damned Rebels,* p. 276.

[27]Dupuy, *Encyclopedia of Military History,* p. 715.

[28]Palmer, p. 101. See also Willcox, *Portrait of General,* p. 176. Willcox does not cite a figure; however, he cites that "[Sir Henry] achieved nothing beyond the acquisition of some livestock."

[29]Otten, p. 92.

[30]Ibid.

[31]Willcox, *Portrait of General,* p. 178, cites "communication with New York was as slow as it was hazardous." And on p. 184, Willcox cites "Clinton could not establish communication even by messengers."

[32]Palmer, p. 101. Count Grabowski's name has also been spelled as Gabrousky.

[33]Ibid., p. 100.

[34]Fleming, *Liberty! The American Revolution,* p. 268. According to Colonel William A. Ganoe, *The History of the United States Army* (N.Y.: D. Appleton and Co., Inc., 1924) (Reprinted N.Y.: D. Appleton-Century, 1942), p. 48, "Howe moved into Philadelphia and, with 20,000 trained troops, was spending his third winter in the capital of the country."

[35]James Phinney Baxter, *The British Invasion From the North. The Campaigns of Generals Carleton and Burgoyne From Canada, 1776-1777, With the Journal of Lieut. William Digby of the 53rd, or Shropshire Regiment of Foot* (Albany, N.Y.: Joel Munsell's Sons, 1887), pp. 34-36. (Hereafter cited as *The British Invasion From the North*).

[36]According to Lieutenant-Colonel Joseph B. Mitchell and Sir Edward Creasy, *Twenty Decisive Battles of the World* (N.Y.: The MacMillan Company, 1964), p. 208, "Clinton's force was too small to have broken through to Burgoyne at Saratoga." (Hereafter cited as *Twenty Decisive Battles*). Sir Henry also knew that he could not simultaneously occupy New York City and its region and conduct an offensive action toward Burgoyne who was positioned well over 140 miles to the north. Along with encountering difficult terrain and patriot resistance, any weakly manned supply and communication line southward to New York City could easily have been cut by any patriot forces or guerrillas. It was also late in the season and the first snowflakes were coming down in northern New York. Simply put, a major thrust to reach Burgoyne would have placed Sir Henry's command in grave danger.

[37]Willcox, pp. 179-180.

[38]Ibid., p. 180.

[39]According to Palmer, "reports of recent troop arrivals from Europe and persistent indications of an impending military operation alarmed New York's watchful governor. Convinced - rightly so this time - that an attempt was afoot to breach the Highlands, [Governor] George Clinton ordered his colonels to assemble one half of each regiment and march to the Highland forts. The remaining halves were to be ready to march 'on a moment's warning.'" (Palmer, pp. 103-104).

[40]See *the Public Papers of George Clinton*, Vol. II, pp. 348-353.

[41]Ibid.

Chapter 6. Sir Henry Attacks!

[1]The 7th (Royal Fusilier) of Foot was formed as Our Royal Regiment of Fusiliers in 1685. In 1751, it was redesignated as the 7th (Royal Fusilier) Regiment of Foot. In 1773, the 7th Foot was deployed to Canada and stationed in Quebec. However, it was soon

dispersed. 295 soldiers were positioned in St. Johns, 83 in Chambly, and 63 in Quebec proper. (See also Philip R. Katcher, *The Encyclopedia of British, Provincial, and German Army Units - 1775-1783* (Pennsylvania: Stackpole Books, 1973), p. 31). The regiment was committed against the American forces in Canada in late 1775/early 1776. Some of the regiment's personnel were captured but exchanged in the prisoner of war agreement. In December, 1776, the entire 7th Foot was transported to New York City where it was reformed. The 7th Foot fought both at Forts Clinton and Montgomery in October, 1777. Lieutenant-Colonel Clarke assumed command of the 7th (Royal Fusilier) Regiment of Foot in 1777 and commanded it until the end of the war.

[2]Known initially as the Cameronians, the 26th Regiment of Foot was organized in 1689. It received its numerical designation in 1751. In 1767, it deployed to the colonies and arrived to New Jersey in the summer. In April, 1775, the regiment was transferred to Canada. Its companies were stationed in various places such as Montreal, Trois Rivieres (Three Rivers), Chambly, St. John's, Ticonderoga, and Crown Point. As for the companies captured at St. John's, its personnel were released in May, 1776, when the American forces withdrew from Canada. In 1777, the 26th Foot was transferred to New York City. It participated in the raids into New Jersey and, in October 1777, was committed into the Highlands. In late 1777, it was transported to Philadelphia returning to New York City in 1778.

[3]Known as the Royal Inniskilling Fusiliers, the 27th Regiment of Foot arrived to Boston in October, 1775. Parts of the regiment were deployed with General Howe and fought at Brandywine on 11 September 1777; others participated in the attack into the Highlands in October, 1777. In 1778, the entire regiment was transferred to the West Indians where it remained until its return to England.

[4]Initially known as the Oxfordshire and later as the 2nd Battalion Buckinghamshire Light Infantry, the 52nd Foot arrived to Boston in October, 1774. Its flank companies participated in the action at Lexington in April 1775 and later at Bunker Hill. Here, the 52nd Foot took heavy casualties. Its heavy grenadier company, for example,

only had eight soldiers left at the end of the action. Reinforced, the regiment was deployed to New York City in 1776 and until mid-1778, participated in various raids and actions around New York City such as the thrust into the Highlands in October, 1777. In August, 1778, the 52nd Foot returned to the British Isles.

[5]The 57th Regiment of Foot was formed in 1755. At this time, it was numbered as the 59th Regiment of Foot. In 1757, the 59th Foot was renumbered as the 57th Foot. Stationed at Middlesex, England, it deployed from Cork, England, in 1776. That year in May, it arrived to Cape May, North Carolina. The regiment participated in the siege of Charlestown but, in mid-1776, was transferred to New York City. The 57th fought in the battles of Long Island and New York City. Stationed in New York City until 1783, it participated in the attack into the Highlands.

[6]Raised in 1758 in West Suffolk, the 63rd Regiment of Foot was deployed to the colonies in 1775. It arrived to Boston in June, 1775. The regiments flank companies fought at Bunker Hill. Transferred to New York City in 1776, the 63rd Foot fought at Long Island. Its flank companies helped to capture Fort Washington. Dispatched to Newport, Rhode Island, in November 1776, the regiment returned to New York City in May, 1777. The 63rd Foot saw action in the Highlands in October, 1777.

[7]The 71st Regiment of Foot was raised in Inverness, Sterling, and Glasgow, Scotland, in 1775. It contained a tremendously large strength of 2,340 personnel. (Katcher, p. 67). In 1776, the 71st Foot deployed to the colonies. That same year in July, 1776, the regiment arrived to New York City. It fought at Long Island and Fort Washington. In 1777, the entire regiment, minus one company, deployed with Howe to Pennsylvania. As for the company which remained in New York City, it participated in the attacks against Forts Clinton and Montgomery that October.

[8]The 17th Regiment of Light Dragoons, along with the 16th Regiment of Light Dragoons, deployed to North America in 1775. The 17th Light Dragoons was stationed in New York City. In October, 1777, the 17th was dispatched into the Highlands.

[9]Little is known of this unit. Though its origins undoubtedly lay in Germany it is known that by 1777 it had developed into a loyalist unit. Possibly, German advisers remained within the unit. In October, 1777, it was utilized in the attack against the Highlands. Its strength appears to have been only that of one or two companies.

[10]Koehle (also spelled as Koehler) was, until 1777, the 4th Battalion Grenadiere von Koehler and from 1777-1782, the 4th Battalion Grenadiere von Platte. In October 1776, the Battalion arrived to New York City and immediately was committed to the fighting in Fort Washington. In June, 1777, it raided Amboy, New Jersey. In October 1777, along with the Anspach-Beyreuth Regiment, the battalion was committed into the Highlands. The 4th von Koehler fought at Forts Clinton and Montgomery.

[11]Also known as 1st Regiment Anspach-Beyreuth. Formed in Germany, the regiment arrived to New York City in June, 1777. After the attack into the Highlands in October, the regiment was sent to Philadelphia in November, 1777. In 1778, it returned to New York City and, until its surrender at Yorktown in October, 1781, served in various locations throughout the colonies. In May, 1783, it returned to Germany. Its average strength (excluding the artillerymen) was 27 officers and 543 enlisted. An Anspach artillery company also existed and was attached to the regiment. Possessing two cannons, this company was commanded by a captain and included 43 other personnel. (See also Katcher, pp. 108-109).

[12]Officially, the Trumbach Hessian Regiment arose in 1778. Raised initially in Germany as the Grenadiere Regiment von Rall and commanded by Colonel Johann G. Rall, the unit deployed for the colonies in 1776 and that August arrived to New York City.

The von Rall Regiment fought at Fort Washington and White Plains, New York. Posted into Trenton, New Jersey, in 1776 the regiment was surprised on Christmas Day. Annihilated, with its commanding officer killed, its survivors were incorporated into a weak battalion known as the Battalion von Loss and it fell briefly under the command of Lieutenant-General Ludwig von Trumbach. In late December, 1776/early January 1777, Colonel W.F. von Wollwarth assumed command and proceeded to rebuild the regiment with German personnel from various other units. Transforming it again into regimental stren-gth, in 1778 General von Trumbach once again resumed command and he maintained command until 1782.

[13]Christopher Ward, *The War of the American Revolution* (N.Y.: The MacMillan Co., 1952) (Volumes I-II). Vol. II, p. 516, cites only Beverley Robinson's Loyal Americans. For additional information on this unit see Katcher, p. 11. (Hereafter cited *War of American Revolution* with appropriate volume).

[14]Also known as Colonel Beverley Robinson's Loyal American Regiment. This regiment was raised in the fall of 1776 in New York City. Commanded by Colonel Beverley Robinson, it registered a strength of 693 loyalist (tory) volunteers. (Katcher, p. 91). In late July 1777, elements of this regiment deployed with Howe into Pennsylvania to participate in the Philadelphia campaign. The remainder of this regiment remained in New York City and in October 1777, approximately 400 of its personnel, to include Colonel Robinson, participated in the attacks against Forts Clinton and Montgomery.

[15]Commanded by Lieutenant-Colonel Andreas Emmerich, the unit was raised in New York City in the fall of 1776. Utilized as a security force within the city, in October 1777 it participated in the attack on Forts Clinton and Montgomery. Its strength was 250 loyalists wearing a grayish colored uniform. (Katcher, p. 86).

[16]Raised by Major Simon Frazer and Major John Aldington in New York City in the fall of 1776, the Guides and Pioneers, with a strength of 250 loyalists was, on occasion, attached to Colonel Robinson's Loyal American Regiment. In 1776/early 1777, the Guides and Pioneers served at the siege of Newport (currently Newport News) in Virginia. In 1777, the unit participated in Howe's attack into Pennsylvania as part of the Philadelphia campaign. Returning to New York City in time for Sir Henry's attack into the Highlands, the Guides and Pioneers participated in the attack against Forts Clinton and Montgomery.

[17]The King's American Regiment (nicknamed as the "Royal Greens" but not to be confused with Johnson's Royal Regiment of

New York and a unit raised in Canada also known as the King's Royal
Regiment of New York and as Johnson's Royal Greens) was raised in
New York City in December 1776. At first, its volunteers were known
as the Associated Refugees. In 1777 the regiment registered a strength
of 833 (Katcher, pp. 88 and 90). Dispatched to the Highlands, it participated in the capture of Forts Clinton and Montgomery. Colonel
Edmund and Lieutenant-Colonel George Campbell commanded
this regiment. It was also known as the "Royal Greens" because its
personnel wore a green colored uniform.

[18]The King's Orange Rangers was a loyalist horse-mounted rifle
company raised in Orange County, New York, in December 1776. It
was commanded by Captain John Coffin. By the conclusion of 1778,
it had reached a regimental strength of 600 and was commanded by
Lieutenant-Colonel John Bayard. (Katcher, p. 90). In October 1777,
one company of the King's Orange Rangers participated in the attack
against Forts Clinton and Montgomery.

[19]The New York Volunteers was a unit raised in Halifax, Canada,
in the period of January-February 1776 from New York loyalists who
had fled to Canada. In March 1777, it was commanded by Captain
Archibald Campbell; from March-October 1777 by Major Alexander
Grant and from October 1777 until its disbandment in New York
City in August 1782, by Lieutenant-Colonel George Turnbull.
Its strength usually hovered at about 474. (Katcher, pp. 93 and 95).
The New York Volunteers participated in the attacks against Forts
Clinton and Montgomery.

[20]For Mr. Leggett's entire letter, see *The Public Papers of George
Clinton*, Vol. II, pp. 353-355.

[21]Otten, p. 93, cites 40 ships but undoubtedly refers to the river
bateaux. Carrington, *Battles of the Revolution*, pp. 357-358, cites "forty
flat [bateaux] boats besides ships and galleys."

[22]Willcox, p. 180; Ward, Vol. II, p. 516; Henry Harrison, *Battles of
the Republic, By Sea and Land* (Philadelphia, Pa.: Porter and Coates,
1858), p. 76. (Hereafter cited as *Battles of the Republic*). Lossing, *The
Empire State*, p. 283. Otten, p. 93, cites "[Sir Henry] was supported by
Commodore Hotham's navy of 40 ships."

[23]Ward, Vol. II, p. 515, cites "he [Sir Henry] detached 4,000 men, including some of the tory [loyalist] regiments." Willcox, p. 180, cites "some 3,000 troops, covered by a naval force under Commodore Hotham." Harrison, *Battles of the Republic*, p. 76, cites "Sir Henry Clinton embarked 3,000 men in vessels of different descriptions, and, convoyed by some ships-of-war under Commodore Hotham, sailed up the Hudson." Lossing, *The Empire State*, p. 283, cites "between three and four thousand troops, in many armed and unarmed vessels commanded by Commodore Hotham." Otten, p. 93, cites a strength of 3,000 men. According to Ketchum, *Saratoga,* p. 384, in a letter written to Burgoyne on 27 September 1777, Sir Henry cited a strength of 3,000 soldiers would probably attack the Highlands. Dupuy, p. 714, cites "[Sir Henry] took 4,000 men up the Hudson." Lieutenant-Colonel Joseph B. Mitchell and Sir Edward Creasy, "Saratoga, A.D. 1777" in *Twenty Decisive Battles of the World*, p. 208, cite "only 4,000 men." Both Mitchell and Creasy acknowledge that "Clinton's diversion started too late... [the] force far too small to have broken through to Burgoyne at Saratoga." (Ibid.). Fleming, *Liberty! The American Revolution*, p. 256, cites "4,000 men and a Royal Navy escort." John Hyde Preston, *A Short History of the American Revolution* (N.Y.: Pocket Books, Cardinal Edition, 1952), pp. 240-241, cites "3,000 men." And William Seymour, "Turning Point At Saratoga" in *Military History* (December, 1999), p. 50 cites "3,000 troops in 60 vessels." Both Preston and Seymour undoubtedly refer just to the army troop strength and are excluding the strength of the British naval and loyalist personnel. Brendan Morrisey, *Saratoga 1777. Turning point of a revolution* (Great Britain: Osprey Publlishing, 2000), p. 23 cites Sir Henry possessed a strength of around 3,500. (Hereafter cited as *Saratoga* 1777). However, according to Morrisey, this strength did not include the 45th Foot and the German units which soon after followed Sir Henry's initial main force. (See *Saratoga,* 1777, fn. 1, p. 24). According to a German report dated 4 October 1777, a German general named Schmidt brought such units northward: the Emmerich Chasseurs, the Stewart Grenadier Battalion, the Koehler Grenadier Battalion, the 35th Regiment, the Trumbach

Regiment, the York Volunteers, and the newly arrived Hessian Jaegers. (See Burgoyne, *Enemy Views (1777)*, p. 224. As for the Hessian Jaegers, possibly these were from the Hessian Grenadier Battalion No. 4 commanded by Lieutenant-Colonel Johann von Koehler with a strength of 15 officers and 400 enlisted. (See Morrisey, fn. 1, p. 24).

[24]Sir Henry's thrust was supported by a sizable strong naval escort.

[25]Located in the Bronx, New York.

[26]Ward, *War of American Revolution*, Vol. II, p. 515; Carrington, *Battles of the American Revolution,* p. 357.

[27]Ward, Vol. II, p. 516.

[28]Ward, Vol., II, p. 515; Carrington, *Battles of the American Revolution*, p. 357. Some units had been transferred directly to General Washington's Main Continental Army while others had been deployed to other sectors in both New York State and New Jersey. Requests by militiamen to return home in September to harvest crops along with individuals who never reappeared following a furlough, also took its toll. Such factors left the Highlands tremendously weakened.

[29]Palmer, p. 103, refers to this force as a "third force."

[30]For what Governor Clinton reported, see *The Public Papers of George Clinton*, Vol. II, p. 362. See also Palmer, p. 104. In actuality, the governor did not report very much.

[31]Almost directly to the southwest of Verplanck's Point across the Hudson River lies Stony Point.

[32]Ward, *War of American Revolution*, Vol. II, p. 516.

[33]Regarding loyalist ranks, they were not held in the same high esteem as were the British or German ranks. In fact, if a loyalist held the rank of, for example, lieutenant-colonel, the loyalists rank was looked upon as that of a captain or, at best, a major. Rarely did a British or German officer take commands from a loyalist officer. Because by 1777 many British and German officers loathed the loyalists (this was especially true in New York City and its environs), loyalist officers generally received very little respect. According to Palmer, the loyalist force left behind at Verplanck's Point "was a weak element."

[34]Palmer, p. 104, cites the 12-pound cannon was left behind. It had not even been fired.

[35]This figure is cited from a map presented in Palmer's book. The map also depicts Putnam's retreat route. See "The British Maneuver, 5-6 October 1777" map.

[36]According to Otten, p. 96, "the same winds that pushed Sir Henry's fleet northward, prevented him [Governor Clinton] from reaching Fort Montgomery by water, however and unable to find a horse, he walked the last six miles, arriving at Ft. Montgomery."

[37]Where Moore's House once stood presently Lee Road is found along with the Lee housing area. West Point's main hospital is also in the location. This area encompasses the northern portion of West Point.

[38]Personal discussion with Mr. Alan Aimone.

[39]Ibid.

[40]Ibid.

[41]Palmer, p. 104. See also Otten, p. 96. Of the two forts Fort Clinton was near completion but in size was smaller than Fort Montgomery.

[42]Palmer, p. 104, cited "300 Continentals, around 100 Continental artillerymen and fewer than 100 militiamen."

[43]Palmer, p. 109.

[44]Major Moffat's Northern Army scouts operated through a very large region encompasssing the Highlands, the entire Catskill region, the area down to New York City, the Palisades, western Connecticut and north central/eastern New Jersey.

[45]Patriot scouts were even posted along the Palisades and the villages and towns of the modern day cities of Hoboken and Jersey City, New Jersey. See John Hyde Preston, *A Short History of the American Revolution,* p. 199.

[46]Suffern, a town in New York State, is located right over the New Jersey border.

[47]Major Moffat also submitted another immediate follow-up report citing such:

"As for the individual who was killed instantly, he was identified as Micael [Michael?] Brady. In his pocket he possessed a pass procured from a Doctor Joseph Sacket to go to Philadelphia. The pass was dated 17 May 1777."

Moffat also wrote that in addition to the pass, Brady carried a purse. The purse contained: "7 half Joes, 1 whole Joe, 6 Guines, 4 Spanish Dollars and some small Silver' in it; he had also with him a pair of Silver Shoe Buckles and knee Buckles, beside a bundle of Cloaths – they [Moffat's scouts] found One Gun and some other Small Matters – the whole I suppose is worth between 50 and 60 Pounds which I have ordered the Capt. to divide amongst the Men."

Major Moffat also concluded: "It is most probable that he who was Killed Dead was out Inlisting Men as he brough[t] these from Sterling [a forest in southern New York State], Near which he was seen and the Night before was heard to drink a health to King George and Damnation to the Congress. The Name of the other I have forgot."

Moffat's letters to Brigadier General James Clinton are not only interesting but, most importantly, reveal very accurate informational reporting pertaining to British movements such as in the opening hours of their attack upon the Highlands. For the entire letter see *The Public Papers of George Clinton,* Vol. II, pp. 363-367.

[48]Palmer, p. 105.

[49]Ibid.

[50]Stewart's name has also been spelled as Stuart.

[51]Palmer, p. 105. In regard to the chain-of-command and who was the top ranking officer during the combat period of 6-29 October, there appears to be some confusion here. Though officially Putnam commanded the Highlands, Governor Clinton regarded the Highlands as being his jurisdiction in consideration that he, too, was a general but most importantly, was the newly elected governor of New York State. It must also be remembered that Putnam was not a militia commander, but was a regular Continental Army officer. Though in the early night hours of 7 October Putnam resigned his command, by 9 October he had re-established a headquarters and once again proclaimed himself as being in charge; however, because Governor Clinton regarded him as being totally incapable, the governor remained in charge and coordinated his activities with those such as General Gates, the overall commander of the Northern Army.

General Gates also found Governor Clinton to be a far more effective and skilled combat leader.

[52]Palmer, p. 105, cites "a couple of hours after midnight."

[53]Also known as Thunder Hill. As for the present day Bear Mountain, in 1777 it was referred to as Bear Hill. (Personal discussion with Mr. Aimone).

[54]Excluding some old ruins covered by much vegetation and vines, Doodletown no longer exists.

[55]Personal discussion with Mr. Aimone.

[56]Otten, p. 97.

[57]Although Robinson held the highest rank, he was still subordinate to Lieutenant-Colonel Campbell.

[58]Ward, Vol. II, p. 516, cites 900. According to Carrington, p. 358, Lieutenant-Colonel Campbell's force was composed of 500 regulars from the 27th and 52nd Foot Regiments and from Emmerich's Chasseurs and another 400 from Colonel Beverley Robinson's loyalists. (Carrington identified the German commander as Emerick. Various other sources cite a von Emmerich though the name has also been spelled as Emmerick. See also map between pp. 380–381 in *The Public Papers of George Clinton,* Vol. II). According to Harrison, *Battles of the Republic,* p. 78, "Colonel Campbell [was] at the head of 900 men." Although Harrison cites Campbell's rank as "Colonel," all other sources identify Campbell as being in the rank of Lieutenant-Colonel on 6 October 1777. According to Morrissey, *Saratoga 1777,* p. 71, Campbell commanded 1,000 troops.

[59]Ward, Vol. II, p. 516; Carrington, p. 358.

[60]Ward, Vol. II, p. 516; Carrington, p. 358; and Harrison, p. 78.

[61]Ward, Vol. II, p. 516.

[62]Ward, Vol. II p. 516.

[63]A distant blood relationship did exist between the Clinton brothers and Sir Henry. Personal discussion with Mr. Aimone.

[64]In the aftermath of the terrible Wilderness War of 1777, Captain Stewart submitted a testimony report regarding this to a Court of Inquiry. See "Papers of Alexander McDougall" in New York Historical Society, March, 1942, Reel #2.

Otten, a former military lieutenant-colonel, also holds the view that "[Major] Logan could have become a hero. With 100 men in Timp Pass he could have stopped the British in their tracks. A narrow, windy, rocky defile at the crest of a massive mountain, Timp Pass provided the classic location for an ambush." See Otten, Vol. 1, p. 97.

According to Ward, Vol. II, p. 516, "a handful of determined opponents posted at the top of the activity could have held them off." And retired Lieutenant-General Palmer also cites that the pass could have been defended. Palmer strongly implied that Major Logan could have held the British at bay when he wrote: "One wonders how [Sir] Henry Clinton could possibly have passed had the Americans heeded any of George Washington's oft-repeated admonitions to 'secure your flanks and rear. . . by stopping up all roads by which you are accessible in any part.' But they had not. And, what is worse, Logan failed to grasp the significance of the position. Even when some of his officers pointed it out to him." (See p. 108).

And, from the English side in the aftermath of the Revolutionary war, such an observation was heralded:

"As the path would not admit above three men to march abrest, and by its windings would have exposed the troops during their passage to be destroyed at the pleasure of any force stationed at the top of the hill, the most trifling guard would have been sufficient to have rendered the attempt of the British abortive." (Cited also from Palmer, p. 108).

[65]Also known in Dutch as Peploaps Kill.

[66]Sir Henry never fully defined Tryon's role. Basically, his task was to provide support wherever needed. Undoubtedly, Tryon was also brought along for psychological reasons, to maintain the morale of the loyalists, and recruit additional loyalists.

[67]Palmer, p. 106.

[68]Ibid.

[69]Ibid. 9 a.m. is generally the time cited.

[70]Ward, Vol. II, p. 518, identifies a Lieutenant Jackson but cites Jackson had 30 men. Ward agrees that Jackson was dispatched from Fort Clinton to reconnoiter the situation. (Ibid.).

[71]The road was, indeed, very rocky, rutted, and even tortuous. (Palmer, p. 108). A report written at the time even described it as "almost impenetrable." (Ibid.).

[72]Ward, Vol. II, p. 518; Otten, p. 99.

[73]Ibid. Otten also cites 50 militiamen. However, Ward spells McLaughry's name as McLarey. Otten identifies James McLaughry in the rank of colonel rather than as lieutenant-colonel. Otten also cites that the 50 militiamen accompanying McLaughry came from Colonel William Allison's militia regiment.

[74]Although Lamb was in charge, it appears he did not accompany the group. All sources reveal that Major Newkirk, Captain Fenno, and Lieutenant Machin were the most prominent officers of this small group.

[75]See *The Public Papers of George Clinton,* Vol. II, pp. 311-312.

[76]Both the front sides of Forts Clinton and Montgomery faced the Hudson River. Because the British attack was a ground maneuver, both forts were actually attacked from the rear.

[77]Palmer, p. 110.

[78]Today, it is known as Hessian Lake. Another name previously attached to this lake was "Bloody Pond."

[79]This lake lies from a slight northwesterly to southeasterly direction. It would also be the burial ground for many of the troops but especially the German personnel killed in those days. Hence the name "Hessian Lake."

[80]Some have alleged that Waterbury was "highly inefficient." Regardless, even a "highly inefficient" person, noting such a critical situation, would have reacted promptly and properly to it. Undoubtedly, Waterbury was a loyalist and an agent operating for the British. The fact that in the aftermath of the Wilderness War of 1777 he ended up in New York City attests to this. Disappearing in 1783, it is believed he left with the British that year.

As for Livingston's servant who also appeared late, though the possibility exists that he, too, might have been pro-British in actuality, it appears that he simply roved around the countryside looking for General Putnam. Unable to locate the general, the servant decided to obtain some help in some headquarters.

[81]Harrison, p. 79.
[82]Palmer, p. 111.
[83]Ibid.
[84]Ibid., p. 112.

Chapter 7. The Highlands Fall to Sir Henry's Juggernaut

[1]It appears that the Montgomery was the first to engage the enemy.

[2]When Sir Henry attacked on 6 October, the *Congress* was positioned at Fort Constitution.

[3]Palmer, p. 106.

[4]It is not known, however, if this was ever done.

[5]*The Public Papers of George Clinton*, Vol. II, p. 393.

In a report dated 9 October 1777 and written from New Windsor to General George Washington, Governor Clinton cited "... about two o'clock in the afternoon the enemy approached the works and began the attack, which continued with few intervals till about five o'clock, when an officer appeared with a white flag."

Carrington, *Battles of the American Revolution*, p. 359, cites "the attack upon [Fort Montgomery] was maintained until five o'clock, when a flag was sent, demanding a surrender." Lossing, *The Empire State*, p. 284, cites no particular time but implies late afternoon when he wrote: "Lieutenant-Colonel Campbell appeared before Fort Montgomery toward evening." Lossing, however, also cited that "a peremptory demand for the surrender of both posts was made."

This, in itself, is interesting because at the very same moment Campbell and Livingston were negotiating, Fort Clinton was being attacked. However, had Campbell succeeded in inducing Fort Montgomery into surrendering, Fort Clinton, now thoroughly surrounded from all sides, would have had to follow suit and surrender as well.

[6]*The Public Papers of George Clinton*, Vol. II, p. 393. See also Palmer, p. 113; and Otten, pp. 101-102.

[7]Otten, pp. 101-102.

[8]Otten, p. 102. Palmer, pp. 112-113, cites Campbell and Robinson had 900 soldiers. See map "The Assault of Forts Clinton and

Montgomery, 6 October 1777." (Map between pp. 115-116). Harrison, p. 78, cites 900 attacked Fort Montgomery.

[9]At the very moment that Robinson was leading the troops General Putnam's wife lay in Robinson's home suffering from an illness. That day she was also visited by her son, Daniel Putnam, a patriot major who had authorization from the British to visit his mother. Attending to the ill woman was Ivanna Robinson, one of Beverley Robinson's daughters. Despite her father's involvement with the British it appears that his daughter actually harbored a strong pro-patriot sentiment. Possibly, she even spied for the patriots. In the aftermath of the British surrender at Saratoga and the British withdrawal from the Highlands, Colonel Robinson was forced to flee. His daughter, however, remained behind and was never harmed by patriot authorities. After October, 1777, the house was used by various patriot commanders as a command post and headquarters.

[10]Harrison, p. 78, cites "both forts, garrisoned by about 600 men, were attacked at the same time." Palmer, (see map between pp. 115-116), cites 200 plus within Fort Clinton. Ward, Vol. II, p. 59, cites the two forts were defended by "a few Continentals and 600 militia." William P. Cumming and Hugh Rankin, *The Fate of a Nation. The American Revolution Through Contemporary Eyes* (London, England: Phaidon Press, Limited, 1975), p. 163, cites a report submitted by the American surgeon Doctor James Thacher. Although Doctor Thacher was not a participant of this event he wrote "the forts were defended by Governor George Clinton, and his brother James Clinton, of New York, having about six hundred militia men, a force inadequate to the defence of the works." For Thacher's entire report, see pp. 160-162. Fleming, *Liberty!*, p. 256, cites a patriot militia strength of 600 defenders.

[11]Palmer, map pp. 115-116. Harrison, p. 78, cites no less than 1,200 British, German, and loyalist soldiers. Harrison also cites that Fort Clinton was regarded as the strongest of the two forts. But according to Mr. Aimone, "Fort Montgomery was the major fort. It had the biggest cannons directed on the river."

[12]Regarding this, there appears to be some confusion as to how General James Clinton actually escaped. Otten, p. 103, cites he crossed

the river via the chain and rafts. Boynton, *History of West Point,* p. 46, cites "General James Clinton, the commander of the fort bearing his name, forced his way to the rear." (Boynton also wrote "Governor George Clinton escaped by a boat across the river."). Carrington, p. 360, cites "Governor [George] Clinton safely crossed the Hudson in a skiff and joined General Putnam." But Carrington implies that General James Clinton escaped via land when he writes "General Clinton received a bayonet wound, but escaped to the mountains." (Ibid.). Regardless, it appears that both George and James Clinton escaped via the river. Governor Clinton was picked up by a rowboat whereas General James fled over the rafts. After crossing the Hudson onto its eastern bank General James, accompanied with some other fighters, fled northward into the mountains.

[13]Palmer, p. 116.

[14]By midnight, the main activities of the day were over.

[15]From 6-7 October 1777, "Old Put" Putnam maintained no firm command in the Highlands. In late 1777, Putnam was officially removed from command by General Washington himself. Not wanting to discredit his old friend, Washington ordered Putnam to supervise recruitment in the New England region. On 29 May 1790, in Connecticut, Putnam passed away.

[16]To cite an example: on 6 October, the two messengers bound for Putnam reached him late. But why wasn't Putnam dispatching his own messengers? Factually speaking, Putnam should have been dispatching messengers by the hour to determine what, precisely, was going on. By noontime he should have moved a strong reinforcement across the river and, likewise, should have either repositioned himself onto the western side of the Hudson River or, in the least, had appointed a strong commander to assist the Clinton brothers who, in the true sense, were solely directing military operations on that pivotal day.

Sadly for the patriots, throughout that day Putnam moved listlessly and indecisively with no strong concerns and initiative. Though loyal to the patriot cause, Putnam was almost 60 years of age and was a physical wreck. Tremendously obese, he had difficulties in breathing and probably suffered from high blood pressure which explains his constant headaches. Though it is true that Putnam did experience shortages in men, weapons, and material so, too, did many other commanders. Regardless, Putnam should have instilled into the Highlands a stronger spirit of aggressiveness. Had this been done, the Highlands would have been much better prepared for war.

The possibility also exists that on 6 October Putnam might have been suffering from some type of serious health problem. In December 1779, a massive stroke finally terminated his military career. Possibly, Putnam began to experience his very first stroke attacks in 1777. Though minor, they were significant enough to dramatically reduce his performance. And the fact that Putnam's ill wife was dying on that crucial day in Robinson's house was not helping the situation either.

Noteworthy is that when months earlier a number of officers felt that Putnam was incapable of leading effectively and requested that he be removed from command, this criticism reached not only General George Washington, the Commander in Chief but, even, the Continental Congress. Yet, the warnings were discarded.

In this area, Washington himself had failed. Very fond of "Old Put," he insisted on keeping him in command. Though it is now known that shortly before the British invasion of the Highlands, Washington was contemplating removing Putnam, this was not done in time. And for this Washington must be faulted because the fact remains that had a stronger, more capable, assertive, and aggressive, commander been in command, the Highlands' defenses would have been better prepared for an attack and Sir Henry's efforts could have possibly been defeated at the foot of the Highlands.

Finally acknowledging on 16 March 1778 Putnam's failures, Washington relieved "Old Put" from commanding the Highlands Department. (Otten, p. 118). Major General McDougall, a former commander of the Highlands, replaced Putnam. As if not to make Putnam look totally irresponsible Washington "transferred" Putnam to oversee recruitment in Connecticut. (Ibid.).

According to Preston, *A Short History of the American Revolution,* p. 240, General "Old Put" Putnam was "incompetent." Preston also cites faulty leadership when he wrote: "He [Sir Henry] had moved up the

Hudson, attacked blustering old Put and his mongrel incompetents at Fort Montgomery, and carried the place." On p. 241, Preston also faults Putnam's "stupidity" which enabled Sir Henry to so rapidly capture the Highlands.

[17]Palmer, p. 117.

[18]Peekskill was abandoned on 5 October 1777. But since the loyalist force landed at Verplanck's Point as a diversion had not yet advanced to Peekskill, by the late evening hours of 6 October some continental and militiamen had probed their way back into Peekskill. Even Putnam himself approached Peekskill on 6 October.

[19]In itself, Pollepel Island was never manned.

[20]Palmer, p. 118. Otten, p. 103, cites 26 officers and 237 enlisted. 67 various cannons were captured as well. (Ibid.). Carrington, p. 360, cites that 67 cannons were captured in the forts. But in all, 100 cannons had been lost. (Ibid.). These would have also included those on the ships, and in such places as at Verplanck's Point. According to a German report dated 12 October, "about 300 men, including 23 officers, had been made prisoners by us during the capture of this fort." (Burgoyne, *Enemy Views (1777)*, pp. 224-225). Diamant, *Chaining the Hudson,* p. 116, cites "As the undermanned forts were overwhelmed, including the crippled engineer [Lieutenant Machin], managed to stumble off into the gathering darkness. Two hundred and sixty-three Americans – including 26 officers – were killed, wounded, or captured, with the loss of 67 irreplaceable cannon."

In a personal discussion with Grant Miller, historic site manager of Fort Montgomery, a total of 67 cannons, of different calibers, were secured at Fort Montgomery, Fort Clinton, and in the batteries near these forts. The number of 67 did not include the cannons captured at Fort Constitution.

[21]Otten, p. 103.

[22]Ibid.

[23]According to Otten, p. 103, in addition to senior ranking officers such as Colonel Allison, Lieutenant-Colonel's McLaughry and Livingston, and Major Stephen Lush being captured others officers, such as Lieutenants Patton Jackson, John Furman, Samuel Dodge, Alexander Archer, Henry Pawling, Solomon Pendleton, Ebenezer

Mott, Abraham Leggett, Henry Swartwout, and John McClaughry went into captivity as well.

[24]See Otten, p. 103. While in captivity, Lieutenant-Colonel Livingston was robbed.

[25]Palmer, p. 118. McClaughry was also related to the Clinton brothers.

[26]Willcox, pp. 180-181.

[27]Throughout the Revolutionary War both the British and the patriots minimized their own losses and exaggerated the losses inflicted upon the other. See also Palmer, p. 118.

[28]Otten, p. 104.

[29]Otten, p. 104.

[30]Harrison, p. 79.

[31]Bruce Burgoyne, ed., "Activity in the New York Area" in *Enemy Views (1777). The American Revolutionary War as Recorded by the Hessian Participants* (Maryland: Heritage Books, Inc., 1996), p. 217. Captain von Erckert was laid to rest by a Hessian Honor Guard in New York City. (Hereafter cited as *Enemy Views (1777).*

[32]Ibid.

[33]Ibid., p. 219. It appears that this included the losses of not only the Germans but as well the British and loyalists.

[34]Otten, p. 105. A small inn was also located in the Widow Falls House. Hence, it was sometimes referred to as Widow Falls Inn.

[35]This water obstacle, known as "the Great Chain," was stretched across the entire Hudson River from the cliff at the base of Fort Montgomery to Anthony's Nose. (The location of the chain was just north of the present day Bear Mountain Bridge). It had 850 giant links and weighed no less than 35 tons. From one end to the other, the chain stretched 1,650 feet. It floated on rafts built from hundreds of pine logs. To counter the occasional strong tides and currents, numerous anchors, eyelets, cables, and chains kept the chain links securely tied down and in place. For a detailed description of this chain see also Otten, pp. 80-81. According to a German report dated 12 October, "A very strong iron chain had been stretched across the river. This fell

into our hands and was taken to New York." (See Burgoyne, *Enemy Views (1777)*, p. 225).

[36]Indeed, at daybreak, many of those who were stationed in the Highlands even descended down the steep cliff to marvel the patriot obstacle. Prior to attacking the Highlands, for months they had been hearing rumors and stories of such a river obstacle. (See also Palmer, p. 118).

[37]*The Public Papers of George Clinton*, Vol. II, p. 118. This figure did not encompass those who left to enlist in the standing Continental Army, were attached to other units, were on harvesting leave, on teamster duty, or had deserted.

[38]Ibid., p. 126.

[39]Ibid.

[40]Ibid. This figure included those assigned to Fort Constitution but, at the moment, were not on duty.

[41]Major Lewis Dubois is not to be confused with the Colonel Lewis Dubois who commanded the 5th New York Continental Regiment and fought at Fort Montgomery. In fact, despite the same first and last names, neither of the two was related. See Palmer, p. 119; and Otten's Index Section, p. 385, cites under "Dubois, Maj. Lewis (not related to Col. Dubois)."

[42]Palmer, p. 119.

[43]Ibid.

[44]Ibid. Palmer does not cite a strength but a Return of Captain Mott's Company of Artillery at Fort Constitution, dated 3 July 1777, revealed a strength of 1 captain, 1 captain-lieutenant, 3 lieutenants, 2 sergeants, 1 corporal, 1 gunner, and 11 matrosses (assistant gunners) for a total of 14 enlisted and 5 officers. No drummers or fifers are listed. (See *The Public Papers of George Clinton*, Vol. II, p. 67). It may be speculated that on 6 October, no more than 12-15 artillerymen were present at Fort Constitution.

[45]Personal discussion with Mr. Aimone.

[26]Otten, p. 106.

[47]Palmer, p. 119. According to Diamant, *Chaining the Hudson*, p. 118, though the commander of Fort Constitution torched whatever

would burn, he did leave 77 unspiked cannon guns behind. (Personal discussion with Grant Miller, site manager of Fort Montgomery).

[48]A copy of this letter went to General George Washington.

[49]For the entire letter see *The Public Papers of George Clinton*, Vol. II, pp. 380–383.

[50]Indeed, those who were captured and transported downriver to New York City experienced an agony known only to those who ever had the misfortune of being subjected to such a hellish ordeal. Though some of the prisoners were released in 1780 and 1781 on exchanges, most were not. Packed into overcrowded, disease-infested prisons and prison ships, they died by the masses. Hunger also took its toll. For the survivors released in 1783, many experienced health problems for the rest of their lives.

Chapter 8. Sir Henry Consolidates the Highlands But Quickly Retires

[1]Palmer, p. 120.

[2]A German report dated 14 October 1777 acknowledged that Peekskill had been destroyed. "General Tryon had already burned down all the enemy magazines, houses, armories, and barracks at Peekskill." See Burgoyne, *Enemy Views (1777)*, p. 225.

[3]Carrington, p. 360, acknowledged that many supplies were destroyed but also cites "a considerable amount of stores were taken." Undoubtedly, much (if not most) of the captured supplies were removed. It was to Sir Henry's advantage to remove as many of the supplies as possible for near future use. It must be emphasized that some of the raids conducted in 1777 were solely undertaken to secure supplies. And with the patriot defense in shambles, ample time existed to remove the supplies.

[4]Palmer, p. 122.

[5]*The Public Papers of George Clinton*, Vol. II, p. 389.

[6]For Putnam's entire short letter see, *The Public Papers of George Clinton*, Vol. II, pp. 384–385.

[7]For Moffat's entire letter see, *The Public Papers of George Clinton*, Vol. II, p. 386.

[8]This obstacle was positioned on Pollepel Island.

[9]For the entire letter see *The Public Papers of George Clinton,* Vol. II, pp. 387-389.

[10]Lossing, *The Empire State,* p. 285; Otten, p. 106, presents a portion of Sir Henry's response. See also Ketchum, *Saratoga,* p. 385; Willcox, *Portrait of a General, Sir Henry,* pp. 183-184; Baxter, *The British Invasion From the North,* pp. 33-34. On 11 October, Governor Clinton submitted a copy of the entire short letter as proof to the Council of Safety along with his observations. See *The Public Papers of George Clinton,* Vol. II, p. 414.

[11]As for Captain Scott, he never made it. After repeated attempts to reach Burgoyne, Scott was forced to return. Regardless, it did not matter because by now Burgoyne had surrendered and Sir Henry was no longer in the Highlands. In the latter part of October, Captain Scott arrived back to New York City.

[12]Sometimes the name is cited as David Taylor. Regarding his rank, there appears to be some confusion. Otten, p. 106 and Palmer, p. 123, cite Taylor was a lieutenant. Baxter, however, cites Daniel Taylor in the rank of sergeant.

[13]According to Willcox, p. 184, at one time Sir Henry "could not establish communication by messengers, for none of them got through."

It is known that on 31 July 1777, General Burgoyne dispatched a letter to Germain complaining how he (Burgoyne) was having a hard time communicating with Howe in New York City. Burgoyne cited how in recent weeks ten messengers, using ten different routes, had been sent southward and yet, Burgoyne never received a response on any of his ten letters. See also Burke Davis, *George Washington and the American Revolution* (N.Y.: Random House, 1975), p. 208.

[14]From his headquarters on 1 October 1777, Governor Clinton admitted using brute force when he wrote: ". . . and demanded the ball [bullet] on pain of being hung up instantly and cut open to search it. This brought it forth." Clinton also cited that Taylor was "administered a very strong emetic." For Clinton's report regarding Daniel Taylor, see *The Public Papers of George Clinton,* Vol. II, pp. 412-414.

[15]This, in itself, is very interesting. How the governor learned about Captain Campbell is not known. At the very same moment that Taylor was being threatened, Campbell was actually working his way up north and in the late evening hours of 16 October, Campbell delivered Sir Henry's message to Burgoyne. (See Baxter, p. 36, footnote no. 28).

In the aftermath of Burgoyne's surrender, Campbell became a prisoner of war. Surviving the war, upon returning to England he remained in the army. On 1 January 1812, he was promoted to Brigadier General in the British Army.

Is it possible that Governor Clinton had a spy operating within Sir Henry's inner circle? And if so this spy, known solely to the governor, somehow informed Governor Clinton that a British army captain and runner by the name of Campbell was also enroute to Burgoyne. This can only be speculated upon since messengers were only to be known to Sir Henry and, at best, perhaps no more than one or two others (if that) on his staff.

[16]In essence, Taylor's message was such – "Sir Henry is in possession of the Highlands and the passes were dubbed by Sir Henry as the key of America."

[17]On 14 October 1777, Taylor was tried as a spy. Colonel Louis Dubois presided as the president of the military board. Two majors and ten captains also served on this board. (For a list of the twelve officers, see *The Public Papers of George Clinton,* Vol. II, p. 443). Captain Hamtramck was one of those who officiated as a board member. The court martial was ordered by Governor Clinton.

During the trial, Taylor admitted that he was delivering a message from Sir Henry to General Burgoyne. But Taylor vehemently denied that he was a spy. As for being out of uniform, Taylor argued that his mission required him to be out of uniform. Besides, the Americans who had captured him were themselves in British army uniforms. This, in itself, argued Taylor, was a violation. Regardless, Taylor was found guilty and Colonel Dubois stipulated Taylor would "be hanged at such Time and Place as the General [Governor Clinton] shall direct." (See *The Public Papers of George Clinton,* Vol. II, p. 444). On 16 October

1777, Governor Clinton approved the verdict. On 18 October, Taylor was hung. Governor Clinton did, however, permit Taylor to write several letters back home to England. Following the hanging, Taylor was buried in an unmarked grave not far from the ruins of Kingston, N.Y.

[18]Hereafter, Fort Clinton will be referred to as Fort Vaughan.

[19]Willcox, p. 185. Clinton to Howe, October 9, 1777. This letter was addressed directly to General Howe.

[20]For the entire fairly lengthy letter, see *The Public Papers of George Clinton,* Vol. II, pp. 389-395.

[21]For Lieutenant Taylor's entire confession see, *The Public Papers of George Clinton,* Vol. II, pp. 398-399. Taylor, however, got the ranks mixed up. In actuality, Grant was a Major and Campbell was the Lieutenant-Colonel.

[22]According to Palmer, p. 124, the prisoners were moved to Connecticut.

Chapter 9. Sir Henry's Last Attack and the Conclusion of the Wilderness War of 1777

[1]Jill Canon, *Heroines of the American Revolution* (Santa Barbara, CA: Bellerophon Books, 1998), p. 2, cites how Dr. Clarke, in Benson J. Lossing's, *The Pictorial FieldBook of the [American] Revolution* (N.Y.: Harper & Brothers Publishers, 1860), Volumes I – II), cited ". . . in all patriotic enterprises the services of one woman are equal to those of seven men and a half."

[2]Willcox, p. 187. According to Morrisey, *Saratoga 1777*, p. 68, Sir Henry had no formal orders to assist Burgoyne. Though Sir Henry was free to exercise his own personal judgment on what to do regarding Burgoyne, undoubtedly the few messages Clinton received prior to October from Burgoyne is what tempted Sir Henry to attack northward.

[3]In 1777, the 45th Foot was not in full strength. Initially formed in 1741, it received its 45th numerical designation in 1751. In 1776, it participated in the fighting on Long Island and New York City. Afterwards, the 45th Foot provided manpower to various other units and some of its officers, when dispatched to other parts of the colonies, returned directly back to the British Isles without first returning back

to the 45th Foot. This explains why when the 45th was committed into the Highlands in October, 1777, German personnel augmented the regiment. In previous years, Sir Henry had also commanded the 45th Foot.

[4]Diamant, p. 119.

[5]Ibid. The 1,600 troops did not include the German or loyalist strength. According to Morrisey, *Saratoga 1777*, fn. 1, p. 24, the 4th Hessian Battalion registered a strength of 15 officers and 400 troops; the Anspach-Bayreuth Regiment (comprised of two grenadier battalions) had a strength of 28 officers and 511 troops.

[6]Palmer, p. 124; Willcox, p. 187. This information was also immediately pushed on to General Washington, the Main Northern Army Headquarters in Albany and to the Continental Congress.

[7]Copies of this letter went to various regional commanders and probably to Washington himself.

[8]Palmer, p. 124. This figure did not include the bateaux personnel nor the strength of the small naval fleet which would accompany the force. According to Willcox, p. 186, Governor Tryon proposed that Sir Henry use the bulk of his troops to move upriver by land and water to force a junction with Burgoyne with transports following to receive Burgoyne's exhausted army. But realizing the dangers of this, Sir Henry immediately ruled this suggestion out. (Ibid.).

[9]For the entire letter of 13 October see *The Public Papers of George Clinton*, Vol. II, pp. 423-426. A copy was also forwarded to General Washington.

[10]It appears that this delegation never established any contact with General Putnam. Regarding this incident, this was not the very first time that Colonel Robinson had attempted to reach Putnam. In early 1777, Sir Henry Clinton received some news that the commander of the Highlands, General Putnam, was holding the view "that the American revolution was nearly ruined." Though not certain if this was, indeed, true, Sir Henry decided that perhaps, it should be further explored and, if so, exploited to the British advantage; therefore, Sir Henry ordered Colonel Robinson to make contact with Putnam.

Perhaps thought Sir Henry, Putnam would even surrender the Highlands to him. Unfortunately, very little is known of this matter.

Despite Robinson's best efforts, he failed in his mission. It is not even known if Robinson ever met with General Putnam, though it is known that Robinson did make personal contact with Putnam's son, Daniel, serving in the rank of major in the Northern Army at West Point. But even here, nothing positive was gained other than Robinson receiving a very severe tongue lashing from Major Putnam. As for the intrigue found in every war and conflict since ancient times, it, too, factored in during the Revolutionary War's Wilderness War of 1777. Along with the psychological and propaganda war waged in late 1776-1777 various agents, spies, the so-called "eyes and ears" along with arsonists, assassins, and saboteurs, conducted a highly secretive yet critical activity in helping the patriots to achieve a victory in and around the majestic forests of the Highlands region. See also Carl Van Doren, *Secret History of the American Revolution* (N.Y.: Viking Press, 1941).

[11]Palmer, p. 124; Willcox, p. 187; Otten, p. 108. This figure did not include the bateaux personnel nor the strength of the small naval fleet which accompanied the force. Lossing, *The Empire State,* p. 286, cites General Vaughan had 3,600 strong. Undoubtedly, the 3,600 also included the entire British strength found at this time in the Highlands.

[12]Erroneously and probably in a rush, General Gates accidentally wrote "Septr." (September) instead of October on the top of the letter. At this very moment, Generals Gates and Burgoyne were negotiating for the surrender of Burgoyne's army. For the various letters and documents to include the entire "Article of Convention Agreed Upon between Him [General Burgoyne] and Major General Gates" see *The Public Papers of George Clinton,* Vol. II, pp. 428-456. For "Major General Gates' Proposals, together with Lieutenant General Burgoyne's Answers" and the "Articles of Convention Between Lieutenant General Burgoyne and Major General Gates" finally agreed upon see Stone, *The Campaign*, pp. 102-112.

[13]At that time, a small settlement known as Esopus existed. Presently, the town of Esopus is located here.

[14]Palmer, p. 125, cites this action took place at Rondout Creek. Otten, p. 108, cites that it actually took place at Esopus Creek, a creek just south of Rondout Creek. Both creeks flow into the Hudson River. Possibly, one position was erected at Rondout Creek and the other at Esopus Creek.

[15]In a report submitted by General Vaughan on board the ship *Friendship* and dated 17 October, 10 o'clock in the morning, General Vaughan wrote:

"Sir. I have the honor to inform you that on the evening of the 15th instant I arrived off Esopus; finding that the rebels had thrown up works and had made every disposition to annoy us and cut us off our communication I judged it necessary to attack them. . . I accordingly landed our troops, attacked the batteries drove them from their works, spiked and destroyed their guns." For Vaughan's entire report, see *The Public Papers of George Clinton,* Vol. II, p. 458.

[16]The time cited came from a report describing what occurred at Kingston on 16 October 1777. See *The Public Papers of George Clinton,* Vol. II, pp. 457–458.

[17]Otten, pp. 109–110; Diamant, p. 119, cites that "Vaughan and Wallace burnt Kingston to the ground, laying everything in ashes." Hearing of this, on 19 October General Gates sent a letter directly to General Vaughan not only denouncing the destruction of " . . . . the fine village of Kingston to ashes, and most of the wretched inhabitants to ruin" but also denounced the ongoing destruction when Gates wrote:"I am also informed, you continue to ravage and burn all before you on both sides of the river . . . " For Gates' entire letter to include the warning he sent to Vaughan see "Gates to Vaughn, Esopus, October 19, 1777" in *The Public Papers of George Clinton,* Vol. II, p. 459. (General Gates spelled the name as Vaughn).

Of interest is that no one on Vaughan's or Wallace's staff ever herald any outrage or criticism regarding the destruction of Kingston. For such comments see Diamant, pp. 119–120.

[18]Margaret Livingston (nee Beekman) married Robert Livingston III in 1742. In the aftermath of the destruction of her

estate, she continued her work in assisting refugees. What crops not destroyed she helped to gather up and deliver to the Northern Army. After the Revolutionary War she rebuilt the Manor Estate into its original state.

[19]In the aftermath of the Revolutionary War, Mrs. Van Cortlandt also rebuilt her estate.

[20]By and large, river pilots were civilians hired by the British army or navy. In the Wilderness War of 1777, General Vaughan was not the only one to experience hardships because of civilian work personnel. Most of Burgoyne's wagoners were hired civilians as well.

[21]Seymour, *Turning Point at Saratoga,* p. 50, cites "the river pilots refused to take Wallace's vessels farther."

[22]Willcox, p. 188.

[23]Ibid.

[24]According to Fleming, *Liberty!,* p. 262, a combination of "militia swarming both banks - and the navy's doubts about navigating the river - discouraged the British from going further."

[25]From 15-19 October, General Vaughan received various reports as to Burgoyne's fate. This included that he was either negotiating a surrender or had surrendered, was retreating back to Canada, and related. Though there was some truth to all of the information, the message which Vaughan finally received directly on 19 October from Burgoyne via an emissary, Lord Petersham, made it clear that Burgoyne had, in fact, surrendered. (See Willcox, pp. 184-190). After debriefing Petersham, Vaughan immediately sent Petersham downriver to New York City with a message for Sir Henry. Informing Sir Henry that for the time being he would remain in place, Vaughan also requested orders on what he was to do next. "Vaughan to Clinton, no. 1, 10/19/77." (Willcox, fn. 9, p. 188).

[26]Willcox, p. 188. By this action, Howe was only further weakening Sir Henry. And Christopher Ward, *The War of the Revolution,* Vol. II, p. 567, cites such: "The truth is that Howe's entire campaign, from its beginning when he first proposed to himself the capture of Philadelphia, had been a sheer waste of time, of money, and of men."

[27] *The Public Papers of George Clinton,* Vol. II, pp. 459–460.

[28] For the entire letter, see Vol. II, p. 459; and Otten, pp. 109–110.

[29] Fleming, p. 262, cites that from where Vaughan's force stood at Livingston Manor the distance was 45 miles to Albany and 85 to Saratoga.

[30] Palmer, pp. 126–127.

[31] For this and other views see Burgoyne, *Enemy Views (1777),* pp. 221–225. Regarding the officer's view, he was more than correct. With Burgoyne's surrender, even excluding the Northern Army's soldiers and militiamen sent home for furlough, Gates would still have possessed a combat strength of no less than 10,000 to 12,000 troops to immediately march southward. And if other units were brought down from the Schoharie and Mohawk Valley's, New England, and northern New Jersey, this combat strength figure would rise significantly.

[32] A high piece of ground overlooking present day West Point and Constitution Island, Crow's Nest is located on the left - or west - side of the Hudson River.

[33] Some authors have presented that Sir Henry's "little campaign thrust accomplished virtually nothing." See James Kirby Martin, *Benedict Arnold,* p. 393. As for General Vaughan he, too, returned back to New York City.

[34] For a drawing of the beautiful Robinson House see Palmer, p. 279. In the aftermath of the Revolutionary War in 1783, Robinson sailed to England with most of his family. There, until his death in April, 1792, he never found the support or sympathy as he and many of the other loyalists thought they were entitled to and would receive. For most of the loyalists, England turned out to be not only a disappointment but, in actuality, a true hardship. As for Robinson, he had a total of 12 children – 9 sons and 3 daughters – Ivanna, Susannah Maria, and Joanna. In the aftermath of the Wilderness War of 1777, the house was utilized as a hospital, military headquarters, and briefly housed General Arnold and his wife. After the Revolutionary War, various owners owned the property. In approximately 1892, it burned down during a heavy lightning storm.

[35] For the entire letter see *The Public Papers of George Clinton,* Vol. I, pp. 488–489.

Of interest is that as late as 18 October some of the Germans serving in Sir Henry's force ". . . remained aboard ship, not knowing where we should go." The Germans were also informed that they would be "landed on the following day." They believed this would be undertaken ". . . to proceed to a union with the Army from Canada" because they were aware that "General Vaughan's army had pressed on as far as Aesopus [Esopus]." However, by 23 October, it was reported that "Burgoyne and his entire army have been captured." Undoubtedly the reason why the German troops from the period of approximately 14 October until 23 October had been moved farther southward back toward New York City is because someone over them had been informed that Burgoyne was either in the process of retreating or would be surrendering.

As they recorded on 16 October: "We suggested to ourselves that we should march to Albany to join with Burgoyne's army . . ., but were interrupted by an order from General Clinton, which commanded our immediate return down river. We did not know the reason for this order. We ate our noon meal in disgust, because of the retreat. The rebels fired at our ships from the shore with small arms, but to no effect. We sailed down the Hudson River at about four o'clock. Some, in disgust, lay down." (Surely on 16 October, the Germans were not yet aware of Burgoyne negotiating a surrender. Although their force returned southward many might have assumed that within a day or two, they would again be moving northward. The Germans also cited that Commodore Hotham commanded the fleet. Regardless, upon their return to the city, the disembarked troops were never recalled back to duty in 1777). For additional information on the German participation in Sir Henry's force during the Highlands attack see also *Enemy Views, (1777)*.

Chapter 10. African Americans in the Wilderness War of 1777

[1](See Thomas A. Bailey, *The American Pageant. A History of the Republic* (Mass: D.C. Heath and Company, 1975), 5th ed., Vol. 1, p.14), hereafter referred to as *The American Pageant*; "The Slave Trade" in Philip Davies, David Ryan, David Brown, Ron Mendel, *The History*

Atlas of North America. From First Footfall to New World Order (N.Y.: Simon and Schuster MacMillan Company, 1998), pp. 28–29; William H. Watkins, "Slavery in Herkimer County. African-Americans Were Here in the Valley from the Beginning" in *Legacy. Annals of Herkimer County* (N.Y.: Herkimer County Historical Society, Issue No. 3, 1990), pp. 5–7).

[2]Linda Grant DePauw, *Four Traditions: Women of New York During the American Revolution* (Albany, N.Y.: New York State American Revolution Bicentennial Commission, 1974), p. 8. (Hereafter cited as *Four Traditions*).

[3]DePauw, *Four Traditions*, pp. 8–11; and Watkins, *Legacy. Annals of Herkimer County,* pp. 7–8.

[4]Bailey, *The American Pageant*, p. 69; DePauw, p. 7, cites "As late as 1771, [even] after a sharp increase in the white population, slaves still represented almost 12 percent of the total population." In some regions, the black population was very high. In Albany County in the Colony of New York and in the Mohawk Valley the black population exceeded 15 percent. (Watkins, *Legacy*, p. 7). However, the percentage could possibly have been even higher.

[5]Bruce Quarles, *The Negro in the American Revolution* (N.C.: Chapel Hill, 1961), p. 33. (Hereafter cited as *Negro in the American Revolution*).

[6]An exhaustive study of this has been made by Bruce Quarles in *Negro in the American Revolution*).

[7]Jay David and Elaine Crane, *The Black Soldier: From the American Revolution to Vietnam* (N.Y.: William Morrow and Co., Inc., 1971), p. 11. Hereafter cited as *The Black Soldier*. According to the authors, "most [were] from northern states." (Ibid.). Ronald Hoffman and Peter J. Albert, *Women in the Age of the American Revolution* (Virginia: University Press of Virginia, 1989), p. 327, also cite 5,000. The figure of 5,000, however, does not encompass those who served within the militia units, various guerrilla organizations, or as spies. (Hereafter cited as *Women in the Revolution*).

[8]Irving S. and Nell M. Kull, *A Chronological Encyclopedia of American History* (N.Y.: Popular Library, 1969), p. 87.

[9]See "Revolution in Black" in Fleming, *Liberty!,* p. 303.

[10]Quarles, pp. 39–41.

[11]Quarles, p. 40.

[12]Ibid.

[13]Ibid.

[14]Quarles, p. 72.

[15]Quarles, p. 73; Lee N. Newcomer, *The Embattled Farmer: A Massachusetts Countryside in the American Revolution* (N.Y.: 1953), p. 106.

[16]Fleming, *Liberty!*, p. 302.

[17]According to Sylvia R. Frey, "Between Slavery and Freedom: Virginia Blacks in the American Revolution" in *Journal of Southern History* (History Journal 49, 1983), pp. 383-391, black slaves which sought British refuge were not always granted refuge.(See also Black, p. 31).

[18]Quarles, p. 156; Frey, p. 391; Hoffman and Albert, p. 327.

[19]See also "Negroes In the American Revolution" in Boatner, *Encyclopedia of the American Revolution*, pp. 775-777.

[20]Fleming, *Liberty!*, p. 303.

[21]At this time, integration existed in all of the Continental Armies. See David and Crane, *The Black Soldier*, p. 12.

[22]Richard M. Ketchum, *Saratoga. Turning Point of America's Revolutionary War* (N.Y.: Henry Holt and Company, 1997), pp. 111-112. (Hereafter cited as *Saratoga, Turning Point*).

[23]North Callahan, *Flight From the Republic. The Tories of the American Revolution* (N.Y.: Bobbs-Merrill Co., Inc., 1967), p. 137; Donald Barr Chidsey, *The Loyalists*, p. 167.

[24]Watkins, *Legacy*, p. 9.

[25]According to Jeptha R. Simms, *The Frontiersmen of New York* (N.Y.: George C. Riggs, publisher, 1882), p. 259, the Johnsons were large slave owners.

[26]Watkins, *Legacy*, p. 9.

[27]According to DePauw, *Four Traditions*, p. 35, "even black women made some gains from the [American Revolutionary] war."

Chapter 11. Women Fighters in the Wilderness War of 1777

[1]For excellent accounts of how women were involved in 1777 and throughout the Revolutionary War see Canon, *Heroines of the American Revolution*; Karen Zeinert, *Those Remarkable Women of the*

American Revolution; Elizabeth F. Ellet, *The Women of the American Revolution* (N.Y.; Baker and Scribner, 1849) (Reprinted Massachusetts: Corner House Publishers, 1980), Vol. I-II; David J. Harkness, *Northeastern Heroines of the American Revolution* (Tennessee: University of Tennessee, 1977); Paul Engle, *Women in the American Revolution* (Illinois: Follett Publishing Company, 1976); and Lucille Recht Penner, "Women at War!" in *The Liberty Tree: the Beginning of the American Nation* (N.Y.: Random House, 1998). Ronald Hoffman and Peter J. Albert, ed's, *Women In the Age of the American Revolution* (Virginia: University Press of Virginia, 1989), p. 13, cite that around 20,000 American women served in the patriot armies during the war. For an interesting study of women in combat during the Revolutionary War see Patricia Edwards Clyne, *Patriots In Petticoats* (N.Y.: Dodd, Mead and Company, 1976) and David E. Jones, *Women Warriors. A History* (Virginia: Brassey Publishers, 2000), p. 220. (Hereafter cited as *Women Warriors*). Jones acknowledges that patriot women established the so-called 'Daughters of Liberty' which, along with the 'Sons of Liberty', espoused freedom from British rule. (Ibid.).

[2]Jeanne Meader Schwarz and Minerva J. Goldberg, *New York State in Story* (N.Y.: Frank E. Richards, 1962, Books I-II), Book 2, p. 64. At this time, many women were involved in the fur trade.

[3]Ibid.

[4]Ibid.

[5]According to *Linda Grant DePauw, Four Traditions,* pp. 5 and 30, "Rape was one of the grievances that made patriots out of neutrals." Mark M. Boatner, "Rawdon-Hastings, Francis," in *The Encyclopedia of the American Revolution* (N.Y.: David McKay Co., Inc., 1966), pp. 918-919, cites Lord Rawdon's writings describing the amusement of rape. And Robert Leckie also acknowledged that rape even turned female and male tories (loyalists) into patriots. (See *The Wars of America*, pp. 162-163). As Leckie cited "His Lordship [Rawdon] also found the ravishing of American women highly entertaining." (Ibid.). See also John C. Miller, *Triumph of Freedom, 1775-1783* (Boston: Little & Brown, 1948), pp. 165-166). Various

British officials and officers acknowledged that rape was rampant. See George Scheer and Hugh Rankin, *Rebels and Redcoats,* back cover of book.

[6]See Oscar Barck, p. 58.

[7]See also "New York City, 1776-1780: Sanctuary or Trap?" in Robert McCluer Calhoon, *The Loyalists in Revolutionary America, 1760-1781* (N.Y.: Harcourt Brace Jovanovich, Inc., 1973), p. 371; Wallace Brown, *Tories In the Revolution* (Fort Ontario Archives, Oswego, N.Y.); and Thomas Jones, *History of New York During the Revolutionary War* (N.Y.: 1879), Vol. I, pp. 136-137.

[8]Personal discussion with Mr. William "Bill" Nasi, a New York City historian.

[9]Discussion with Mr. Nasi.

[10]Ibid.

[11]Jeptha R. Simms, *History of Schoharie County and Border Wars of New York* (Albany: Munsell and Tanner, 1845), p. 267.

[12]Oscar Theodore Barck, *New York City During the War For Independence* (N.Y.: Columbia University Press, 1931) (Reprinted in 1966 by N.Y.: Ira J. Friedman, Inc., 1966), p. 57.

[13]For an excellent study of this entire problem see "Keeping the Peace In the War-Time City," in *New York City During the War For Independence,* Chapter III, pp. 49-73. DePauw, pp. 30-31; Leckie, *The Wars of America,* p. 162; and General (Ret'd) Dave Richard Palmer, *The River and the Rock. The History of Fortress West Point, 1775-1783* (N.Y.: Greenwood Publishing Corp.), p. 63.

[14]See William P. Cumming and Hugh F. Rankin, *The Fate of a Nation. The American Revolution Through Contemporary Eyes* (London, England: Phaidon Press Limited, 1975), p. 115.

[15]DePauw, *Four Traditions: Women of New York,* p. 32.

[16]DePauw, *Four Traditions: Women of New York,* p. 32.

[17]Benson Bobrick, *Angel In the Whirlwind,* p. 481.

[18] Ibid., pp. 290-291.

[19]DePauw, pp. 36-37.

[20]See also DePauw, p. 32.

[21]For an interesting study of this see Karen Zeinert, "In the Army" in *Those Remarkable Women of the American Revolution* (Connecticut: The Milbrook Press, 1996), Chapter 2, p. 16.

[22]Ibid., p. 17. Such possibly was the case with Molly Meeker who hailed from Fairfield (now in the Town of Westport). Enlisting early in the war, Molly was discharged honorably from the army on 24 April 1780.

[23]Ronald Hoffman and Peter J. Albert, ed's, *Women In the Age of the American Revolution* (Virginia: University Press of Virginia, 1989), p. 13.

[24]Ibid.

[25]Alexander Rose, *Washington's Spies. The Story of America's First Spy Ring* (N.Y.: Bantam Dell, 2006).

[26]To this day, the U.S. Army honors the services of these very first volunteers. The women of 1777 also established a foundation for military service for future female generations.

Chapter 12. New York State's Political Election During the Wilderness War of 1777

[1]Lossing, *The Empire State: A Compendious History of the Commonwealth of New York* (Hartford, Connecticut: American Publishing Co., 1888), pp. 257-259. (Hereafter cited *The Empire State*); Harry F. Landon, *History of the North Country. A History Embracing Jefferson, St. Lawrence, Oswego, Lewis and Franklin Counties* (Indiana: Historical Publishing Co., 1932), p. 91. For additional information see also Lossing, *The Empire State. New York: Settlement Through 1875* (Conn.: American Publishing Co., 1888).

[2]Lossing, *The Empire State,* p. 262.

[3]Lossing, p. 257. A copy of the state constitution was soon submitted to the American Continental Congress.

[4]George Bancroft, *History of the United States, From the Discovery of the American Continent* (Boston: Little, Brown, and Company, 1875) Vol. IX , 5th ed., p. 262.

[5]Ibid.

[6]Lossing, pp. 260-261.

[7]Ibid.

[8]Ibid.

[9]Lossing, *The Empire State*, p. 261.

[10]Don R. Gerlach, *Philip Schuyler and the American Revolution in New York, 1733-1777* (Nebraska: University of Nebraska Press, 1964), p. 309. (Hereafter cited *Philip Schuyler . . .*).

[11]Lossing, fn. P. 260.

[12]Gerlach, *Philip Schuyler . . .*, p. 309.

[13]Gerlach, p. 309.

[14]Ibid, pp. 309-310.

[15]Lossing, *The Empire State,* p. 262.

[16]Ibid.

Bibliography

John Adams, *Papers of John Adams* (Cambridge, Mass.: Harvard University Press, 1983). Edited by Robert J. Taylor.

John R. Alden, *A History of the American Revolution* (N.Y.: Alfred A. Knopf, Inc., 1969).

Robert B. Asprey, *War in the Shadows* (N.Y.: Doubleday & Company, Inc., 1975), Volume I.

Thomas A. Bailey, *The American Pageant. A History of the Republic* (Massachusetts: D.C. Heath and Company, 1975), 5th Edition, Volume I.

John Bakeless, *Turncoats, Traitors and Heroes* (N.Y.: J.B. Lippincott Company, 1959).

George Bancroft, *History of the United States, From the Discovery of the American Continent* (Boston: Little, Brown and Company, 1875). (Volume IX, 5th edition).

_____, *The American Revolution* (Boston: Little, Brown, and Company, 1875). Volumes I-V).

Oscar Theodore Barck, Jr., *Colonial America* (N.Y.: The MacMillan Company, 1958).

_____, *New York City During the War For Independence* (N.Y.: Columbia University Press, 1931). (Reprinted: N.Y.: Ira J. Friedman, Inc., 1966).

Dr. Ian Barnes, *The Historical Atlas of Native Americans. 150 maps chronicle the fascinating and tragic story of North America's indigenous peoples* (N.Y.: Chartwell Books, Inc., 2009, reprinted 2011).

James Phinney Baxter, *The British Invasion From the North. The Campaigns of Generals Carleton and Burgoyne From Canada, 1776-1777, With the Journal of Lieut. William Digby of the 53d, or Shropshire Regiment of Foot* (Albany, N.Y.: Joel Munsell's Sons, 1887).

Charles A. Beard and Mary R. Beard, *A Basic History of the United States* (N.Y.: Doubleday, Doran & Company, 1944).

Carol Benkin, *Revolutionary Mothers Women in the Struggle for America's Independence* (N.Y.: First Vintage Books, 2005).

Fred Anderson Berg, *Encyclopedia of Continental Army Units. Battalions, Regiments and Independent Corps* (N.Y.: Stackpole Books, 1972).

Major Tharratt Gilbert Best, *A Soldier of Oriskany* (Boonville, N.Y.: The Willard Press, 1935).

"Biography of Colonel Peter Schuyler." (From: Documents Relative To the Colonial History of the State of New York). (Oswego, N.Y.: Fort Ontario archives).

Jeremy Black, *War for America: The Fight for Independence, 1775-1783* (Great Britain: Sutton Publishing Company, 1998).

Paul E. Blackwood, *The How and Why Wonder Book of North American Indians* (N.Y.: Wonder Books, 1965). (5th Printing).

Bruce Bliven, *New York. A Bicentennial History* (W.W. Norton and Company, Inc., 1981).

Mark M. Boatner, *Landmarks of the American Revolution. People and Places Vital to the Quest for Independence* (Harrisburg, Pa.: Stackpole Books, 1992).

_____, *Encyclopedia of the American Revolution* (N.Y.: David McKay Co., Inc, 1966).

Benson Bobrick, *Angel In the Whirlwind. The Triumph of the American Revolution* (N.Y.: Simon & Schuster, 1997).

Nikolai N. Bolkhovitinov, *The Beginnings of Russian-American Relation, 1775-1815* (Massachusetts: Harvard University Press, 1975).

Captain Edward C. Boynton, *History of West Point, and Its Military Importance During the American Revolution; and the Origin and Progress of the United States Military Academy* (Freeport, N.Y.: Book for Libraries Press, 1863). (Reprinted 1970).

John Brick, *The King's Rangers* (N.Y.: Doubleday & Company, Inc., 1954).

Peter Brock, *Pacifism In the United States: From the Colonial Era to the First World War* (N.J.: Princeton University Press, 1968).

Richard Brookhiser, *Alexander Hamilton - American* (N.Y.: The Free Press, 1999).

Wallace Brown, *Tories In the Revolution* (Oswego, N.Y.: Fort Ontario Archives).

James W. Burbank, *Cushetunk, 1754-1784. The First White Settlement in the Upper Delaware River Valley* (N.Y.: Sullivan County Democrat, 1975) (3rd Printing).

Bruce Burgoyne, ed., *Enemy Views, (1777). The American Revolutionary War as Recorded by the Hessian Participants* (Maryland: Heritage Books, Inc., 1996).

General John Burgoyne, *A State of the Expedition from Canada as Laid Before the House of Commons* (N.Y.: New York Times & Arno Press, 1969). (Reprinted).

_____, *Thoughts for Conducting the War from the Side of Canada* (New York: Oswego Fort Ontario Archives).

H.C. Burleigh, *Captain MacKay and the Loyal Volunteers* (Ontario, Canada: Bayside Publishing Company, 1977).

Martha Byrd, *Saratoga: Turning Point In the American Revolution* (England: Auerbach Publishers, Inc., 1973).

A.L. Byron-Curtiss, *The Life and Adventures of Nat Foster, Trapper and Hunter of the Adirondacks* (Utica, N.Y.: Thomas J. Griffiths Press, 1897) (Reprinted 1976 by Harbor Hill Books, Harrison, N.Y.).

Robert M. Calhoon, The *Loyalists in Revolutionary America, 1760-1781* (N.Y.: Harcourt Brace Jovanovich, Inc., 1973).

North Callahan, *Flight From the Republic. The Tories of the American Revolution* (N.Y.: Bobbs-Merrill Co., Inc., 1967).

Colin G. Calloway, *The American Revolution in Indian Country. Crisis and Diversity in Native American Communities* (N.Y.: Press Syndicate, 1995).

The Campaign of 1777 (Unpublished text). (Oswego, N.Y.: Fort Ontario Archives).

Eugenia Campbell Lester and Allegra Branson, *Frontiers Aflame! Jane Cannon Campbell, Revolutionary War Heroine when America Only Had Heroes* (N.Y.: Heart of the Lakes Publishing, 1987). Reprinted.

William W. Campbell and William L. Stone, *Siege Fort Stanwix [Schuyler] & Battle of Oriskany* (N.Y.: Bropard Company, Inc., 1977) (Reprinted).

Jill Canon, *Heroines of the American Revolution* (Santa Barbara, Ca.: Bellerophon Books, 1998).

Henry B. Carrington, *Battles of the American Revolution, 1775-1781. Historical and Military Criticism, with Topographical Illustration* (N.Y.: S. Barnes and Company, 1877).

Adrian G. Ten Cate, *Pictorial History of the Thousand Islands of the St. Lawrence River* (Canada: Besancourt Publishers, 1982).

Bruce Catton, *The American Heritage History of the American Revolution* (N.Y.: American Heritage Publishing Co., 1971).

Donald Barr Chidsey, *The Loyalists. The Story of Those Americans Who Fought Against Independence* (N.Y.: Crown Publishers, Inc., 1973).

George Clinton, *The Public Papers of George Clinton* (N.Y.: Albany, 1904. Published by New York State, Volumes 1-10).

Patricia Edwards Clyne, *Patriots In Petticoats* (N.Y.: Dodd, Mead and company, 1976).

Hubbard Cobb, *American Battlefields. A Complete Guide to the Historic Conflicts in Words, Maps, and Photos* (N.Y.: Simon & Schuster Macmillan Company, 1995).

William Colbrath, *Days of Siege. A Journal of the Siege of Fort Stanwix in 1777* (N.Y.: Publishing Center for Cultural Resources, 1983).

William T. Couch, ed., *Collier's Encyclopedia* (N.Y.: P.F. Collier and Son Corporation, 1955).

William P. Cumming and Hugh Rankin, *The Fate of a Nation. The American Revolution Through Contemporary Eyes* (London, England: Phaidon Press, Limited, 1975).

Edward E. Curtis, *The Organization of the British Army in the American Revolution* (N.Y.: Ams Press, 1969). (Reprinted from 1926 edition).

Anthony D. Darling, *Red Coat and Brown Bess* (Canada: Museum Restoration Service, 1970).

Jay David and Elaine Crane, *The Black Soldier: From the American Revolution to Vietnam* (N.Y.: William Morrow and Co., Inc., 1971).

Philip Davies, *The History Atlas of North America. From First Footfall To New World Order* (Simon & Schuster Macmillan Company, 1998).

Burke Davis, *George Washington and the American Revolution* (N.Y.: Random House, 1975).

Linda Grant DePauw, *Four Traditions: Women of New York During the American Revolution* (Albany, N.Y.: New York State American Revolution Bicentennial Commission, 1974).

"Description of the Country Between Oswego and Albany - 1757. (Paris Doc. XIII)." (Oswego, N.Y.: Fort Ontario Archives).

Lincoln Diamant, *Chaining the Hudson. The Fight for the River in the American Revolution* (N.Y.: Carol Publishing Group, 1989).

Lieutenant William Digby, *The British Invasion From the North: Digby's Journal of the Campaigns of Generals Carleton and Burgoyne From Canada, 1776-1777* (Albany, 1887). (Edited by James Phinney Baxter).

Richard M. Dorison, ed., *Patriots of the American Revolution. True Accounts of Great Americans from Ethan Allen to George Rogers Clark* (N.Y.: Gramercy Books, 1998).

Lieutenant-Colonel Fairfax Downey, *Indian Wars of the U.S. Army, 1776-1865* (N.Y.: Doubleday and Company, 1962).

R. Ernest Dupuy and Colonel Trevor N. Dupuy, *The Encyclopedia of Military History From 3500 B.C. to the Present* (N.Y.: Harper and Row, Publishers, 1977) (Revised Edition).

Trevor N. Dupuy, Curt Johnson, and David L. Bongard, *The Harper Encyclopedia of Military Biography. An Invaluable Compilation and Assessment of the 3,000 Most Important Worldwide Military Figures From Earliest Times to the Present* (N.Y.: Castle Books, 1995).

Allan W. Eckert, *The Wilderness Empire* (Boston: Little, Brown and Company, 1969).

_____, *The Wilderness War: A Narrative* (Boston: Little, Brown and Company. 1978).

Edward K. Eckert, *in War and Peace. An American Military History Anthology* (Ca.: Wadsworth Publishing, Co., 1990).

Elizabeth F. Ellet, *The Women of the American Revolution* (N.Y.: Baker and Scribner, 1849). (Reprinted Massachusetts: Corner House Publishers, 1980), Volumes I-II.

David M. Ellis, *New York State, Gateway to America. New York State, Revolutionary Cockpit, 1763-1789* (N.Y.: Windsor Publications, 1988).

The Encyclopedia Americana. International Edition (Danbury, Conn.: Grolier Inc., Publishers, 1982).

The Encyclopedia Americana. International Edition. U.S. Constitution Bicentennial Commemorative Edition (Connecticut: Grolier Incorporated, 1988), Volume 21.

Paul Engle, *Women in the American Revolution* (Illinois: Follett Publishing Company, 1976).

Colonel Vincent J. Esposito, ed., *The West Point Atlas of the Civil War [Adapted From the West Point Atlas of American Wars]* (N.Y.: Praeger Publishers, 1962).

Excelsior Studies in American History (N.Y.: William H. Sadlier, 1921).

Cyril Falls, ed., *Great Military Battles* (London, England: The Hamlyn Publishing Group Limited, 1969).

Colonel Kevin W. Farrell, "The [American] Revolution's Boldest Venture" in *Army. The Magazine of the Association of the U.S. Army* (Arlington, VA: July, 2014).

John C. Fitzpatrick, *The Writings of George Washington, from the Original Manuscript Sources, 1754-1799* (Washington, D.C.: U.S. Government Printing Office, 1931-34) (39 Volumes).

Thomas Fleming, *Liberty! The American Revolution* (N.Y.: Viking Publishers, 1997).

The Forts of Oswego (Unpublished text) (Oswego, N.Y.: Fort Ontario Archives).

_____, (Updated Text) (Oswego, N.Y.: Fort Ontario Archives).

Sylvia R. Frey, "Between Slavery and Freedom: Virginia Blacks in the American Revolution" in *Journal of Southern History* (History Journal 49, 1983).

Rear Admiral Rea Furlong, Commodore Byron McCandles, Harold D. Langley, *So Proudly We Hail. The History of the United States Flag* (Washington, D.C.: Smithsonian Institution Press, 1981).

Robert Furneaux, *The Battle of Saratoga* (N.Y.: Stein and Day, 1971).

———, *The Pictorial History of the American Revolution* (Chicago: J.G. Ferguson Publishing Co., 1973).

Colonel William A. Ganoe, *The History of the U.S. Army* (N.Y.: D. Appleton and Co., Inc, 1924).

Charles Gehring, *Agriculture and the Revolution in the Mohawk Valley* (N.Y.: Fort Klock).

Don R. Gerlach, *Philip Schuyler and the American Revolution in New York, 1733-1777* (Nebraska: University of Nebraska Press, 1964).

Major Tharratt Gilbert, *A Soldier of Oriskany* (Boonville, N.Y.: The Willard Press, 1935).

Henry F. Graff, *America: The Glorious Republic* (Boston: Houghton Mifflin, Co., 1990).

Barbara Graymont, *The Iroquois in the American Revolution* (Syracuse, N.Y.: Syracuse University Press, 1972).

Donald A. Grinde, Jr., *The Iroquois and the Founding of the American Nation* (New York: Indian Historian Press, 1977).

Edward A. Hagan, *War In Schohary, 1773-1783* (The Middleburgh News Press, 1980).

Robert E. Hager, *Mohawk River Boats and Navigation Before 1820* (Syracuse, N.Y.: Canal Society of New York State, 1987).

Reginald Hargreaves, *The Bloodybacks. The British Serviceman in North America and the Caribbean, 1655-1783* (N.Y.: Walker and Company, 1968).

David J. Harkness, *Northeastern Heroines of the American Revolution* (Tennessee: University of Tennessee, 1977).

Henry Harrison, *Battles of the Republic, By Sea and Land* (Philadelphia, Pa.: Porter and Coates, 1858).

Hugh Hastings and J.A. Holden, ed's., *The Public Papers of George Clinton, First Governor of New York, 1777-1795, 1801-1804* (N.Y.: AMS Press) (Volumes 1-10).

Carlton J.H. Hayes, *A Political and Social History of Modern Europe* (N.Y.: Macmillan Company, 1916), Volume I.

"Herkimer Home" in *State Historic Site, Little Falls, New York, Central Region* (N.Y.: Office of Parks, Recreation and Historic Preservation).

History of Civil Affairs (Ft. Bragg, N.C.: U. S. Army John F. Kennedy Special Warfare Center and School, October, 1992).

Ronald Hoffman and Peter J. Albert, ed's., *Women In the Age of the American Revolution* (Virginia: University Press of Virginia, 1989).

James A. Huston, *The Sinews of War: Army Logistics, 1775-1953* (Washington, D.C.: U.S. Government Printing Office, 1966).

Islands. A Description. (Oswego, N.Y.: Fort Ontario Archives).

Mary Jemison, *The Life of Mary Jemison* (N.Y.: James D. Bemis, Publishers, 1823).

Crisfield Johnson, *History of Oswego County, New York, 1739-1877* (N.Y.: 1878).

Lieutenant-Colonel James M. Johnson, "Staff Rides and the Flawed Works of Fort Constitution" in *Engineer. The Professional Bulletin for Army Engineers* (October, 1990).

Crisfield Johnson, *History of Oswego County, New York, 1739-1877* (N.Y.: 1878).

David E. Jones, *Women Warriors. A History* (Washington, D.C.: Brassey's, 2000).

Thomas Jones, *History of New York During the Revolutionary War* (N.Y.: 1879), Volumes I-II.

Philip R. Katcher, *The American Provincial Corps, 1775-1784* (N.Y.: Osprey Publishing, Ltd., 1973).

_____, *The Encyclopedia of British, Provincial, and German Army Units, 1775-1783* (Pennsylvania: Stackpole Books, 1973).

John Keegan, *Warpaths. Fields of Battle in Canada and America* (Canada: Vintage Books, 1996).

Alan Kemp, *The British Army In the American Revolution* (Great Britain: Almark Publishing Co., Ltd., 1973).

Richard M. Ketchum, *Saratoga. Turning Point of America's Revolutionary War* (N.Y.: Henry Holt and Company, 1997).

_____, *The Winter Soldiers. The Battles For Trenton and Princeton* (N.Y.: Henry Holt and Company, 1973).

Irving S. Kull, Nell M. Kull, Stanley H. Friedelbaum, *A Chronological Encyclopedia of American History* (N.Y.: Popular Library Press, 1952).

Mark V. Kwasny, *Washington's Partisan War, 1775-1783* (Ohio: Kent State University Press, 1996).

Richard B. LaCrosse, Jr., *The Frontier Rifleman. His Arms, Clothing and Equipment During the Era of the American Revolution, 1760-1800* (Union City, Tennessee: Pioneer Press, 1989).

_____, *Revolutionary Rangers. Daniel Morgan's Riflemen and Their Role on the Northern Frontier, 1778-1783* (Bowie, Maryland: Heritage Books, Inc., 2002).

_____, *Daniel Morgan's Riflemen on America's Northern Frontier, 1778-1783* (Unpublished text. Oswego, N.Y., Fort Ontario Archives).

Roger Lamb, *An Original and Authentic Journal of Occurrences During the Late American War from its Commencement to the Year 1783* (Ireland: Dublin, 1809) (Reprinted by New York Times & Arno Press, 1968).

Bruce Lancaster and J.H. Plumb, *The American Heritage Book of the Revolution* (N.Y.: Dell Publishing Co., Inc., 1981).

Harry F. Landon, *History of the North Country. A History of Embracing Jefferson, St. Lawrence, Oswego, Lewis and Franklin Counties* (Indiana: Historical Publishing Company, 1932), Volumes I-III.

A.J. Langguth, *Patriots. The Men Who Started the American Revolution* (N.Y.: Simon and Schuster, Inc., 1989).

Harold D. Langley, *So Proudly We Hail. The History of the United States Flag* (Washington, D.C.: Smithsonian Institution Press, 1981).

Robert Leckie, *The Wars of America (Updated Edition)* (N.Y.: HarperCollins Publishers, 1992).

Eugenia Campbell Lester and Allegra Branson, *Frontiers Aflame! Jane Cannon Campbell. Revolutionary War Heroine When America Had Only Heroes* (N.Y.: Heart of the Lakes Publishing, 1987).

Michael O. Logusz, *With Musket & Tomahawk. The Saratoga Campaign In the Wilderness War of 1777* (PA: Casemate Publishers, 2008. Reprinted 2012).

————————, *With Musket & Tomahawk. The Mohawk Valley Campaign In the Wilderness War of 1777* (PA: Casemate Publishers, 2012).

Phillip Lord, Jr., *War Over Walloomscoick. Land Use and Settlement Pattern on the Bennington Battlefield - 1777* (Albany, N.Y.: State University of New York, 1989).

Benson J. Lossing, *The Empire State: A Compendious History of the Commonwealth of New York* (Hartford, Connecticut.: American Publishing Co., 1888).

————————, *The Empire State. New York: Settlement Through 1875* (Conn.: American Publishing Co., 1888).

————————, *The Pictorial Field-Book of the [American] Revolution* (N.Y.: Harper & Brothers, Publishers, 1860), Volumes I-II.

The Loyalist Papers (N.Y.: New York Public Library). (Oswego, N.Y.: Fort Ontario Archives).

Christine Lunardini, *What Every American Should Know About Women's History. 200 Events that Shaped Our Destiny* (Massachusetts: Bob Adams, Inc., 1994).

John Luzader, *The Saratoga Campaign of 1777* (Washington, D.C.: National Park Service Publications, 1975).

John Luzader, Louis Torres, Orville W. Carroll, *Fort Stanwix: Construction and Military History, Historic Furnishing Study, Historic Structure Report* (Washington, D.C.: U.S. Government Printing Office, 1976).

Mary C. Lynn, ed., *The Sprecht Journal. A Military Journal of the Burgoyne Campaign* (Contributions in Military Studies, Number 158, 1995).

Piers Mackesy, *The War for America, 1775-1783* (Nebraska: University of Nebraska, 1993).

John K. Mahon and Romana Danysh, *Army Lineage Series: Infantry Part I: Regular Army* (Washington, D.C.: 1972).

James Kirby Martin, *Benedict Arnold, Revolutionary Hero. An American Reconsidered* (N.Y.: New York University Press, 1997).

Joseph Plumb Martin, *Private Yankee Doodle. Being a Narrative of Some of the Adventures, Dangers and Sufferings of a Revolutionary Soldier* (Boston: Little, Brown and Company, 1962).

David McCullough, *John Adams* (N.Y.: Simon & Schuster, 2001).

Ann McGovern, *The Secret Soldier: The Story of Deborah Sampson* (N.Y.: Scholastic Press, Inc., 1975).

Edgar J. McManus, *A History of Negro Slavery in New York* (N.Y.: Syracuse University Press, 1966).

Mary McNeer, *The Hudson, River of History* (Illinois: Garrard Publishing Co., 1962).

Roy Meredith, *The American Wars: A Pictorial History from Quebec to Korea 1755-1953* (N.Y.: The World Publishing Co., p. 1955).

The Military Journals of Two Private Soldiers, 1758-1775, with Numerous Illustrative Notes (N.Y.: Poughkeepsie: 1845).

Charles E. Miller, Jr., Donald V. Lockey, Joseph Visconti, Jr., *Highland Fortress: The Fortification of West Point During the American Revolution, 1775-1783* (West Point: Unpublished text at the United States Military Academy (USMA) Library).

Lieutenant-Colonel Joseph B. Mitchell and Sir Edward Creasy, *Twenty Decisive Battles of the World* (N.Y.: The MacMillan Company, 1964).

Barbara Mitnick, *New Jersey in the American Revolution* (New Brunswick, NJ: River Gate Books, 2005).

Lynn Montross, *The Reluctant Rebels. The Story of the Continental Congress, 174-1789* (N.Y.: Harper & Brothers Publishers, 1950).

Frank Moore, *The Diary of the American Revolution* (N.Y.: Washington Square Press, Inc., 1968).

Samuel Eliot Morison and Henry Steele Commager, *The Growth of the American Republic* (N.Y.: Oxford University Press, 1952). (3rd Printing).

Richard B. Morris and James Woodress, ed's., *Voices From America's Past. 1-The Colonies and the New Nation* (N.Y.: E.P. Dutton and Company, Inc., 1961).

Brendan Morrisey, *Saratoga 1777. Turning point of a revolution* (Great Britain: Osprey Publishing, 2000).

Jim Murphy, *A Young Patriot. The American Revolution as Experienced by One Boy* (N.Y.: Clarion Books, 1996).

David Saville Muzzey, *An American History* (Boston: Ginn and Company, 1911).

Brigadier General Harold W. Nelson, Major General Bruce Jacobs, Colonel Raymond K. Bluhm, *The Army, United States Army* (VA: The Army Historical Foundation, 2012).

Lee N. Newcomer, *The Embattled Farmer: A Massachusetts Countryside in the American Revolution* (N.Y.: 1953).

New York State Preservationist (Fall/Winter),Volume 2/Number 2, 1998.

James F. O'Neil, *Their Bearing is Noble and Proud. A Collection of narratives regarding the appearance of Native Americans from 1740-1815* (Dayton, Ohio: J.T.G.S. Publishing, 1995).

Oswego Palladium Times, Tuesday, November 20, 1945.

Lieutenant-Colonel William L. Otten, Jr., (Ret'd), *Colonel J.F. Hamtramck. His Life and Times Volume One (1756-1783) Captain of the Revolution* (Port Aransas, TX, 1997).

_____, *Colonel J.F. Hamtramck, His Life and Times Volume Two (1783-1791) Frontier Major* (Port Aransas, TX, 2003).

General Dave Palmer, *The River and the Rock. The History of Fortress West Point, 1775-1783* (N.Y.: Greenwood Publishing Co., 1969).

Rod Paschall, "George Washington, the Father of U.S. Intelligence" in *Spies and Secret Missions. A History of American Espionage* (Newtown, Pa.: 2002).

Michael Pearson, *Those Damned Rebels. The American Revolution As Seen Through British Eyes* (N.Y.: G.P. Putnam's Sons, 1972).

Lucille Recht Penner, *The Liberty Tree: The Beginning of the American Nation* (N.Y.: Random House, 1998).

Deborah Pessin, *History of the Jews in America* (N.Y.: The United Synagogue Press of America, 1957).

Walter Pilkington, *The Journal of Samuel Kirkland, 18th - century Missionary to the Iroquois, Government Agent, Father of Hamilton College* (Clinton, New York: Hamilton College Publishing, 1980).

John A. Pope, Jr., ed., *Strange Stories, Amazing Facts of America's Past* (Pleasantville, N.Y.: Reader's Digest Press, Inc., 1989).

Arthur Pound, *Lake Ontario. The American Lakes Series* (N.Y.: The Bobbs-Merrill Company Publishers, 1945).

John Hyde Preston, *A Short History of the American Revolution* (N.Y.: Pocket Books, Cardinal edition, 1952).

Proceedings of the New York State Historical Association. The Fifteenth Annual Meeting, With Constitution, By-Laws and List of Members (N.Y. :State Historical Association, 1914),Vol. X111).

Benjamin Quarles, *The Negro in the American Revolution* (N.C.: University of North Carolina Press, 1961).

Emily Raabe, *Ethan Allen. The Green Mountain Boys and Vermont's Path to Statehood* (N.Y.: Rosen publishing Group, Inc., 2002).

Willard Sterne Randall, *George Washington: A Life* (N.Y.: Henry Holt and Company, 1997).

Hugh F. Rankin, *The Fate of a Nation. The American Revolution Through Contemporary Eyes* (London, England: Phaidon Press limited, 1975).

George Reed, *Fort Ontario* (Unpublished Text).

"Revolutionary Vet's Grave Found in Montezuma" in The Post-Standard (Syracuse, N.Y.: June 24, 1998).

Revolutionary War Dates Relating To Oswego (Unpublished text) (Oswego, N.Y.: Fort Ontario Archives).

Revolutionary War Diaries Relating to Oswego (Unpublished text) (Oswego: N.Y.: Fort Ontario Archives).

George W. Roach, *Colonial Highways in the Upper Hudson Valley* (N.Y.: New York State Historical Association,April, 1959).

Lemuel Roberts, *Memoirs of Captain Lemuel Roberts* (N.Y.: New York Tmes & Arno Press, 1969). (Reprinted).

Alexander Rose, *Washington's Spies. The Story of America's First Spy Ring* (N.Y.: Bantam Dell, 2006).

Clinton Rossiter, *The Federalist Papers* (N.Y.: The New American Library, Inc., 1961).

Lorenzo Sabine, *The American Loyalists, or Biographical Sketches of Adherents to the British Crown in the War of the Revolution;*

Alphabetically Arranged; with a Preliminary Historical Essay (MA: Boston Publishers, 1847). (Republished 1864 in 2-volumes).

Barnet Schecter, *The Battle for New York. The City at the Heart of the Revolution* (N.Y.: Walker Publishing Company, Inc., 2002).

George F. Scheer and Hugh F. Rankin, *Rebels and Redcoats* (N.Y.: The New American Library, Inc., 1957).

Elizabeth Eggleston Seelye, *Hudson, Mohawk, Schoharie. History From America's Most Famous Valleys and the Border Wars* (N.Y.: Dodd, Mead and Company, Publishers, 1879).

William Seymour, "Turning Point at Saratoga" in *Military History* (December 1999).

Victoria Sherrow, *The Iroquois Indians* (N.Y.: Chelsea House Publishers, Inc., 1992).

Jeanne Meader Schwarz and Minerva J. Goldberg, *New York State in Story* (N.Y.: Frank E. Richards, 1962), Books I-II.

Jeptha R. Simms, *History of Schoharie County and Border Wars of New York* (Albany: Musell and Tanner, 1845).

_____, *The Frontiersmen of New York* (Albany, N.Y.: George C. Riggs, 1882).

Anthony M. Slosek, *Oswego, New York and the War of 1812* (Oswego, N.Y.: Heritage foundation of Oswego), 1989.

Ted Smart, *Colonial Virginia. A Picture Book To Remember Her* (N.Y.: Crescent Books, 1979).

Linda Spizzirri, ed., *Northeast Indians* (South Dakota: Spizzirri Publishing, Inc., 1982).

"St. Leger's Attack on Ft. Stanwix in 1777 Proved Fiasco" *(Oswego Palladium-Times,* Tuesday, November 20, 1945).

William Leete Stone, *Life of Joseph Brant - Thayendanegea: Including the Border Wars of the American Revolution, and Sketches of the Indian Campaigns of Generals Armar, St. Clair, and Wayne* (N.Y.: George Dearborn and Co., 1838), Volume I.

_____, *Life of Joseph Brant - Thayendanegea Including the Indian Wars of the American Revolution* (N.Y.: H.&E. Phinney, 1845).

_____, *The Campaign of Lieut.Gen. John Burgoyne and the Expedition of Lieut.Col. Barry St. Leger* (N.Y.: Da Capo Press, 1970) (Reprinted).

Stephen G. Strach, *Some Sources For the Study of the Loyalist and Canadian Participation In the Military Campaign of Lieutenant-General John Burgoyne 1777* (Eastern National Park and Monument Association, 1983).

James Sullivan, *The Papers of Sir William Johnson* (Albany, N.Y.: University of New York State, 1922).

Hallie DeMass Sweeting, *Pioneers of Sterling, N.Y. (Cayuga County)*. (Red Creek: Wayuga Press, 1998).

Howard Swiggert, *War Out of Niagara* (Port Washington, N.Y.: Friedman Publishers, 1963).

Syracuse Herald-American, Sunday edition, July 2, 2000. "The Battle of Oriskany" in *The Herald-American, Sunday, July 4, 1999.*

The Papers of Sir William Johnson (N.Y.: Albany University, 1922).

Lowell Thomas and Berton Bradley, *Stand Fast for Freedom* (Philadelphia, Pa.: The John C. Winston Company, 1940).

Colonel Robert L. Tonsetic, *Special Operations during the American Revolution* (PA: Casemate Publishers, 2013).

Barbara W. Tuchman, *The First Salute* (London, England: Penguin Group Publishers, 1989).

Colonel Stanley M. Ulanoff, ed., *American Wars and Heroes. Revolutionary Through Vietnam* (N.Y.: Arco Publishing, Inc., 1985).

Highland Commanders (Unpublished text at West Point Archives).

Carl Van Doren, *Secret History of the American Revolution* (N.Y.: Viking Press, 1941).

Dale Van Every, *A Company of Heroes. The American Frontier, 1775-1783* (N.Y.: William Morrow and Company, 1962).

Wendy Van Wie, *The Homestead At 188 Cross Highway In Its Historical Context.* (Westport, CT: 2014).

Baron Friedrich Adolph Von Riedesel, *Letters and Journals Relating to the War of the American Revolution* (Albany, N.Y.: Joel Munsell, 1867). (Translated by William L. Stone). (Reprinted, N.Y.: New York Times & Arno Press, 1968).

John G. Waite and Paul R. Huey, *Herkimer House. An Historic Structure Report* (N.Y.: 1972).

Christopher Ward, *The War of the Revolution* (N.Y.: The Macmillan Co., 1952) (Volumes I-II).

George Washington, *Papers of George Washington* (Virginia: University of Virginia Press, 1983). Edited by W. W. Abbot.

_____, *Writings of George Washington from the Original Manuscript Sources, 1745-1799* (Washington, D.C.: Government Printing Office, 1931-1944), 39 Volumes. Edited by John C. Fitzpatrick.

William H. Watkins, "Slavery in Herkimer County. African Americans Were Here in the Valley From the Beginning" in *Legacy. Annals of Herkimer County* (N.Y.: Herkimer County Historical Society, 1990). (Issue Number 3).

Richard Wheeler, *Voices of 1776* (N.Y.: Thomas Y. Crowell, Co., 1972).

David C. Whitney, *The People of the Revolution: The Colonial Spirit of '76* (1974).

William B. Willcox, *Portrait of a General. Sir Henry Clinton in the War of Independence* (N.Y.: Alfred A. Knopf, 1962).

William M. Willett, *A Narrative of The Military Actions of Colonel Marinus Willett, Taken Chiefly From His Own Manuscript* (N.Y.: G.&C.&H. Carvill, 1831).

T. Harry Williams, *The History of American Wars. From Colonial Times to World War I* (N.Y.: Alfred A. Knopf, Inc., 1981).

John E. Wilmot, ed., *Journals of the Provincial Congress of New York* (Albany, 1842), Vol. 1.

Thomas G. Wnuck, "The Last Offensive of the American Revolution" in *The Dispatch* (Summer '80) (Oswego, N.Y.: Fort Ontario Archives).

James Albert Woodburn and Thomas Francis Moran, *American History and Government*.

A Text-Book on the History and Civil Government of the United States (N.Y.: Longmans, Green, and Co., 1907).

Wallace F. Workmaster, *The Forts of Oswego: A Study in the Art of Defense* (Oswego, N.Y.: Fort Ontario Archives).

Esmond Wright, ed., *The Fire of Liberty. The American War of Independence seen through the eyes of the men and women, the statesmen and soldiers who fought it.* (N.Y.: St. Martin's Press, 1983).

George M. Wrong, *Canada and the American Revolution. The Disruption of the First British Empire* (N.Y.: Cooper Square Publishers, Inc., 1968).

Philip Young, *Revolutionary Ladies* (N.Y.: Alfred A. Knopf, Inc., 1977).

Brian Kilmeade and Don Yaeger, *George Washington's Secret Six. The Spy Ring That Saved the American Revolution* (NY: Sentinel Publishers, 2013).

Karen Zeinert, *Those Remarkable Women of the American Revolution* (Connecticut: The Millbrook Press, 1996)

About the Author

MICHAEL O. LOGUSZ served in both the Regular and Reserve branches of the U.S. Army. He is a graduate of various military schools including the U.S. Army's Military Police (MP) Academy, the Non-Commissioned Officer's (NCO) Academy, Officer Candidate School (OCS), the Combined Arms and Services Staff School, and the Command and General Staff College. He has served throughout the United States, Asian, Pacific, European, and Southwest Asian Theaters. A qualified parachutist, he served with the U.S. Army's elite 18th Airborne Corps Rapid Deployment Force (RDF). Logusz holds a B.A. in Social Sciences from Oswego State College and an M.A. in Russian Area Studies from Hunter College in New York City. In the civilian sector, he possesses an extensive law-enforcement background including Probation Officer in the New York City Department of Probation. In his continuous interest in military-political historical events Logusz authored *The Galicia Division. The 14th Waffen SS Grenadier Division, 1943-1945* and two books on the American Revolutionary War specifically pertaining to the year 1777: *With Musket & Tomahawk: The Saratoga Campaign in the Wilderness War of 1777* and *With Musket & Tomahawk: The Mohawk Valley Campaign in the Wilderness War of 1777*. A veteran of "Operation Iraqi Freedom," Lieutenant-Colonel Logusz served from June 2007 to May 2008 in Kuwait-Iraq. Upon his return, Logusz immediately resumed his writing on military-political events.

Index

Robinson's Landing, 78, 81–82,
   90, 99, 102
Romans, Bernard, 16–18, 19,
   172n–173n, 175n, 177n
Rondout Creek, 127, 224n
Rosekrans, James, 47
Roundout Creek, 126
Royal Navy, 27, 60, 94, 104
Rye Neck, Connecticut, 29

S
Salisbury Island, 93
Salzburg, Colonel August Voit
   von, 122
Sampson, Deborah ("Robert
   Shurtleff"), 33
Saratoga, 42, 51, 53, 123,
   125–126, 133, 134, 141
Saratoga's region, 4
Savannah, 144
Schoharie Valley, 5, 14, 45,
   167n, 226n
Schuyler, General Philip, 38, 42,
   45, 141, 148, 154, 157,
   158–159, 190n
Schwarz, 150
Scott, Captain, 117, 219n
Scott, General John Morin, 20,
   21, 158–159
Scott, John Morris, 156
Sela, Major, 120
Shark, 37, 46, 93–94, 100
Shepherd, Colonel, 46
"Shurtleff, Robert"
   (Deborah Sampson), 33
Sill, Major, 104
Silliman, Gold S., 28–30
Simms, Jeptha R., 151
Six Nation Iroquois Indian
   Confederacy, 35

Skene, Philip, 145–146
Skenesborough, 145
"Skinners" gang, 25, 26, 32–34,
   34–35, 183n
Smith, William, 156
Snyder, Colonel, 42, 46
Snyder, Colonel Johannis, 46
soldiers: English, 5; German, 5;
   loyalist, 5
Spitfire, 121, 136
Springster, Brom, 76, 78
Spuyten Duyvil Creek, 60
St. Lawrence River, 14, 195n
St. Leger, General Barry, 5, 9,
   49, 50, 135–136, 146–148,
   167n, 197n, 247n
Staten Island, 5, 9, 59, 151, 158
Stedman, Charles, 100
Stewart, Captain, 67, 73–74,
   186n
Stewart, William, 2, 33, 186n
Stony Point, 62, 65, 67–70, 74,
   76–79, 134
Suffern, 66, 206n
"Sugar House Period," 184n
Susquehanna Company, 35, 36
Susquehanna River, 35
Swarthout, Captain Abraham,
   24, 180n
Swift, Colonel, 46

T
Tallmadge, Major Benjamin,
   2, 154
Tappan Zee (Tarrytown Bay),
   61, 62
Tappen, Doctor Peter, 120
Tarrytown, 60, 61
Tarrytown Bay, 61, 62
Tartar, 59, 61, 123, 134